Understanding Mozart's Piano Sonatas

D0531968

JOHN IRVING
University of London, UK

ASHGATE

Published by
Ashgate Publishing Limited
Wey Court East
Union Road
Farnham
Surrey, GU9 7PT
England

Ashgate Publishing Company
Suite 420
101 Cherry Street
Burlington
VT 05401–4405
USA

www.ashgate.com

British Library Cataloguing in Publication Data
Irving, John, 1959–
    Understanding Mozart's piano sonatas.
    1. Mozart, Wolfgang Amadeus, 1756–1791. Sonatas, piano. 2. Sonatas
    (Piano) – History and criticism.
    I. Title
    786.2'183'092–dc22

Library of Congress Cataloging-in-Publication Data
Irving, John, 1959–
    Understanding Mozart's piano sonatas / John Irving.
        p. cm.
    Includes bibliographical references and index.
    ISBN 978–0–7546–6769–8 (hardcover : alk. paper) – ISBN 978–1–4094–1023–2
    (ebook)
    1. Mozart, Wolfgang Amadeus, 1756–1791. Sonatas, piano.
    2. Sonatas (Piano) – History and criticism.
    I. Title.
    ML410.M9I75 2010
    786.2'183092–dc22   2010010027

ISBN 9780754667698 (hbk)
ISBN 97814094102329 (ebk)

© Mixed Sources

Printed and bound in Great Britain by
MPG Books Group, UK

Contents

List of Music Examples

Preface

Some 25 years ago, when I was a young and idealistic PhD student in the University of Sheffield, I had a conversation with one of my fellow students there (a clarinettist) about music's purpose in our lives. Basically, we were debating a question going more or less: 'What's the *point* of studying music?' Being in those days a trainee musicologist, I said something like 'of course, the point of studying music is to *study* it in and of itself' (it was meant quite sincerely; whether I grasped the sheer pretentiousness of that remark, I don't recall – probably not). Being a trainee performer (she has excelled and continues to excel in that profession, notably in Mozart's music), she disagreed, and did so with directness and clarity: 'No: the point of music is to *play* it.' I have reflected on that conversation many times over the years, and on what the consequences of our disagreement might be. In fact, since I spend much of my life involved with Mozart's music, I reflect upon our conversation specifically in relation to his compositions. I think we were both a bit wrong – certainly so far as Mozart is concerned. I also like to think that we've each grown up musically during the passing years and have met in the middle somewhere in our strivings to understand the 'point' of studying music (and particularly Mozart's music). Despite our disagreement then, the student with whom I had that conversation did eventually consent to marry me and I owe so many of my discoveries about Mozart's music to her, whether in her observations on its notation, or in her characterful and moving interpretations in performance. Dedicating this little book to Jane is a small token of my thanks and love.

Happily, I have not yet discovered how to reconcile *studying* and *playing* Mozart's music. Were I to do so, the enjoyment of trying would have ended, and the provisionality of meaning that inhabits every page of Mozart's sonatas would have been missed. Consequently, this book is an attempt to take that journey a little further, but it is expressly not my intention to reach the end of the path; I make no claims here for comprehensiveness. Indeed, I deliberately introduce a quite broad range of contexts within which I try to understand Mozart's piano sonatas, and the focus deliberately shifts radically and often (sometimes abruptly). In particular, I want to try to explore within this book some ways in which Mozart's piano sonatas might be understood through performance. To put it another way, I'll try to explore how performance enables understandings (the plural is deliberate) of Mozart's piano sonatas.

We know Mozart's music through his notated texts. But how his texts function depends on how we approach them. I believe that we should approach Mozart's texts as *Tools* enabling musical expression, rather than as *Rules* constraining us to behave towards Mozart's music only in certain ways. Many of Mozart's piano works began as improvisations; their notation cannot therefore be paramount.

How are we to approach it? I would claim that we should treat Mozart's scores as provisional, not as definitive. If they objectify anything, that is not an *authorial intention* but a *potential for action*. If we claim that his notation encodes anything, then I would rather it were a *conversation* than an *intention*: a dialogue between the performer and the composer. And a dialogue isn't static, of course: it's not a freeze-frame; it's a living process, and it belongs in the realm of performance. *The Music is not the Score.* I want to develop that idea of performance as creative engagement throughout the following pages. By all means, let us have respect for Mozart's texts, but let us remember to treat them as just one component within our toolkit for understanding his music. Mozart's musical texts are not Mozart's *music*. I would rather think of Mozart's Texts as *Contexts* – one element among several that enable us to bring Mozart's music to life (that is, in performance). That means that as performers, we need to perform his texts *contextually* alongside other components within our musical toolkit, including an awareness of his composing habits as revealed in his autograph scores; contemporary textbooks on performance practice of the late 18th century, and what they have to tell us about texts and their physical expression; and crucially, a knowledge of the sound world and technical capabilities of contemporary instruments (and how these two things relate).

The book is in two parts. In Part I ('Reading Texts'), I look at some ways in which the texts of Mozart's piano sonatas might be conceptualised (namely, how they acquire identities and meanings *conceptually*), and in Part II ('Playing Texts') I consider some ways in which their various identities and meanings might be expressed in performance.

Acknowledgements

First of all, I should thank Heidi Bishop at Ashgate for commissioning this book and for steering it efficiently through its various stages of development. I am grateful for fruitful discussions with colleagues in the School of Advanced Study, University of London, who have suggested valuable interdisciplinary insights during the later stages of the book's preparation. Previously, my students at the University of Bristol patiently indulged my passion for combining music history and historical performance practice in these works, and I am grateful to them for contributing to the development of several strands of the section on expression within Part II. The book was begun during a timely period of research leave granted by the University of Bristol; I am indebted also to colleagues in the Department of Music there for opportunities to trial ideas in seminars and recitals. Financial support from the British Academy and from the Arts and Humanities Research Council for related recording and editorial projects provided extended opportunities to deepen my understanding of the relationships between texts and their expression on appropriate historical instruments. My understanding of Mozart's sonatas has deepened enormously through many conversations with Ronald Brautigam, and from his live and recorded interpretations. Discussions with Robert Levin, Tom Beghin, Alexei Lubimov, Daniel Grimwood and Gary Cooper have also contributed in different ways to the development of my ideas. For unearthing some recordings that were influential on my views in Part II ('Playing Texts') I wish to thank Stefan Bown. The musical examples were typeset by Stephen Rockey.

List of Abbreviations

Briefe
Mozart: Briefe und Aufzeichnungen Gesamtausgabe, ed. Wilhelm A. Bauer, Otto Erich Deutsch and Joseph H. Eibl, Internationale Stiftung Mozarteum, Salzburg, 7 vols (Kassel, Basel, London and New York: Bärenreiter, 1962–75). [References in the form 1: 1 cite letter number and line number.]

NMA
Wolfgang Amadeus Mozart: Neue Ausgabe sämtliche Werke, series IX, *Klaviermusik*, Werkgruppe 25, ed. Wolfgang Plath and Wolfgang Rehm, Internationale Stiftung Mozarteum, Salzburg (Kassel: Bärenreiter, 1986). [Also available as *Wolfgang Amadeus Mozart: Neue Ausgabe sämtliche Werke: Taschenpartitur-Ausgabe*, vol. 20: *Klaviermusik*, and as a two-volume sheet music edition.]

Where references to pitches within specific octaves (for clarification or comparison, rather than generically as note-names) are indicated in the text, these are given by Helmholz's system of notation, c′ being 'middle C' on the piano.

Chapter 1

Pretexts

Mozart's piano sonatas form a rich and diverse oeuvre. Yet they remain somewhat in the shade of his concertos for that instrument. Just a handful of the sonatas are at all regularly performed, and they suffer from a mindset that regards them as mere prefaces to the much more rewarding sonatas of Beethoven. One world-famous pianist, in a masterclass for some of my students at Bristol University about fifteen years ago said that Beethoven's sonatas were more rewarding to play than Mozart's because their left-hand parts were more interesting. As with all that pianist's comments, there is a challenge about that remark intended to stimulate further thought, and it was not meant to be derogatory towards Mozart in any way. But it was a bit of a double-edged sword nevertheless, reinforcing for some of the participants on that occasion, I think, the suspicion that Charles Ives was right to pigeon-hole Mozart's sonatas as 'lady finger music'.[1]

I have begun by establishing a context for the sonatas because context is what this study attempts to address in understanding Mozart's sonatas. Performing these pieces requires some prior investigation of their materials, possibly including detailed analysis not only of those materials in themselves (and not just pitches and durations, but also articulation marks, textures, dynamics, tempos …), but also of how they interact with each other to create continuities which the performer might express. That forces one to assess what context(s) are being assumed *a priori* (especially analytical contexts), sometimes with uncomfortable results. Lately, in approaching Mozart's piano sonatas as a music historian and performer, rather than as a theorist, I have regularly been shocked to realise how slender is the *a priori* foundation for what I thought I understood about how the music works.

---

[1]   At first glance, Ives's comment seems thoroughly obnoxious now. He may not have intended any specifically gendered offence, however. The performance of 'genteel' piano music (Mozart's, for instance, with its *apparently* simple tunes above an *apparently* routine and harmonically predictable Alberti bass pattern in the left hand) by ladies was a practice associated with the expectations of a certain social class – entirely normal, rather than freakish. If 'lady finger music' seems offensive today, then the offence is perhaps triggered by a hyper-sensitivity towards a particular context in which, historically, ladies are thought to have been treated as musical inferiors or, worse, wholly ignored (interestingly, though, some of the finest pianists of Mozart's own time – and his best early interpreters – were women). A raft of post-war scholarship, recovering the feminine in every walk of society, has arguably institutionalised that hyper-sensitivity to such an extent that it now has the unintended effect of 'making' offence, rather than taking it. Context has a lot to answer for, and Mozart's sonatas are no exception.

Even though I have previously written about these works,[2] I now see that there is value in approaching these pieces once again, this time with a focus on the plurality of contexts within which they may be understood – and most especially performance contexts.

Understanding Mozart's piano sonatas might mean lots of different things. Whatever it means, it depends on relating them to surrounding and supporting contexts. In my previous study of these works, I attempted to combine reception perspectives with one particular theoretical model derived from contemporary understandings of musical rhetoric. These twin paths towards the music depended critically upon relating historical and theoretical claims to texts (whether autograph manuscripts, first or early editions, or various primary or secondary documentary writing about the sonatas, including the Mozart family correspondence). My approach now is somewhat different, since it invokes performance rather strongly as a tool for reaching an understanding of the sonatas. And a performance is a rendering of a text in a certain way, according to certain conditions. That is not the same thing as a text. In a performance, the text is enacted somehow. It is this context (in a literal sense of doing something 'with the text') that will occupy much of this book.

It seems fitting, then, to begin by establishing a context for myself as its author. I have a passion for Mozart's music that stretches back over 40 years and that originated in early piano lessons. During that time, my attachment to Mozart's music has deepened and has been inflected by my awareness not only of other music contextualizing Mozart's own, but of other arts aspiring to express similar facets of the human condition, and also of philosophical reflections on the music's potential for meaning. Crucially, it has been challenged and developed by fruitful discussions with performers, and in the act of performance. But the root of that attachment has never changed, and that is the physicality of my relationship to Mozart's piano music – how it *feels* (literally) to play it and to express it with ten fingers and two knees (on a fortepiano; and with two feet if one still strives to play these pieces on a modern piano). Primarily, that means not simply playing the 'right' notes (though that helps, naturally), but playing them in an articulate fashion – which is not how I remember being taught to play Mozart as a youngster (it resonates in the memory still: 'legato and cantabile, dear, legato and cantabile ...'). Reflecting on that advice now (I did not, as a child, think to challenge it), one cannot help but consider a context. Why legato, and why cantabile? Well, the answer, in part, is the (ultimately late nineteenth-century Russian) tradition from which my early teacher came, the schooling that she and her teachers in turn had received. Breaking with tradition is bravely to deny a part of one's own identity too, and there was no reason to suppose that a local piano teacher in the north of England would break with tradition in teaching a young boy to play a tiny Minuet in F major K.2 by Mozart on a large and imposing upright piano, probably dating from c.1910. So legato and cantabile it was. I realized none of that then, of course.

---

[2]   John Irving, *Mozart's Piano Sonatas: Contexts, Sources, Style* (Cambridge, 1997).

But what I did realize was that there was some quality contained in this composer's short piece that was lacking in everything else I had learnt up to that point (which was not very much). I doubt whether I played it particularly well, but the utterly joyful experience of learning it, and especially the feeling that it seemed to open up new vistas of musical expression and consequently to call for yet more effort every time I thought I had mastered it, has never left me. Nor would I wish it to.

As a fortepianist who is also a music historian with an interest in reception, I find that the issue of a text to be somehow represented beyond the circumstances of its notation on a page – in written or spoken prose or else in performance – is never far away from my mind. None of the tools I have for doing that can operate beyond the controlling embrace of a context. If I play a sonata by Mozart, then I do so using a particular instrument. I do so in a particular place, at a particular time, either alone or in front of listeners (who will bring their own contexts of expectation to the setting). I choose specific tempos which have consequences for the clarity of passagework, ornaments and textures (as do acoustical factors and the particular instrument). I may attempt faithfully to represent a particular text; or (more usually) to *work with* that text, adding my own humble contributions to the creative act in the form of embellishments, particular profiling of the slurring, staccatos and so forth – the ongoing progress of the articulations through a movement, unfolding in a kind of narrative counterpoint to the actual notes. How much of that is successfully conveyed depends on a huge number of variables constituting the environment within which the music has its being in performance. Reflecting on the ontological status of, for instance, the Andante of Mozart's Sonata in F K.533 and 494 draws into play a range of tools for the understanding, such as:

- Analysis (of tonality, of structure, of motive, rhythm and harmony, and of intellectually constructed patternings such as theme, accompaniment, counterpoint, exposition, development, episode, recapitulation, contrast, closure …).
- Theoretical propositions for how these analyses might operate in a systematically satisfying way (for instance, Schenkerian approaches, or readings influenced by Réti, or the more flexible – and brilliant, though forbiddingly complex – recent typological project of Hepokoski and Darcy).[3]
- The recovery of historical modes of theorizing music, especially from Mozart's own time and involving then-current models such as *Affektenlehre* (by then becoming rather old-fashioned), rhetoric and topics.
- Philosophical perspectives, both recent and from the Age of Enlightenment itself.
- Knowledge of performance practices which have a crucial bearing on the way this music speaks.

---

[3] James Hepokoski and Warren Darcy, *Element of Sonata Theory: Norms, Types and Deformations in the Late-Eighteenth-Century Sonata Form* (Oxford, 2006).

- most crucial of all, perhaps, the *sound* – in particular the realisation that modern pianos are inadequate vehicles for capturing Mozart's musical language and that if we seek as performers to enable an understanding of this language that imposes the barest minimum of historical anachronisms in the listener's way then we should abandon compromise and play Mozart's sonatas on a fortepiano.[4]

None of these operates in a vacuum. Their individual and collective meanings (the way they influence our understanding of Mozart's sonatas) are contextual. And that belief underpins the whole of this book. While some relevant theoretical models will from time to time be discussed in relation to particular cases, this is not a book on theory, and I shall promote no particular theoretical model for understanding Mozart's sonatas. On the contrary, I take a quite empirical approach, drawing especially on performance perspectives as tools for understanding these works.

Performance, I believe, is a vital historical context for analysing Mozart's piano sonatas. Mozart was born into the world of composer-performers, his earliest role-model in this respect being his father, who published a seminal treatise on violin playing in the very year of Wolfgang Mozart's birth.[5] Especially because Mozart was a composer-performer, the creative act of composing such a piece did not end with a notated text but extended yet further into a performance given (often) by the composer himself. Composing extended into performing; both were stages of a work's 'coming-into-being'. That may also be true of later cultural traditions within which Mozart's sonatas have belonged at various times, of course, but the relation is a different one in which the subsequence of performance in relation to the text-cum-work is quite literally that: *sub*-sequent, lower in the hierarchy of values to the authorial intention that the notated text is thought to enshrine.[6] Regarding any one of

---

[4]   Some discussion of the background to such a choice will be attempted in Chapter 6. For now, notice that my recommendation is 'a fortepiano' not '*the* fortepiano'. Whereas the modern piano is indeed a generic machine which presumes to be able to play any and all keyboard repertoire from Scarlatti to Messiaen and beyond in a single recital, the fortepiano in Mozart's day was an instrument still in considerable flux and by no means an entity capable of adequate description by the definite article.

[5]   *Versuch einer gründlichen Violinschule* (Augsburg, 1756), trans. Editha Knocker as *A Treatise on the Fundamentals of Violin Playing*, 2nd edn (Oxford and New York, 1985).

[6]   On the other hand, within traditions of virtuosity that emerged in the early to mid-nineteenth-century pianism, the relationship of performance to composition was curiously inverted, the performance becoming itself a kind of text enshrining the intention of the virtuoso performer which was to astonish the audience with seemingly impossible feats of digital skill. Here the composition recedes somewhat into the background, becoming something of which a 'reading' or 'interpretation' is given by the virtuoso. In the case of Thalberg or Liszt, we are again talking of composer performers, though here the letter of the score counts absolutely: the notation is of a precisely crafted and usually very difficult technical refinement; and in order to be able to reproduce it you have not only to be able to play all the notes, but also to control finely graded dynamics, pedallings,

the sonatas as a definitive statement enshrined in a 'fixed' textual presentation that stabilizes the work, in a way allowing it to be measured (albeit in differing ways, reflecting different analytical systems), is an attitude that somehow diminishes, or even misses altogether, the vital ingredient of provisionality, within which performance as an element of the creative act is crucial. An analytical approach which treats Mozart's sonatas as being hermetically sealed against historical forces that diversely illuminate them for different times and places risks constructing these pieces in narrowly materialistic terms. While such a materialistic approach might be more defensible in relation to works of the nineteenth century that appear to achieve a degree of stability in the course of historiographical narratives such as stylistic development, the tracing of influence, emergent cultures of virtuosity and concomitant hero-worship (placing music history firmly in the sociological sphere) or institutionalization (concert societies such as the Gesellschaft der Musikfreunde, the establishment of professional orchestras at the Gewandhaus in Leipzig or the Concertgebouw in Amsterdam, the professionalization of the discipline of musicology in universities and conservatoires and so on),[7] it is every bit as blunt an object for understanding Mozart's sonatas as a modern concert grand piano is as a medium for their performance.

By contrast, I shall regard Mozart's sonatas as works which celebrate the absence of separation between a creative act of composition and a creative act of performance. Both these qualities originally merged in the person of Mozart himself (his letters from the autumn of 1777 repeatedly refer to his own performances of the early sonatas K.279–84, for instance, and at least the rondo finale of the Sonata K.309 began life as an improvisation in one such performance). If modern-day 'historically informed' performances of these pieces on original or reproduction fortepianos by players such as Andreas Staier, Ronald Brautigam and Robert Levin (which refreshingly attempt to reflect that merging of creative forces) seem odd in daringly situating themselves in the mêlée of creativity, engaging with Mozart's notes as something to be treated as starting-points rather than objects of reverential and passive worship, then that is because of an intervening culture that has little or nothing to do with Mozart's likely expectations, but everything to do with constructing these pieces in the light of later nineteenth- and early twentieth-century attitudes towards art objects and representational practices.[8]

---

legatos, staccatissimos, etc. strictly according to the notated score. True, it is often possible, after much practice, to represent the appropriate effect, but that is not really the point. Faithfulness to the score is the absolute touchstone of the virtuoso tradition.

[7] I am indebted here to the work of Jim Samson, specifically 'The Musical Work and Nineteenth-Century History', in Jim Samson (ed.), *The Cambridge History of Nineteenth Century Music* (Cambridge, 2002), pp. 3–28; and 'Analysis in Context', in Nicholas Cook and Mark Everist (eds), *Rethinking Music* (Oxford, 1999), pp. 35–54.

[8] Among the most familiar paradigms here is that of the 'aura', as characterized by Walter Benjamin in his famous 1936 essay *Das Kunstwerk im Zeitalter seiner technischen Reproduzierbarkeit*; for a recent edition, see Walter Benjamin, *The Work of Art in the*

At the beginning of the twenty-first century, we can all too easily recognize the social contingency of those former attitudes, which, in their train, encouraged the formulation of certain analytical responses to music presuming a stable identity for the Work definitively represented by its notated score (indeed, overtly substituting the latter for the former). Moreover, we can nowadays recognize that Mozart's sonatas epitomize an earlier and contrasting set of attitudes celebrating the fusion of compositional creation and representation in performance: a live, evolving and above all *provisional* activity that inhabits virtually every page of eighteenth-century manuals on performance. Given this scenario, performance emerges not as an adjunct, but as a vital historical context for the understanding of Mozart's sonatas. Exploring performance considerations as strategies for the understanding can therefore help us to recover that vital ingredient of Mozart's sonatas that so precisely defines them as products of the classical age, as opposed to the nineteenth century or later: namely that they are a space in which compositional creation and representation in performance are not separate spheres of activity,[9] but contemporaneous fusions of the creative imagination.

Age of Mechanical Reproduction, trans. J. A. Underwood (London, 2008). According to Benjamin, the identity of the art work inheres not so much in its material properties (for instance, the notes in a composition) as in the sense of awe and reverence that attends its perception (principally the conditions within which it is represented – on a stage framed by a proscenium arch, for instance, raised above the level of the audience, upon which a soloist sits or stands centrally as a focus; or in a handsomely bound printed score with an elaborate title page and perhaps containing a portrait of the composer). The aura is a magical, ritual space into which the perceiver is not permitted to intrude; Benjamin felt that mechanical reproduction freed both art work and perceiver from this stasis. Modern historically informed performances of – say – Mozart's piano sonatas likewise transgress the barrier of the 'aura', substituting the paradigm of creative engagement with the musical material for that of deferential adoration.

[9]   It is not fanciful, I would argue, to draw a parallel between the construct of a work of music existing as a product that is subsequently and separately consumed in performance and the construct of a physical product that emerges from a factory and is subsequently and separately displayed in a shop and ultimately consumed by a purchaser. Such a mindset developed apace in the industrial age of mass production and consumption and may have influenced patterns of musical production and consumption as the nineteenth century progressed. One influential medium for this mindset of separate production and consumption was the musical periodical (for instance, *The Musical Times*, beginning in 1844), in which one could not only read analysis or criticism of music – which tends in any case to configure it as an object whose form lies equally in a musical text or else a literary text that describes it at second hand – but see musical products such as sheet music advertised for sale. Such historical narratives powerfully shape our views of what music is and how it may be understood. Equally, because they develop certain agendas while marginalizing others, these accounts give us a clue as to how music was no longer understood (for instance, performance understood as part of the ongoing creative process in musical composition). Nineteenth-century materialistic views of the music of its own or earlier times are vital to balanced reception histories (themselves essential contexts for

Like analysis, performance relates to a text. We might say of their common characteristics that they each refer to an object. Analysis conceives of that object as something sufficiently fixed in nature as to allow systematic investigation of it according to the chosen methodology, leading to verifiable conclusions publicly demonstrated. The usual presumption of performance is also of a text that is studied and then exhibited to public scrutiny through the agency of the performer. The nature of the object is subtly different in each case, though. A historically-informed performance of a piano sonata by Mozart will pay particular attention to the means by which its vocabulary might be spoken through a creative application of relevant performance practices recorded in contemporary treatises taken alongside the sound world and sound production of – say – a Viennese fortepiano of the 1780s (or, more practically, a good modern copy). Necessarily, then, it will conceive of its object (the text) rather flexibly, incorporating an intellectual grasp and expression of sound as well as notation, viewing Mozart's notation indeed as a basis for negotiation (rather than an end-point to be passively accepted). Its methods of engagement with that object are not by nature systematic, though the process still ultimately results in a public demonstration. It will accept Mozart's notation as a challenge to be engaged with in order to achieve its completion, not as something 'definitive' in the sense that some interpreters have taken it to be, arguably applying a tradition of performance that grew up in the wake of a nineteenth-century construct that Lydia Goehr has so memorably characterized as the 'Work Concept'.[10] Works in this sense achieve the status of icons, objects of definitive generic identity, meaning, value – above all, individuality. According to Goehr, music around 1800 attained a status analogous to that of literature, the visual arts and sculpture in that one might now regard it as a finished embodiment of a musical thought. It changed from being an occupation or skill which was first and foremost a *practice*, leading to no fixed product, to being instead an art form that was ultimately objectified and thus capable of placement within a philosophical arena alongside those other arts that invoked in the beholder the attitude of reverence.[11] That translates, in the sphere of performance, into a conception of the text representing that *Work-with-a-capital-'W'* as being on the one hand definitive in every detail (so the performer must not alter its content at

---

analysis) of course. But they should stand alongside, rather than supersede, contrasting traditions, especially those which offer an appropriately contemporaneous historical context for the analysis of Mozart's sonatas. See Samson, 'The Musical Work and Nineteenth-Century History'.

[10]   See her groundbreaking study *The Imaginary Museum of Musical Works: An Essay in the Philosophy of Music* (Oxford, 1992). Subsequent contributions to this area include Michael Talbot (ed.), *The Musical Work: Reality or Invention?* (Liverpool, 2000), including specifically Reinhard Strohm, 'Looking Back at Ourselves: The Problem with the Musical Work-Concept', pp. 128–52, and Michael Talbot, 'The Work-Concept and Composer–Centredness', pp. 168–86.

[11]   Goehr, *The Imaginary Museum of Musical Works*, pp. 150–60.

all), and on the other as something containing within it a mystery to be revealed. It is revealed in interpretation. The Great Work is interpreted by the Great Performer, who at the same time becomes a kind of custodian for the Work.

Without a doubt, a performance is surely something more than a simple playing of the notes. It presumes an element of communication, of making something happen, a 'public exhibition or entertainment'.[12] But nor is it necessarily synonymous with an 'interpretation'. Sadly, the meaning of 'interpretation' has become entangled for many people with the concept of allusion to an iconic object of reverence (namely the Work Concept): 'So-and-so's interpretation of Mozart (Beethoven, Wagner, Liszt, Mahler, Shostakovich …).' Among the agencies responsible for this state of affairs are the growth of a public concert culture in the nineteenth century and later, the training of performers for a professional career within this culture, radio and CD broadcasting and recorded distribution of music, closely allied to marketing strategies built on the cult of 'greatness', and, crucially, reviewing of concerts and recordings in newspapers or specialist journals. A performance may be an interpretation of this sort, in which case it will typically be hailed in reviews as possessing a quality of wholeness and/or unity which is meant to suggest a profound empathy of the performer with the message of the Work, a capturing of the totality of its expressive purpose. But an interpretation need not be thus. An interpretation of a Mozart piano sonata might take the view that there is no such singular message to be revealed, but that Mozart's notation of the sonata is an attempt at encoding ways in which the classical musical language might be put to work were the piece to be performed. That demands creative engagement from the performer, who is required, therefore, to ask certain questions of the notation, which may by turns be suggestive, prescriptive or proscriptive on the level of the motive, phrase, section or movement. Notational clues may suggest an optimum speed (which in turn may limit or enable both the player's ability to communicate, and the listener's ability to hear certain chord progressions or textures; instruments and room acoustics likewise play a part, of course), or a particular emphasis or impetus relating to a dance metre or *topos*; or it may suggest local or global musical architecture through the separation or interactions of patterns such as articulations and dynamics. Interestingly, differently notated texts of the same piece stemming from different times, places and traditions may offer clues about the contrasting ways in which Mozart's sonatas were represented within alternative historical settings. An analysis of, say, the opening movement of the A minor Sonata K.310 which takes as a starting-point the iconic status of this Work as revealing Mozart's darker side (perhaps even influenced by his mother's illness and death in Paris in 1778), laden with emotional tumult expressed in pithy motivic workings-out, will necessarily be different from one that approaches it as containing rather few

---

[12]   According to Robert K. Barnhart (ed.), *The Chambers Dictionary of Etymology* (New York, 2005), p. 777, this sense is first recorded in English in 1709 in the magazine *The Tatler*. The etymological origin of the term 'perform', according to the same source, lies around 1300: '*parfourmen* to do, carry out go through or render'.

but tellingly placed articulations and dynamic indications that are mainly, but not always, coordinated with shifts of texture and register and suggestive of a particular way of appreciating large-scale structure. Different again would be an interpretation following the arrangement of K.310 published in c.1860 as No. 7 in the series 'Morceaux characteristiques et brillantes' by Cramer & Co. as *Sonate sentimentale, pour le piano-forte ... revisé par J[ohann] B[aptist] Cramer* and preceded by an introductory Adagio by Cramer (1771–1858) himself. Performance as an analytical context is a means both of recognizing and of appreciating the difference between contrasting historical constructs of musical understanding.

So much – for now – for the historicity of performance as a context within this book. What of the history to which that context points? If the understanding (for instance, a specifically analytical understanding according to method) happens 'in context', then a key aspect is its location as a *social practice* – that is, something having a social cause, leaving in its wake a social trace which in turn (as a consequence of its reception) produces meanings that are socially constructed too. The (intellectually imagined) sense of a trajectory behind this process is perhaps defined by the word 'history'. If that is so, then one important backdrop to this study of Mozart's piano sonatas is indeed a historical one, namely a shift in the intellectual construction of sonata form (most typically used in first movements) during the half-century following Mozart's death from something in two parts to something in three parts, the middle part being designedly developmental. The contemporary writings in which that paradigmatic shift was enshrined, and which gave it its authority, will be examined in more detail below. In outline, that progression of thought from Koch through Reicha and Czerny to Marx leaves a social trace of an important revision to the cultural situation of music that occurred in the aftermath of the Enlightenment and which involved the (retrospective) construction of a musical classicism – a language against which the new products of the early nineteenth century might be expressively situated. A two-part concept of sonata form extends the prevailing binary form that had accounted for the design of a tonally-rounded movement within a dance-suite. Thus the pattern of tonal organization that prevails in a two-part conception of a classical sonata form had a social cause: its structure arose within an environment in which the binary form exercised a near-irresistible organizational control, for instance over dance-types as diverse as the allemande, gavotte and gigue, but also over a variety of textures (while sarabandes are typically melodic, with chordal support, gigues tend to foreground imitative counterpoint). The tendency of binary-form movements to 'resolve' dominant-key material from part 1 within the tonic in part 2 is noticeable even within broader ritornello designs, most especially, perhaps, in Bach: one thinks of such works as the first movement of Brandenburg Concerto No. 1 BWV1046, or the first movement of the Orchestral Suite No. 3 BWV1068, or the 'St Anne' Prelude BWV552. That diversity suggests in its turn that the influence of binary-form thinking extended beyond the borders of genre too. Given the ease with which such borders are crossed, one might with justification begin to suspect that genre is not self-defining but socially constructed, the stable binary-form foundation being a social trace of a functional and largely domestic identity for music within a particular political system of values characterized by princely patronage, symbolizing, perhaps, the orderly resolution of individuality within a containing societal regime.

A two-part concept of sonata form extends that thought, expressing on a musical level a perceived generic ancestry of the sonata within the suite, but additionally that it is a social trace of the continued hegemony of patronage (in other words, the genre of sonata does not escape the prevailing political mould). By contrast, the three-part sonata concept may be seen as a social trace of *individuation* in that, by recasting the sonata form as a ground for the statement of material and equally of the working-out of its developmental potential within itself and in relation to its surroundings (sometimes prefiguring a dramatized moment of thematic return), several new and inter-related issues present themselves:

- The impression of an individual working with musical material, of penetrating enquiry into its inner shape and relation to what lies outside it, expressed in an extended development section within the sonata.
- By implication, an aesthetic valuation of the act of expressing such materials and relations which reconfigures the sonata as an art form.
- Finding an appropriate setting for such an expressive act, namely the public recital (rather than domestic entertainment), in which an individual, and perhaps virtuoso, performer acts out this exploration of materials and relations before an audience, whose view is inevitably coloured by this particular mode of presentation.
- Validating these modes of expression in public commentary (in analytical textbooks).

Whether we read a Mozart sonata-form from the standpoint of the two-part or the three-part model, we impart a socially-produced set of analytical meanings for it. Our activity of analysing Mozart's music from these contrasting perspectives is *intentional*, either illuminating some facet of the music or else refining an analytical method in the process. But we are simultaneously behaving *historically* by acting out such analytical practices, leaving behind in the process our own traces within Mozart's texts, glossing in our present interventions what was previously a developing historical identity of Mozart's piano sonatas as it was being steadily constructed in social practices of analysis, c.1775–1830.

In this attempt at 'understanding' Mozart's piano sonatas I will myself leave a social trace, of course. The remainder of this book is organized in two large parts: 'Reading Texts' and 'Playing Texts', with an epilogue devoted to what happens when we listen to Mozart's sonata texts. 'Reading Texts' will attempt to contextualize our understanding of Mozart's piano sonatas by selectively investigating reading strategies; the reception perspectives offered by some early editions; and some specific case-studies. 'Playing Texts' will first look at Mozart's sonata texts from the point of view of strategies for their expression in performance and how these affect, enable and characterize our understanding; secondly, performance practice; and finally sound. All in all, this is an empirical survey, though it will draw upon a framework of influences which include the writings of Gadamer, Jauss, Iser and Fish,[13] coalescing in a perspectival understanding that, I hope, respects the responses of a variety of readers (analysts, performers, listeners) in coming to a provisional view. That my view remains provisional is the only claim I would defend in this book, since Mozart's texts of his piano sonatas are themselves provisional, gloriously resisting theory's cold, constricting grip. If we accept these wonderful pieces as texts that release, rather than confine, the imagination of the reader, we may instead aspire to embrace them.

Why not Theory?

This is expressly *not* a theoretical study of Mozart's piano sonatas. I have no pretensions as a theorist, and while some theoretical claims and applications may illuminate Mozart's music, they do so only indirectly (see below) and mostly tell us about the workings of the particular theories concerned. That observation is not intended to be arrogant, or dismissive of recent trends in music theory (on which I am certainly not qualified to pronounce). Rather, it is offered as a caution against equating theoretical rigour with musical understanding. Experience of Mozart's music – especially, experience of it in performance – tends to deepen one's intuitive awareness of its unsystematic nature, and equally to reinforce one's sense of the futility of expecting systematic theoretical approaches to contain its wilful capriciousness. Empirical approaches (especially, these days, positivist ones) will leave some unsatisfied and thirsting for a methodologically rigorous demonstration of what or how Mozart's music might mean anything at all or communicate that meaning.[14] A book that is empirical and unashamedly positivist probably therefore requires some contextual placement *vis à vis* theory. First, let us consider a definition:

---

[13] Hans-Georg Gadamer, *Truth and Method*, 2nd rev. edn, trans. J. Weinsheimer and D. G. Marshall (New York, 1989); Hans-Robert Jauss, *Aesthetic Experience and Literary Hermeneutics*, trans. Michael Shaw (Minneapolis, 1982); Wolfgang Iser, *The Act of Reading: A Theory of Aesthetic Response* (Baltimore, 1978). Stanley Fish, *Is There a Text in this Class? The Authority of Interpretive Communities* (Harvard, 1980) and Stanley Fish, 'Interpreting the Variorum', *Critical Inquiry*, 2 (1976), pp. 465–85.

[14] For two recent examples of critical approaches to Mozart's instrumental music that succeed extraordinarily well in illuminating his compositional craft through the application of common-sense, expressed in clear English prose and without resorting to theoretical abstraction see Simon P. Keefe, *Mozart's Piano Concertos: Dramatic Dialogue in the Age of Enlightenment* (Woodbridge, 2001), and *Mozart's Viennese Instrumental Music: A Study of Stylistic Re-Invention* (Woodbridge, 2007).

> **Theory** [a] supposition or system of ideas explaining something, esp. one
> based on general principles independent of the facts, phenomena, etc., to be
> explained ... the sphere of abstract knowledge or speculative thought.[15]

Central to this are two related conditions: first, the notion of a mental construction
following from the observation of something, and according to which the structure
of that something (whether its external appearance or its internal workings) is
represented schematically; and second, that *something* which the theory purports
to explain. Separately, each of these conditions is easy and reasonable to justify. It
is when we consider their necessary relationship which the activity of music theory
entails that problems develop. Principally, the problem is, I would claim, that theory
requires a text upon which to operate (since it cannot properly deal with the music
that lies behind that text, but only with the encoding of that music in a notated
score). We can imagine several theoretical explanations of how a passage such as
the central development (bars 40–55) of the first movement, Allegro con spirito,
of the D major Sonata K.311 might be organized conceptually, and that these may
offer contrasting and intriguing insights according to, say, Schenkerian principles
of voice-leading or thematic relationships and derivations tracing back to the work
of Rudolph Réti. Such explanations might go a long way towards illuminating the
visual, textual appearance of the music that fills this space within the movement.[16]
But their concern is capturing and demonstrating in a systematic form a mental
construct prompted by detailed consideration of the textual material. Purely as a
mental abstraction, we can well imagine the following thematic similarities:

- Between bar 40 and bar 38.
- Between bar 38 (descending quaver pairs connected by slurs) and bar 17
  (ascending slurred quaver pairs).
- Between bar 42 (just a single slurred quaver pair on beat 1, repeated on
  beat 3) and bar 40 (four successive slurred quaver pairs, descending, rather
  than ascending).
- Between bar 40 and bar 43 (constructed thus: two bars filled with successive
  slurred quaver pairs – the second placed in an initially dissonant harmonic
  context; one bar in which that succession is fragmented with single slurred
  quaver pairs on beats 1 and 3 (and the shape inverted); and a final cadential
  succession returning to the original descending form, and transferred to the
  bass), and a sequential repeat of all this in bars 44–7.
- Between the four-bar phrase successions of bars 40–43 and 44–7 and the
  two-bar phrase successions in bars 48–51.

---

[15]   J. B. Sykes (ed.), *The Concise Oxford Dictionary of Current English, Based on the
Oxford English Dictionary and its Supplements*, 6th edn (Oxford, 1980).

[16]   For instance, a view deriving from Réti might go beyond the rather obvious
relationship of this section to the final two bars of the exposition and look for an origin of
the slurred quaver pairings within the secondary idea which enters at the upbeat to bar 17.

- Between either bars 40–43 and 44–7 or bars 48–51 and bars 52–3, in which there is a further phrase contraction to just a single bar.
- Finally, there is the further relationship between the slurred quaver patterns, viewed as thematic units and a perception of this section as a teleological process of successive repetition and contraction as we approach a point of cadential arrival on B minor at bar 55.

All these relationships stem from the abstract notions, 'independent of the facts' (facts here being this particular passage and its material contents), that the nature of the material Mozart uses (not just here, but generally within the classical musical 'language') might, either in his intentions or else in our imagined processes for organizing experience, lend itself to local similarities in appearance (in this case, thematic similarities), and, moreover, that this potential might be deliberately harnessed in order to create the semblance of organization, both on an immediate local level and structurally. In other words, this is an example of applying a theory – a 'supposition or system of ideas explaining something, esp[ecially] one based on general principles independent of the facts'. But the business of theory here is sight, not sound. The system of organization that it constructs mentally traces back only as far as the notated score, not to the music of which that score is a visual representation. Interestingly, the etymology of 'theory' traces back to the Greek *theōríā*, meaning contemplation or speculation, deriving from *theōrós*, a spectator, in turn deriving from a combination of *théā*, a view, and *horós*, seeing or looking.[17] The *degree to which* bars 44–7 are sequential with bars 40–43 (the notion of sequence, of course, existing purely as a concept lying within 'the sphere of abstract knowledge or speculative thought', a way of expressing the apparent relatedness between the phrases as notated) exists differently in theory as compared with practice. In theory, the sequential relation is either there or not.[18] In performance, you might express that degree of relatedness in several subtly different ways, for instance in the shading-off of any one or more of the individual slurred pairs, especially, perhaps, the pair occurring against the *fp* chord in bar 45, compared with the pair in bar 41. Or you might point up this relationship by pausing slightly on the first beat of bar 45 in order to highlight its particular dissonance more prominently at the start of that sequential phrase. Or you might decide that, after all, *fp* in this context means not a local accent but a gradual decrescendo throughout the bar, in which case the degree of sequential relatedness between bars 40–43 and 44–7 might be determined in performance by shading off each of these bars differently as the phrase unfolds.

What all this seems to suggest is that ultimately, what theory engages with is a particular textual representation of Mozart's piano sonatas, enabling us *as*

---

[17] See Barnhart (ed.), *The Chambers Dictionary of Etymology*, 'Theory'.

[18] Sequence within a diatonic tonal context assumes a certain amount of acceptable intervallic adaptation, or adaptation to the chord-spacing, within the analogous passages, of course.

readers of his texts to construct models of how these might function as schematic structures on a variety of complex and sometimes interacting levels. But we should remember that it is his *Texts* that are being modelled in various ways into theoretical explanations, not his *Music*. That is a seemingly obvious point perhaps, and is not meant to denigrate theoretical approaches to Mozart's sonatas, from whatever perspective. What I am attempting to contextualize here by relating theory to text as opposed to music is first, the absence from this book of any particular theoretical modelling of Mozart's sonatas; and second, the schematic grounding for all of my own purely empirical observations, claims and suggestions relating to the sonatas in subsequent chapters. We now need to devote some attention to the status of these texts, these *things which stand for his music*, and which are in turn the objects of our theoretical engagement.

Text as textus

The Latin *textus* means 'the wording of anything written ... [a] written account, content, characters used in a document ... style or texture of a work'.[19] The text, in this sense is a repository for our thought or imagination (including musical thought and imagination), enabling its transmission, presupposing accuracy (of transmission, but also of an ability to read what is notated) and requiring a social transaction in which what is notated is regarded as being in some sense a 'true' or 'authentic' presentation of the original thought which caused it to be recorded at all, and what is subsequently read is read sincerely by whoever decodes it for whatever purpose. The text here is the material content (or, at least, stands for it in a notated presentation), and upon this objectified form we base our understanding of Mozart's sonatas, according to one or other strategy. One such strategy would be the 'organic' model, in which a sonata's material content is understood as an objectified whole built from inter-related parts. The nature of these relationships is claimed to be so strong – indeed intentional on the part of the composer – and so deeply embedded in the score itself that meaning derives from (depends on?) the capacity for one motive to be explicitly related to another. For such a mode of understanding, not only is the functionality of the composition reducible to this level, but the goal – success? – of the analysis is to perform this very act of reducibility. Moreover, the analytical approach is attractively – seductively? – verifiable in 'hard' terms (one can exemplify by extracting brief snippets from the score that motive -z- is a transposition of -y- which in turn is an inversion of -x-). The concrete exhibition of a densely-packed network of material inter-relationships suggests that Mozart's music is amenable to such systematic modes of representation.

But it may be taking things too far to claim of this bricks-and-mortar approach that this is what the composer actually meant or did when he composed his piano sonatas; that the text on the page displays a particular kind of work whose meaning

---

[19]   See Barnhart (ed.), *The Chambers Dictionary of Etymology*, 'Text'.

resides specifically (or even exclusively) in the close inter-relation of its thematic materials – still less that the exhibition is simultaneously a guarantor of value. A consequence of such an approach is that the role of analytical enquiry becomes very precisely configured indeed, namely to demonstrate how Mozart's 'musical language' functions effectively as a *language* to the degree that seemingly diverse thematic patterns distributed across a sonata-form movement, as here, are actually all derived from common stock. But that restricts both Mozart's musical language and the practice of analysis.[20]

Such is the traditional way in which texts have been viewed within literary theory and theatre studies (and within the study of music too, to a large extent). That model has historically presupposed that the text (for instance of a play) is primary and that a performance on the stage is a (subsidiary) agency for its realization. The text is conceived as having a primary value through its assumed stability (for instance, within a tradition of source filiation and editorial methodology) and permanence (as an entity to be represented), whereas the performance is only one of many that might be imagined which, coupled with its transience, establishes it lower down the scale of relative values. The same separation between a 'primary' text and a 'secondary' performance can easily be imagined in music.

More recently, theatre practitioners have departed from these traditional assumptions in an attempt to disengage performance from its historically dependent relationship to text. The notion of a 'text' is extended beyond the written or spoken word to include the use of movement, of the body or bodily gesture, sound, light and space on the stage – a paradigm shift that has liberated performance from its subservient role.[21] Instead, the activity of performance is established alongside the text as an equal element within the whole theatrical experience in its capacity to communicate as a social practice (rather than simply a means of representation and expression). This important critical and aesthetic revaluation has given performance a vital hermeneutic role too. Performance becomes a tool for illuminating possible aspects of meaning within a work.[22] Because this book is

---

[20] For a further exploration of this territory, see my review of William Kinderman, *Mozart's Piano Music* (New York and Oxford, 2006) in *Music and Letters*, 89 (2008): 467–72.

[21] A valuable recent volume exploring similar trends in musical performance and performativity is Anthony Gritten and Elaine King (eds), *Music and Gesture* (Aldershot, 2006).

[22] Recent relevant literature includes Philip Auslander, *From Acting to Performance: Essays in Modernism and Postmodernism* (London, 1997); Marvin Carlson, *Performance: An Introduction* (London, 1996); Colin Counsell and Laurie Wolf (eds), *Performance Analysis: An Introductory Coursebook* (London, 2001); Adrian Heathfield, *Live: Art and Performance* (London, 2004); Mike Huxley and Noel Witts (eds), *The 20th Century Performance Reader* (London, 2002); Nick Kaye, *Postmodernism and Performance* (London, 1994); Nick Kaye, *Site-Specific Art: Performance, Place and Documentation* (London, 2000); Peggy Phelan, *Unmarked: The Politics of Performance* (London, 1993).

not a manifesto for any particular theory, though, I shall not abandon the historical view of the text as something grounded in historical or analytical perspectives in favour of these more recent practices of text-as-performance, but will draw on both traditional and performative models as ways of attempting to understand Mozart's piano sonatas. Texts are central to an understanding of these works, and they will be treated in this study under two main headings: 'Reading Texts' and 'Playing Texts'.

Text as téchnē

So much for the traditional boundaries inhabited by the *textus* and their transgression in recent performative practices. There is a special etymological sense, too, in which text goes beyond the level of documentary repository. *Textus* derives from the verb *texere* (to weave) and 'is cognate with Greek *téchnē* art, skill, craft'.[23] Here, the text is at one and the same time the object through which representation occurs and the artistic entity so represented (what you might think of as the *action* and also the *documentation of that action*). How might this be true for Mozart's piano sonatas?

We might suppose that on the level of musical *process* we find simultaneously action and documentation of that action (in the notation). Consider again bars 40–55 of the first movement of K.311. The Réti-inspired theoretical construct of thematic inter-relationship and derivation as a connecting thread for this passage considers pitch as the essential ingredient in a succession of slurred quaver pairs. But what of those slurs? The slur is a gesture: both an action and a documentation of that action. Slurring is a behavioural constant here, present throughout the entire passage and unchanging in its intended effect, namely a slight accentual emphasis on the first note of the slur and a decrescendo onto the last note[24] (in this case always the second of a pair). Although the precise management of the relative accentual and dynamic gradations between adjacent quavers and adjacent quaver pairs (whether in purely local successions or on the level of the bar or phrase) lies beyond the power of a text to document, what is documented here beyond a doubt is the presence of the gesture of slurring as a factor in the narrative shaping of these bars. Assuming for the moment that we are reading Mozart's text as a remarkably consistent and continuous succession of one kind of gestural behaviour (namely the slur) and that it functions here not just as a document, but also as an act, we might infer from a departure from this textual consistency a

---

[23]   Barnhart (ed.), *The Chambers Dictionary of Etymology*, 'Text'.

[24]   For instance, Leopold Mozart's *Versuch einer gründlichen Violinschule* (chapter 7, part I, § 20) states that 'the first of such united notes [i.e. connected by a slur] must be somewhat more strongly stressed, but the remainder slurred on to it quite smoothly and more and more quietly'; see *A Treatise on the Fundamental Principles of Violin Playing*, pp. 123–4. See also Antony Pay, 'Phrasing in Contention', *Early Music*, 24 (1996): 291–321.

change also in function and moreover that beyond that point the text can no longer be regarded as *téchnē* but once more as the more usual *textus*. That would imply a kind of 'modulation' (in the sense of a transition from one behavioural mode to another). In the case of this rather extraordinary sonata-form movement, in which themes from the exposition recur in reverse order in the recapitulation, such an event might be of significance in determining the point at which the recapitulation begins. Certainly there is a transition following the cadence in B minor at bar 55 into a different kind of behaviour (the quaver slurring now departs the stage, being replaced temporarily by a different process of three successive cadential steps, each on the half-bar), and perhaps therefore a case for regarding the reprise of the theme originally from bar 28 (in bar 58) as a new beginning of some kind, either within what we construe as a development section or else on a larger level of sonata-form recapitulation. This is a particularly thorny issue, in fact, one recently described as 'the most structurally problematic of Mozart's piano-sonata movements'.[25]

---

[25] See, for instance, Hepokoski and Darcy, *Elements of Sonata Theory*, p. 262. In footnote 11 on that page I am taken to task for claiming that the recapitulation ('Reprise') begins at the upbeat to bar 58 (which, *pace* Hepokoski and Warren Darcy, is not an upbeat to bar 59, as the three-beat slur confirms). For them, the recapitulation begins at the upbeat to bar 79, the prior appearance of substantial elements of the exposition within the subdominant region (including a subsidiary theme and a transitional passage), belonging instead to the 'developmental space'. Be that as it may, what neither Hepokoski and Darcy nor I adequately reflect in our varying interpretations of where the recapitulation begins is the extent to which this sonata movement is inflected by episodic rondo procedures. The return of the opening theme at bar 99 is not, of course, a conclusion the first time it is heard, for its cadential resolution proceeds back to a repeat of bars 40–55 (as usual, Mozart specifically marks the repeat in his autograph); bar 99 for the second time sounds, therefore, somewhat like a concluding rondo statement; indeed, from a rondo perspective, the successive reappearance of the thematic material of bar 28 at bar 58, once again at bar 91 and twice more if the repeat is observed also provides strong grounds for thinking of this movement more in terms of a structure comprising episodes and reprises than as a sonata form (or even as a hybrid of two typologies, with a diversion during the statement of the secondary theme beginning in bar 79, as Hepokoski and Darcy claim).

Part I
Reading Texts

Chapter 2
Contexts

Perhaps the first thing we do with a text (including a text of a Mozart piano sonata) is to *read* it. But of what does reading consist? We might, for instance, read a text to ourselves from the score as an act of introspection, in silent contemplation of the symbols on the page, forming as we go a mental illusion of the sound it could make if performed. Or we might 'read aloud', in other words, play it (not necessarily the same thing as a performance, but a conversion of the symbols into sounds nonetheless). In either case, we might take the text at 'face value', assuming that its content is simply what we see on the page, nothing more, nothing less, and imagining that the crotchets and quavers included there function as quantifiable materials making up the piece. Or we might 'read between the lines', taking notice of the potential for certain details in the score to function not quantifiably (as if a fixed statement of material fact with no meaning beyond its simple presence) but suggestively, as a foundation for creative interpretation. We might read Mozart's texts as representing a structure consisting of parts relating to wholes (for instance, we might read a particular passage against a mental construct such as sonata form, explaining it in terms of its transitional function between important key-areas. Or we might read a particular passage in narrative terms: for instance, a developmental episode running its own course by means of a particular handling of theme and or tonality, while also postponing or preparing for the return of refrain material (by temporarily withholding its arrival, the episode justifies its presence). Narrative may be local or long-range. We might read a sonata-form movement as falling into two or three sections, drawing, respectively, on eighteenth- or nineteenth-century principles of *Formenlehre* (and whichever approach we take, our choice betrays an interface of analytical and historical reading).

In most of the above reading scenarios, we are reading *interpretively*. We derive a meaning (not necessarily an authorial intention) from what we read, applying, consciously or not, agendas deriving from our own experience as previous readers. Reading in this sense is an active, not passive, discipline. Reading the text of a Mozart sonata conflates several different kinds of activity including:

- Linguistic competence.
- Notions of authorship and the construction of meaning.
- The authority of readerships (reader-response criticism).
- The application of memory and experience.

The assumed linguistic competence of a reader approaching a particular text underlies a relatively traditional, structuralist view of how texts work. When we decode a particular text – the central developmental section in the first movement of Mozart's A minor Sonata K.310, for example – we might imagine that Mozart's text requires of us competence in how the musical materials encoded within his text work: that is, how they combine on local and extended levels to create intelligible designs. Those designs might be regarded as being built upon well-defined inter-relations among types of material such as themes and harmonic progressions (but also processes for handling and discriminating among these, such as contrast and repetition). In such a system, the implication is that the material and perhaps also the processes have objective status and are manipulated and recognized according to socially embedded sets of conventions. The social aspect is important; agreed meaning (here referring to agreement about the identity and function of the materials) emanates from a shared competence to which the text appeals and which enables meaningful responses to that text's structures and practices. Within the development section of K.310, for instance, the material content that the text portrays (according to a structuralist perspective) includes a characteristic dotted-rhythm pattern (recognizably derived from the opening bar of the movement by means of its rhythm and its repeated single pitch) situated at the top of the texture and driving the music forwards thematically; and the counterpoint within the right hand featuring an extended pattern of suspended dissonances and resolutions over a pedal point. The processes include repetition of the theme and dotted-rhythm pattern and transposition through carefully regulated tonal degrees, forming a circle-of-fifths progression founded successively on B, E and A (and leading to a breach in this texture when the music arrives at D minor); from this point to the return of the opening theme there are different applications of dotted rhythm (fragmentation of the original theme), circles of fifths at quicker harmonic pace and texture-inversion. Note that the derivation of a structural meaning for this section of the movement from these particular contents and processes is possible because of a shared agreement about their identity and function, and not because of some absolute property inhering in the materials themselves. Even the status of a theme or rhythm pattern underlying this section results from the reader mapping a socially conceived set of values onto the text being read. Evidently the text's nature is something more complex than just 'being there'.

Following Roland Barthes's essay 'The Death of the Author' in his collection of essays *Image, Music, Text*,[1] modernist schools of critical thought have tended towards the view that a text is divorced from its author, and that any meaning it is believed to have arises in relation to other texts, 'intertextually', rather than 'essentially'. Drawing on the work of Ferdinand de Saussure,[2] modernist criticism

---

[1]   Roland Barthes, 'The Death of the Author', in *Image, Music, Text*, trans. Stephen Heath (New York, 1977), pp. 142–8.

[2]   Ferdinand de Saussure, *Cours de linguistique générale*, ed. C. Bally and A. Sechehaye with the collaboration of A. Riedlinger (Lausanne and Paris, 1916); trans. W. Baskin as *Course in General Linguistics* (Glasgow, 1977). On Saussure generally, see C. Sanders (ed.), *The Cambridge Companion to Saussure* (Cambridge, 2004).

has developed the idea that meaning in a written text derives not from single words but from their local grammatical contexts (that is, syntactically) and also contextually, namely in relation to other words that mean something else. Meaning thus emerges not from defined and isolated quantities, each possessing a certain and fixed identity, but instead relationally, within a 'field of meaning' in which individual terms acquire meaning in part by being different from other terms with which they come into close local contact. Texts continue to have meaning(s), but they do so not through authorial intention, but instead through their existence within a culturally acquired framework of language use. The language within which a text is written operates as a reservoir of cultural understanding through which the meaning of any particular text arises. So a text such as a Mozart piano sonata acquires a meaning not through Mozart's supposed 'intention' but because it operates within the culturally configured and understood framework that is the classical musical language. It has meaning because the individual terms it contains operate within (and against) the prevailing conventions of the classical musical language, in relation to what we might call an 'archive' (existing in our training, experience and memory) of cultural meanings within that language, in relation to the habits of that language use (for instance, opening gestures such as those found at the start of K.284 or K.309; rapidly shifting and contrasting textures; and cadence-formation …), even in relation to previous specific pieces. Its meaning is necessarily *intertextual*, residing between the totality of texts comprising the classical musical language, as a result of interconnections across boundaries, rather than in isolation, and existing within a play of language.

What authority do readerships possess, against which they construct meanings for texts (including Mozart's texts)? Reader-response criticism claims that texts do not exist without a reader and, by implication, that a text acquires meaning through the purposeful act of reading (and consequently, interpreting) it. Thus it is in the act of reading that the writer (composer) is empowered to speak. Reading is a transaction between the author and the reader mediated by the text. Different readers will render certain aspects of a work more significant than others, according to the particular experience brought to the act of reading. This may be a memory of a particular melodic figure, harmonic progression, texture, procedure of thematic or harmonic development (such as a 'circle of fifths'), or a transition or preparation for climax or return; in such cases meaning stems from an interpretation that refers to a network of associations personal to that particular reader. Thus the reader is an agent in the production of a text's meaning, which suggests in turn that the activity of reading a text is, in a sense, a performance. That performative act of reading (decoding) Mozart's texts can be either private or public, and in each case the text exerts some degree of control over the reader, defining boundaries within and outside which meaning either is or is not sustainable. For Hans-Robert Jauss,[3] the reader brings an individual 'horizon of expectations' ('Erwartungshorizont') to the act of reading. The horizon is formed from experience of reading works from the

---

[3] Jauss, *Aesthetic Experience and Literary Hermeneutics*.

period in question (the classical period, for instance), and it is from this perspective that each reader reads. Alternatively, reading might take place according to a shared set of values, in which case the interpretation is socially rather than individually situated (this is what Stanley Fish argued was an 'interpretive community'; see below). For instance, I might take a somewhat controversial (bizarre, some would say) approach to identifying the location of the recapitulation within the first movement of the D major Sonata K.311, reading it in a way that seems to some critics – Hepokoski and Darcy, for instance – to be extreme in its departure from a shared view within broader scholarship that Mozart is simply reversing the order of his themes within the recapitulation here. Their alternative view is that this movement is evidence of migration en route between two different species of sonata cycles that they itemize in their treatise, and is also a departure from the common ground inhabited by the 'interpretive community'. In all these cases, though, the act of reading, because it engages with the notated signs to be found in Mozart's text – because it *interprets* – is a performance out of which meaning flows. Underlying that meaning is a tension between the subjectivity involved in a private act of reading and the presumed objectivity attaching to a 'community' view. For instance, an interpretive community that examines the first movement of K.311 from a Schenkerian analytical perspective will tend to privilege certain features such as voice-leading and nested hierarchies of dissonance–consonance relations, and it is not at all obvious how such benchmarks may be regarded as subjective, whereas a view that treats the arrival of a particular texture associatively as a sign of recapitulation might be felt to lack objectivity. Both extremes are evidence-based assertions, though one tends towards an objective, the other towards a subjective rationale.

In reading Mozart's sonata texts, then, it seems that we navigate between subjective and objective approaches. It is only really when we regard these two as opposing poles that (usually negative) ideological conflicts arise, according to which one or other approach is felt to be inappropriately theorized, for instance, or else too narrowly materialistic, lacking a sufficiently social arena of mediation. In fact, aside from an ideological interpretation of these two terms, we can apply them cooperatively and fruitfully as agencies in our investigations. This is implied in the writings of Hans-Georg Gadamer and more recently Wolfgang Iser. For Gadamer,[4] the interpreting of a text catalyses in the reader a 'fusion of horizons' in which the text's historical setting is articulated according to the reader's own background of experience and association. Though readers are enmeshed in the particular history and culture that shaped them, their particular historical or cultural approach to a text encoding a style of the past is neither a barrier to interpreting and understanding that text, nor indeed a threat to correct understanding, but instead a creative force. Gadamer's 'fusion of horizons' is effectively the bridging of a historical or cultural gap in the act of reading. Within such a 'fusion of horizons', the text being read acquires both subjective and objective characters. The nature

---

[4]   Gadamer, *Truth and Method.*

of the terms constituting the text is not separate from the act of reading (i.e. having objective status) but is identified in the course of the transaction (i.e. subjective). Yet the focus for the present reader's attention is something from the past. However strongly the interpretation stems from the present reader's historical or cultural perspective, a residue of the past persists, constructed within the act of reading, to be sure, but constructed from *something other than* the act of reading in itself. Some feature of the text – however its terms are identified – always constrains and controls the reader's response. That quality of constraining a reader's activities is addressed in the writings of Wolfgang Iser,[5] for whom the text creates its own possibilities for interpretation by a reader whose field of travel is set by terms operating within the text. The reader's viewpoint may adapt as he or she wanders through the text, seeing its terms from different and changing perspectives, but only within limits. Again reading is a transaction between subjective and objective approaches: the text may be interpreted differently as one moves through it (one is expected to negotiate creatively with the text in the act of reading), but that which is being interpreted nevertheless exerts limitations on the interpreter. Iser's notion of a text is a produced effect arising in the act of reading. Once again reading becomes a *performance*.

Bearing such varied perspectives in mind in our reading of Mozart's sonata texts, let us proceed to read a selection of these texts, unconstrained by strong ideological positions and positively welcoming a blend of subjectivity and objectivity in our interpretations.

Gadamer's pivotal study *Truth and Method* problematizes conditions of being. Clearly, since we may perceive an object (whether a physical one, such as a printed musical score, or a conceptual one, such as a piece of music like the Andante of Mozart's F major Sonata K.533 and 494), it must enjoy an existence of some sort ('Truth'). But when we come to examine, and attempt to explain, the conditions of its being (its ontology), we do so by applying tools such as description, analysis and synthesis – viewing the object in terms of shape, size, relation of parts to wholes, similarities and discrepancies, recognizable and measurable patterns ('Method'). These are our ways of perceiving it, but they are all conditional. They do not inhabit the object perceived but are categories applied in the act of our perception. Consequently, the object becomes an intellectual construct: our formation of its possibility of existence stands within categories of perception innate to us, not it. We hold it together. Moreover, we do so historically. Gadamer claimed that our consciousness is a 'historically produced' phenomenon ('wirkungsgeschichtliches Bewußtsein') and that when we perceive, we do so contextually, within the particular history and culture that have shaped us. When we interpret an object such as a text, the process engages a 'fusion of horizons' ('Horizontverschmelzung') in which we discover ways in which the text's history articulates with our own background: 'The horizon is the range of vision that includes everything that can

---

[5]   Iser, *The Act of Reading.*

be seen from a particular vantage point.'[6] In other words, the work becomes a meeting-point for the different reception perspectives from which it is approached (for example, history, analysis, performance and listening). Furthermore, its identity assumes a social context in which meaning stems from the reader's negotiation with the text (similar in kind to what happens when one is involved in a conversation – though the particular language uses may be different in each case), rather than mere passive acceptance of it. Readers and listeners interpret the text's meanings from the particular standpoint of their personal cultural backgrounds and experiences. Consequently, the text's meaning rests not within the text itself, but within the interface between the text and the reader. Meaning is completed through interpretation, constructed as a consequence of Method, rather than inhering *a priori* or *ad infinitum* as a Truth. A further consequence is that a text (including a musical text) may be regarded as a performing art in which each reader (be it an analyst, performer or listener) becomes actively *involved*, creating a unique, text-related performance of that text in the act of interpretation, a performance which, while absolutely requiring that the reader understands the musical language within which the 'conversation' takes place, will relate strongly to the cultural background of that individual.

By extension, the meaning of a specific text may be socially, rather than individually, constructed when a group of readers shares a cultural background, driving a similar interpretation of that text. The literary theorist Stanley Fish has examined how one's interpretation of a text is to some degree dependent upon shared intellectual values which he attributes to an 'interpretive community' (to which one belongs or subscribes somehow – whether consciously or not). Instead of the individual reader making the text, he or she acts as an agent for a community view to which he or she belongs. Meaning therefore derives from a sociological claim towards interpretive authority.[7] The meaning of a text within such a sociological framework is limited to a particular set of cultural assumptions underlying the meaning and interpretation of individual terms and their inter-relation within the text. Being part of an interpretive community gives the reader a particular way of reading a text. Applying that does not negate the possibility of authorial intention, but locks the text (and the possibility of its meaning *something*) into a relationship with a contextually enlightened reader. Meaning stems from the relationship between text and reader, and does not inherently and exclusively reside within the text.

Gadamer's claim for the reader as creative rather than passive respondent has its own contextual origin, of course. He was a pupil of Martin Heidegger at the

---

[6]   Gadamer, *Truth and Method*, pp. 302–5 A similar point is made by Hans-Robert Jauss, for whom readers bring a certain mental framework – what he calls a 'horizon' of expectations ('Erwartungshorizont') – to the practice of reading; in other words, a historically dependent perspective from which an individual reader forms an interpretation at any given time in history.

[7]   Fish, 'Interpreting the Variorum', pp. 483–5.

University of Freiburg. Gadamer's own mindset cannot have escaped the influence of one of the twentieth century's most powerful and controversial thinkers on ontology. Most provocatively, Heidegger's quest for a grasp of what it is to *be* rested on an appeal to 'authority' or 'authenticity' – of fully inhabiting the present in which we live.[8] For most critics, that claim was fatally undermined because Heidegger's own living of it expressed itself politically in the Nazism that swept through the University of Freiburg in the 1930s, which he never renounced to the end of his life. But the principle itself retains a nobility of thought that goes beyond the merely political. I would like to propose that in the realm of music, performance carries that authority – that *Urempfinding* – that Heidegger claimed. Performance is something that exists in relation to a text. But it is a particular expression of that relationship that exists continually in the present: an *inhabiting* of that present. It is a spiritual action – a full believing in the Truth of the object in the moment of its presentation to perception, free from the categorical description and classification that is Method. That possibility encourages me to believe in turn that performance as a tool for understanding may offer a perspective of value in trying to understand Mozart's piano sonatas. That is why I have not hesitated to invoke it in this book, even though, through the medium of print, it will lose some of its immediacy.

---

[8] Principally to be found in Heidegger's groundbreaking *Sein und Zeit* (1927), in *Martin Heidegger: Gesamtausgabe*, vol. 2, ed. F.-W. von Herrmann (Frankfurt am Main, 1977); trans. John Macquarrie and Edward Robinson as *Being and Time* (London, 1962).

Chapter 3
Horizons of Understanding

K.533 Andante: History and Form

As an example of the constructed nature of the object suggested by Gadamer's 'fusion of horizons' (or Fish's 'interpretive communities') we might take the Andante of Mozart's F major Sonata K.533 and 494 (1788). The Andante, in B flat, is in sonata form. How we understand the outline of that form (its overall shape, in other words) derives arguably from the method by which we attempt to discern it rather than from an essential existence of a form within the music. Let us take two contrasting 'horizons' in exploring the movement.

We might view it as a two-part form, its section divisions (each marked by repeats) consisting of bars 1–46 and 47–122. Such a conception would accord with most late eighteenth-century descriptions of sonata form as exemplified, for instance, by Heinrich Christoph Koch's *Versuch einer Anleitung zur Composition*.[1] Koch focuses on the harmonic rather than the melodic aspects of the form in which a key is established and then departed from (part 1); that broad gesture is then counterbalanced by part 2, which restores the tonic. part 1 is regarded as a single action; part 2 as subdivided:

> … the opening allegro … comprises two sections and these may be played with
> or without repetition. The first section contains just a single main period and is
> the outline for the symphony ['symphony' meaning here the symphony genre
> as such, but simply a movement]; thus, the main melodic phrases are sounded
> here in their original sequence and later some of these are subdivided … The
> second section contains two main periods; the first is diverse in its structure
> [what we would perhaps term the 'development'] … The [third and] last period
> of the opening allegro holds in the main to the home key, and normally begins
> with the [opening] theme in this key, but sometimes starts with another main

---

[1]   Heinrich Christoph Koch, *Versuch einer Anleitung zur Composition*, 3 vols (Leipzig and Rudolstadt, 1782, 1787, 1793). The treatment of sonata form is found in vol. 2, p. 223, and vol. 3, pp. 301 ff. and 344 ff. Other contemporary accounts configuring sonata form as a two-part design include Johann Portmann, *Leichtes Lehrbuch der Harmonie, Composition, und des General-basses* (Darmstadt, 1789), p. 50; Georg Löhlein, *Clavier-Schule*, 5th edn, rev. J. G. Witthauer (Leipzig and Züllichau, 1791), pp. 182 ff.; Francesco Galeazzi, *Elementi teorico-practici di musica* 2 vols (Rome, 1791, 1796), vol. 2 (1796), pp. 253 ff.; and August C. F. Kollmann, *An Essay on Practical Musical Composition* (London, 1799), p. 5.

melodic idea instead … Finally, the second half of the first main period which [had previously] continued after the dominant-phrase in the fifth [what we would think of as the 'second subject' in the dominant key], returns in the home key and this is how the allegro ends.[2]

Koch makes no prescription here as to the number of themes to expect, simply stating that part 1 will replace the tonic key with a contrasting, and usually related, key and that part 2 will (i) begin by exploring that new tonal space and (ii) conclude with a restatement of the earlier material (perhaps in its entirety, but not necessarily so), holding this time to the tonic. While the generating element of the form here is the contrast of tonality (key area) rather than theme, eighteenth-century sonata-form theory did not overlook the importance of melody. Koch, in his description quoted above, explains that part 1 contains the plan of the movement, outlining the principal themes in their 'original sequence', and that in part 2 the last period will normally start with the opening theme, and implies that material formerly in the dominant will recur in the tonic in a form allowing that fact to be recognized. Moreover, he assumes a degree of thematic contrast within such a movement when he notes the arrival of a singing theme ('cantabler Satz') when the dominant key arrives.[3] A more explicit view of melodic content is given by Francesco Galeazzi (1796), who refers to a characteristic passage ('passo caratteristico') in the new key, preceding the cadence in that key 'introduced for the sake of greater beauty, towards the middle of the first part'. Normal practice in the second main section would be to coordinate the return of the tonic with a restatement of the opening theme, 'but if one does not want to make the composition too long, then it shall be enough to repeat instead the Characteristic Passage transposed to the fundamental key'.[4]

The distinction between tonality and theme as formal generator here is really one of degree. Theme is not irrelevant by any means; it is simply subordinate to tonality. Theme was crucial to the concept of the form, but primarily on the level of local contrast, articulating, perhaps, the stages in the outline, rather than as a determinant of its outline. That was the business of tonality.

---

[2]   Further on this, *Heinrich Christoph Koch: Introductory Essay on Composition – The Mechanical Rules of Melody, Sections 3 and 4*, ed. and trans. Nancy K. Baker (New Haven and London, 1983), pp. 199–200.

[3]   Koch, *Versuch*, vol. 3, pp. 304 ff., 364 and 385. Also his *Musicalisches Lexicon* (Frankfurt am Main, 1802), p.746 notes that musical material should consist of a main thought and related accessory thoughts which, by means of contrast, will reinforce that main thought, though in such a way that the unified *Affekt* of the movement will not be disturbed.

[4]   *Elementi*, vol. 2, pp. 253–60. This translation is from Bathia Churgin, 'Francesco Galeazzi's Description (1796) of Sonata Form', *Journal of the American Musicological Society*, 21 (1968): 181–99 (at 195–6).

Looking at the Andante of K.533 in this light, we might foreground the following:

Part 1 (bars 1–46)

- Establishment of the tonic, B flat major, bars 1–10, consisting of a contrasting antecedent–consequent phrase pair (bars 1–4, 5–10) and leading to an imperfect cadence on the dominant, F in bars 9–10.
- A subsequent modulation into the dominant involving sequential progressions in bars 19–21 and reinforced by another imperfect cadence in that key at bars 21–2.
- Further exploration of the new tonal space by means of sequence (bars 23–4, 25–6, 27–8) and chromatic harmonies (bars 28–30) resolving into a strong perfect cadence finally and firmly establishing the dominant, F major, in bar 33.
- Introduction of a contrasting theme coordinated with the arrival of the dominant key, F major (Koch's 'cantabler Satz', Galeazzi's 'passo caratteristico'), and confirmation of this new key area by regular periodic phrase and cadence patterns (bars 35, 37, 38, 39, 41–2, 43–4, 45–6), including a prominent chromatic digression to A flat and a so-called Neapolitan preparation (bars 40–41) for the perfect cadence at bars 41–2).and subtle chromatic enhancement of the bass line's cadential motion as the end of the section is reached (bars 44–5).

Part 2 (bars 47–122)

A (bars 47–72), characterized by:

- Diversity of key, touching on D minor and G minor in bars 47–59, though without ever firmly establishing these (and leaving ambiguous the status of the A major chord in bar 59); bars 60–70 move exclusively in sequence, hinting at keys (G minor? in bars 61–2, C minor? in bars 64–5, F minor? in bars 67–8) but always in transit, withholding any cadential resolution, making the eventual arrival of a dominant seventh chord in bar 71 (timed with the arrival of the highest pitch, E♭‴) seem a dramatic point of furthest extension, heralding the return of the tonic, B flat major at bar 73.[5]
- Diversity of texture, counterpointing an adaptation of the movement's opening melodic and rhythmic idea against a row of sextuplet semiquavers (bars 47–50, inverted in the following phrase and continuing in phrases

---

[5] Kollmann, *An Essay on Practical Musical Composition*, p. 5, describes this part of the sonata form as 'consisting of digressions to all those keys … besides that of the fifth (or third) [dominant or relative major]; and being the place for those abrupt modulations or enharmonic changes which the piece admits or requires'.

of half length to bar 59); this extreme contrast of note-values between the hands is followed by a passage more uniformly in quavers, and in a thicker texture confined to octaves, sixths and thirds (always two notes per strand). The breaking of this texture at bar 71 (along with the cascading arpeggio covering almost the whole of Mozart's five-octave instrument, and the protracted silence of bar 72) is coordinated with the arrival of the preparatory dominant seventh, reinforcing the over-riding importance of tonality in the structure.

B (bars 73–122):

- Return of the tonic key, coordinated (following Koch's normal procedure) with the return of the opening theme (bar 73).[6]
- The restriction of the tonal space following the reprise of the opening theme to the tonic area, B flat (conforming to Koch's prescription that 'the second half of the first period which followed the dominant-phrase in the fifth, is repeated in the main key and with this the allegro ends'). The repeat is not literal – though seen as a relation to the 'plan' set out in part 1 it is simply a repeat – but incorporates texture inversion at bar 82, beat 3 – bar 85 (compare bar 10, beat 3 – bar 14) and bars 91–4 (compare bars 23–7); the omission of bar 14, beat 3 – bar 18); and the addition of a coda (bars 114–22).[7]

That is a possible representation of Mozart's Andante. It is not what the Andante actually *is* – merely how it might seem when interpreted according to one historically situated collection of analytical precepts comprising a 'fusion of horizons'. Alternatively, we might pursue an interpretation of this movement from a different 'horizon', a three-part view of the sonata form that developed after Mozart's death, and which assumed an increasingly prominent role in nineteenth-century music theory as developed by Reicha, Czerny and Marx.

The idea of sonata form as comprising a division into three sections, rather than two, was established gradually during the 1820s and 1830s. In the second volume of Antoine Reicha's *Traité de haute composition musicale* (1826) the large-scale division of a sonata-form movement is expressed as a 'grande coupe binaire'.[8] But it is already clear that Reicha is really conceiving the layout in *three* parts, since he elaborates at length on a central section of such movements devoted

---

[6]   Likewise Galeazzi, *Elementi*, states that at the reprise in long movements, 'the true Motive [namely, the opening theme] in the principal key is taken up again' (Churgin, 'Francesco Galeazzi's Description', pp. 195–6).

[7]   Koch, *Lexicon*, p. 345, explains the addition of a coda as a device giving a fuller sense of conclusion to a movement.

[8]   Antoine Reicha, *Traité de haute composition musicale*, 2 vols (Paris, 1824–6), vol. 2, p. 300. Further on the 'grande coupe binaire', see Peter A. Hoyt, 'The concept of

specifically to the 'développement' of the musical materials. His famous diagram of the 'grande coupe binaire', for all that its designations are 'Première partie ou exposition des idées' and 'seconde partie' (the latter subdivided as 'Première section' and 'seconde section'), is visually displayed on three diagrammatic levels, the middle level of which ('Première section de la seconde partie') is specifically to do with development and has two functions: 'DÉVELOPPEMENT principal, en modulant sans cesse' and 'ARRÊT sur le dominante primitif'. By contrast with earlier theoretical descriptions, Reicha's account gives considerable weight to thematic functions ('MOTIF ou première idée mère; PONT ou passage d'une idée à l'autre; SECONDE IDÉE MÈRE dans la nouvelle tonique; IDÉES ACCESSOIRES et conclusion de la première partie'), giving rise to a degree of tension between a bipartite tonal concept and a tripartite thematic concept, within which *development* of theme is crucial.

The practice that Reicha attempts to encapsulate in his 'grande coupe binaire' is one in which, following the exposition of the thematic materials at the start of the movement, their subsequent development was so significant an act as to require a dedicated section in which to dissect these materials, minutely examining their individual and inter-related functions and potentialities. That process of close inspection completed, the rest of the movement functioned as a modified restatement of the exposition material (albeit now understood in a new light), but aimed at convincing tonal closure towards the end of the movement (the 'PONT' of the 'première partie' appearing as 'Quelques modulations passagères avec les idées du pont', and the 'SECONDE IDÉE MÈRE' as 'Transposition de la seconde tonique dans la tonique primitive, avec des modifications'). Thus Reicha's 'Seconde section' of the 'seconde partie' (which we would typically understand as a recapitulation) balances the tonal exploration of the 'Première partie ou exposition des idées' and 'Première section de la seconde partie' (our exposition and development). Among the particular ways of treating the material of the 'Première partie ou exposition des idées' he lists developing ideas, fragmenting them, presenting them in different ways and in various interesting combinations, and producing out of these same ideas effects that are unexpected and novel ('développer ses idées, ou en tirer parti (après les avoir faites précédement entendre), les présenter sous différentes faces, c'est les combiner de plusieurs manières intéressentes, c'est enfin produire des effets inattendus et nouveaux sur des idées connues d'avance').[9]

Seen in relation to Koch's account above, in which there was no attempt to prescribe what the composer should do with the materials of part 1 of the binary view in the first section of part 2 (i.e. immediately after the central double bar), the range of procedures outlined by Reicha in his *Traité* represents a substantial conceptual shift. All in all, it is overwhelmingly clear that, within Reicha's 'grande coupe binaire', there lurked a three-stage pattern of exposition, development and

'Développement' in the Early Nineteenth Century', in Ian Bent (ed.), *Music Theory in the Age of Romanticism* (Cambridge, 1996), pp. 141–62.

9   Reicha, *Traité*, vol. 2, p. 240.

recapitulation, which was steadily to become the norm for nineteenth-century conceptions of sonata form. Carl Czerny's translation of Reicha's *Traité* into German, published in 1834,[10] may well have been influential in promoting the idea of a three-part sonata form comprising a central development framed by sections which stated and restated materials whose nature was coalescing as objectified and measurable entities with classified and separated functions ever more suitable for the thematic manipulation expected within the development section.[11] This is the layout codified a few years later in volumes 2 and 3 of Adolph Bernhard Marx's *Die Lehre von der musikalischen Komposition, praktisch-theoretisch*, in which 'sonata form' appears to have been used terminologically for the first time.[12]

Marx inherited a conception of the sonata form in which the external shape seemed ideally wedded to the internal content. The concept of a three-part progression within a sonata-form movement:

statement–development/conflict–restatement/resolution

becomes for Marx an epistemological tool for justifying the organic growth of musical materials such as themes and phrases from fundamental particles or

---

[10]   As *Vollständiges Lehrbuch der musikalischen Composition*, 4 vols (Vienna, 1832–4). Reicha's *Traité* appeared as vols 3 and 4 in 1834.

[11]   Reicha was not the first to classify thematic and phrase functions, of course. Joseph Riepel (*Anfangsgründe zur musikalischen Setzkunst*, 1752–68), Koch (*Versuch*) and Joseph-Jérome de Momigny, *Cours complet d'harmonie et de composition*, 1803–6) among others do so. The difference in Reicha is not one of degree so much as one of effect. The earlier authors tend to view the resulting categories within the expressive context of musical rhetoric as a means of showing pedagogically how the underlying affective nature of music (which appears as a spontaneous whole) may be represented categorically in terms of discrete parts interacting with each other in order to make up the expressive whole. Koch, *Versuch*, vol. 1, p. 4, specifically comments that music 'expresses feelings through the relationships between the notes'. His terminology in the *Versuch* is an attempt to express those relationships. For Reicha, by contrast, categorization supports an overt process of dissection into components – building, perhaps, on the sophisticated analytical hierarchies introduced in his *Traité de mélodie* (1814): the 'grande' (or 'petite') coupe binaire' (or 'ternaire'), containing several 'périodes', which in turn contain two or more 'rhythmes' or 'membres'; and finally the 'dessin', the smallest unit. While the principle of categorization is similar (and though Reicha's terms might at first glance seem interchangeable with 'Satz' or 'Einschnitt' in Riepel or Koch), it is not aimed at explaining expressivity, but is rather a blueprint for construction, representing the systematic logic with which melody is built. It is not without significance that Reicha describes his analyses (of the opening of the finale of Mozart's 'Hunt' Quartet K.458 in *Traité de mélodie*, p. 61, and his Planche 46, mus. ex. B3), for instance) as 'décomposition du thème'.

[12]   Leipzig, 1838 and 1845 respectively; see vol. 2, pp. 482, 497; vol. 3, p. 195. For a partial English translation see Scott Burnham (ed. and trans.), *Musical Form in the Age of Beethoven: Selected Writings on Theory and Method* (Cambridge, 1997).

motives. Main and subsidiary themes of a sonata-form movement[13] are designed such that they are suited to being pulled apart into their constituent units within the central development section, whose rationale within the whole is precisely as an arena within which this action may take place. Within Marx's theoretical model, content and its formal expression are not only in equilibrium they enable each other, as the following two excerpts show:[14]

[1] A middle section (interposed between the first and last sections of the sonatina form [which Marx had described in the previous section of the treatise]) is indispensable to the sonata form; it must be in three parts ... the second [middle] section must hold fast to the material of the first section.

[Die Sonatenform kann einen mittlern Theil (zwischen dem ersten und letzten der Sonatine) nicht entbehren, sie muss dreitheilig werden ... muss der zweite Theil der Sonatenform den Inhalt des ersten Theils festhalten.]

[2] Fundamentally, the second section in a sonata form, which is pre-determined, brings in no new material.

Consequently, it must occupy itself with the materials of the first section, [*viz.*]

- with the principal theme
- with the subsidiary theme
- by the same token with the closing theme

or else with one or two of these themes, or even with all of them.

[Der zweite Theil, das steht bereits fest, erhält in der Sonatenform in Wesentlich keinen neuen Inhalt.

Folglich muss er sich wesentlich mit dem Inhalte des ersten Theils,

- mit dem Hauptsatze
- mit sem Seitensatze
- auch wohl mit dem Schlusssatze

---

[13]   Which Marx famously described as 'Hauptsatz' and 'Seitensatz', the latter being the 'Weibliche' (feminine) in relation to the 'Männliche' (masculine) opening. For a subtle reconsideration of Marx's intended meanings, see Scott Burnham, 'A. B. Marx and the Gendering of Sonata Form', in Ian Bent (ed.), *Music Theory in the Age of Romanticism* (Cambridge, 1996), pp. 163–86.

[14]   These two excerpts are from the 5th edn (Leipzig: Breitkopf & Härtel, 1879), vol. 3, pp. 221 and 225 respectively.

beschäftigen, und zwar entweder nur mit einem, oder mit zweien dieser Sätze oder gar mit allen.

Applying the three-part model, the Andante of Mozart's K.533 and 494 might appear thus:

Exposition (bars 1–46)

First subject (bars 1–22?):

The first subject is an antecedent–consequent design, bars 1–4 being answered by bars 5–10. While asymmetrical (4 + 6 bars) on the level of the phrase, it may easily be resolved into a succession of two-bar segments, the antecedent consisting of 2 + 2 bars, the consequent of 2 + 2 + 2 bars. There is also an element of complementarity, the upbeat scansion of the consequent contrasting with the antecedent. Within the consequent, there is already the suggestion of a thematic approach to phrase extension, the cadential approach phrase of bars 8 and 9 being derived from the right hand's falling-step quaver pairs, b♭'–a' and c''–b♭', in bar 6. In the repetition of the opening theme which follows (bars 11–21), there is a further illustration of this tendency towards thematic building-blocks: the material of bars 18–22 may be interpreted as consisting entirely of repetitions and transpositions of falling-step quaver pairs derived from bar 16 (and ultimately, from bar 6). Incidentally, such an approach to interpreting the surface continuity presumes that some value is attached (whether in the composer's mind or the analyst's) to unification of musical space – interrelation between themes and indeed specific derivation of thematic elaborations from underlying motives being purposeful elements of design.

Transition (bars 23–32?):

Following the arrival at an imperfect cadence on the secondary dominant, C in bar 22, is the restatement of the opening theme in the dominant key at bar 23 to be regarded as the 'second subject' (in which case, we would have an example of monothematicism)? Or is this the beginning of the 'transition', connecting the first subject group to the second subject group? Thematically, there is nothing conclusive to guide us either way, since sequential repetition is characteristic both of thematic statement and of modulatory process. The dissolution into chromatic harmonic progressions in bars 28–30 and the subsequent return to diatonic cadential writing perhaps convinces us that bars 23–32 are transitional, and that the F major theme announced in bar 33 is the 'true' second subject.

Second subject (bars 33–46):

Assuming that to be the case, this section is actually a 'second subject *group*', since it consists of two dominant-key themes at bars 33 and 42, the latter serving a closing function. The initial second subject once again displays a tendency towards motivic extension, its sextuplet line actually being generated 'from within' by repetition and transposition within bar 34 of the interval patterns of bar 33, beat 3.

In summary: the exposition, when viewed from the thematic standpoint, is strongly suggestive of a compositional approach in which concrete musical ideas (identifiable patterns of intervals, specific pitch-orderings, rhythms and lengths) might have a dual function, either as something to be stated in their own right or else as progenitors for further elaboration. While the conventions of good part-writing, harmonic progression and tonal succession are still essential, they occupy a secondary place to composition as *thematic* process. This process will become even more significant in the development section proper, as we shall see.

Development section (bars 47–72)

This section is quite clearly segmented into two thematically distinct parts, each of which is notable for its concentrated, even obsessive motivic working-out. The two segments display similar techniques of elaboration, principally repetition and sequential extension of figures which are isolated from their original exposition context and objectified as motivic 'cells' used as building blocks. Examples:

- Beginning at bar 47, the first four notes of the Andante are separated from their original four-bar melodic profile and reconfigured as a generative pattern positioned at the start of a chain of two-bar sequential periods (later involving texture inversion).
- The spun-out sextuplets in counterpoint to this cell are internally modelled from threefold repetition within each bar of a six-note pattern (in itself a development of the similar generation of the right-hand line beginning at bar 34).
- The first five notes of the themes beginning on the upbeat to bar 5 (in sixths) and bar 7 (in thirds) are similarly detached in bars 60–72 and extended sequentially and in chromatic harmonic progressions, avoiding cadential repose and creating a deliberate instability, contrasting with the diatonic original, which served to mark out the tonic, B flat, clearly in the Andante's opening phrase.

In each of these cases a short and specific succession of pitches of finite length is treated as a unit (a 'cell') from which, by repetition in a fairly strict intervallic relation, longer segments are derived. Moreover, these are not just any motivic cells, but are each drawn from a kind of 'memory bank' of material stated near the beginning and thus describing a particular kind of relation of parts and wholes in which the identity, status and function of certain surface attributes trace back in organic fashion to one or two fundamental roots.

Such thematic inter-relation can be straightforward or more complex. For instance, the opening of the development section (bars 47–59) refers back to two points of the exposition: the texture is clearly enough derived from the transitional pattern of bars 23 ff., though the precise shape of the filigree passagework is derived from the sextuplets of the second subject (bars 33 ff.). The continuation beyond this point combines in counterpoint the patterns of bar 5 and bar 7, which were originally successive points along a melodic line. By uniting diverse elements of the exposition material in novel combinations and exploring previously unrealized potential of the earlier thematic content (including harmonic and textural potential), thematic process creates a narrative logic for the unfolding of this section and conforms to early nineteenth-century models of development.

Recapitulation (bars 73–122)

In terms of its thematic content and ordering, the recapitulation largely replicates the exposition, Mozart's adjustments following the reprise of the opening theme ensuring that the continuation remains in the tonic area, as follows:

- Mozart retains the repeat of the main theme (bars 83–6; compare bars 11–14), though he inverts the texture and introduces a new contrapuntal strand.
- He subsequently omits the material of bar 14, beat 3–bar 18, perhaps because it played an extended role in the development section, and continues instead with a downward transposition of bars 19–22, ending with an imperfect cadence on the dominant, F.
- Allowing for the texture inversion of bars 91–100, the music then proceeds exactly as in the exposition until bar 114, from which point the original cadence is replaced by a coda returning to the sextuplet idea introduced in the development section.

Beyond the straightforwardly factual listing of materials, procedures and functions within the Andante, what these two contrasting accounts show is that since both of them are possible, defensible explanations of the piece, that piece cannot exclusively inhere in either account. Instead, what the Andante *is* arises afresh in each new interpretive encounter. Its text is a partner within the encounter, but not the whole story. The Music is not the Score. Whatever it is, it becomes in that encounter. I wrote earlier of one important consequence of Gadamer's 'fusion of horizons', in which we actively engage with a text in a performative act. The text is not frozen symbols on the page but something that objectifies a state of existence for the piece that only comes alive – and comes alive differently – whenever such a performative act of interpretation occurs. The differences involved here are primarily the contrasting interpretive perspectives (the 'fusion of horizons': in this case, the two-part and three-part analytical models for understanding sonata form), but also the reception perspectives – in this case, not only the historical situation for those two-part and three-part models, but also our implication within the act of applying them: for instance, our motivation for doing so, which could be a desire to understand historical processes; or to understand analytical systems; or to perform the piece; or to listen to it – or prepare someone else to – in a particular way. The objectified text potentially acquires a plenitude of identities from the performative act. Those identities are both historical and contemporary: we too leave behind a trace of our particular social context, a context from which a meaning for the text arises as a by-product of our negotiating with it in interpretation.

K.310 Allegro maestoso: Ethics and Pedagogy

Having introduced the notion of a 'fusion of horizons' in a fairly formalistic way, reading the Andante of K.533 as being implicated in a historical succession of approaches to understanding sonata form between c.1785 and c.1835, let us now turn our attention to a different work and to different horizons: the opening Allegro maestoso of the A minor Sonata K.310 (composed in Paris in the summer of 1778), which inhabits the intersection of late eighteenth-century and early nineteenth-century theory and piano pedagogy. Such an encounter raises, as we shall see, some important ethical considerations in relation to what and how we understand (and what we subsequently do about that).

As we have seen, by 1826, Antoine Reicha, writing in his *Traité de haute composition musicale*, describes sonata form in a way that presumes the separation of different functional categories, principally the outlining of thematic material and its subsequent treatment. Among the particular ways of treating the material he lists developing ideas, fragmenting them and presenting them in different ways and in various interesting combinations, producing out of these same ideas effects that are unexpected and novel.[15] His conception of musical form presumes a kind of organization according to which large, externally recognizable shapes are built from small, internal parts (typically themes) which fit together in certain regular and describable ways. Such a model reflects a certain mindset in which everything must be viewed as part of a hierarchy in order to make sense (perhaps reflecting, in turn a class-tiered conception of society, or a private household with 'everything in its proper place'). In encouraging a particular way of viewing the subdivision of a whole movement, Reicha's model promotes expectations that material (themes, harmonies, patterns of recurrence and contrast and so on) will behave in certain ways. Conversely, it encourages prejudice and bewilderment when things do not apparently conform. And that inevitably prompts consideration of ethical perspectives.

We have already seen that Reicha's model, for all that it advocates still a 'grande coupe binaire', is but a hair's breadth away from a three-stage division of the sonata form since it foregrounds a separate process of development acting as a conceptual grounding of the structure as a whole. What precedes it must logically be a statement (that is, our 'exposition'); what follows it is a modified restatement;

---

[15]   Reicha, *Traité*, vol. 2, p. 240.

and in between these two lies that centrally located process of thematic dissection and reconfiguration. That model conditions our appreciation of the music crucially – not just structurally, but also in terms of material identity. Among its *a priori* assumptions, perhaps the most fundamental is that material will be firstly stated, and secondly developed according to certain processes. Consequently, when we approach the music from this analytical perspective, the choices we make in selecting appropriate material properties for discussion are determined not by any essential qualities residing in that musical material, but by the parameters of the model. Naturally, our appreciation (and that of our readers and/or listeners) is profoundly affected by this. Hence this situation raises an ethical dimension too. By 'ethical' here, I mean that we act in knowledge of two things:

- That we possess the power of choice.
- That the consequences of exercising that choice resonate beyond the *event of choosing*.

So when we choose (either as readers or as players) to apply Reicha's thematically based 'statement–development' model retrospectively to Mozart's sonata forms, we behave in a certain way that should involve first of all the acknowledgement of responsibilities. Most obviously, we are choosing to apply a model developed 40 or 50 years after the music was composed, and in the face of alternative theoretical models known to exist from the composer's own lifetime and against which his music might have been understood, or even conceived. That choice, while perfectly defensible (on the grounds that it could illuminate certain aspects of Mozart's music that the bipartite model of, say, Koch, misses), nevertheless requires some mediation. First and foremost, Reicha's sonata form needs to be understood as a socially located model. On one level, it may be understood teleologically, that is, as a marker on the route to a fully-fledged tripartite model that was ultimately established in the theory of Adolph Bernhard Marx described previously, a model strongly influenced by the sonata forms of mid-period Beethoven. Important organizational properties of Beethoven's piano sonatas (Op. 22, or the three sonatas of the Op. 31 set, for instance) are indeed well served by an analytical model grounded in thematic statement and developmental process. Evidently, the sense in which analytical theory reflects and attempts to account for recent and contemporary compositional practice during the first three decades or so of the nineteenth century is healthy and positive, and possibly representative also of a keen historical awareness of stylistics among theorists (many of whom were also active as musical practitioners, of course, most notably Carl Czerny). On another level, the model was clarified during a period in which musical life in Europe became stabilized as a concert culture increasingly dominated by the notion of canonic masterworks on the one hand, and on the other by virtuoso performers. The former suggests a normative approach to musical understanding and its dissemination in print (whether in theoretical textbooks or periodical literature of the time); the latter focuses on the individuality of musical utterance, privileging dramatic statement of surface detail and physical – indeed, strongly visual – struggling with material and its technical demands in the maelstrom of self-expression before an astounded audience. Both these embodiments of concert culture rest crucially upon the separation of musical statement and musical process that underlies sonata-form theory as it was evolving during the early nineteenth century.

In what follows, I will consider some ethical implications of applying such a sonata form model to the opening movement of Mozart's A minor Piano Sonata K.310 (1778), and most especially the implications for our understanding of its central 'development section', highlighting the potential distortion of Mozart's discourse that privileges a dialectical process of thematic 'statement and development' representative of an individual struggle for self-expression, to the exclusion of other features (harmonic and textural, for instance). Such a reading has ethical implications for the performer too, encouraging the player to behave in a certain way towards Mozart's material, promoting yet further choices, each with its unique ethical consequences (especially for the listener).

When we choose to apply Reicha's statement-process model to the opening Allegro maestoso of K.310, this positions us in a particular way with respect to Mozart's music. In particular, we instantly focus our attention upon the relationship between thematic content and its subsequent developmental usage. Part of that relational equation concerns the suitability of the material for developmental treatment, which is immediately to view it as if its configuration were specifically *designed* for developmental purposes – that is, not as something that 'is', but as something with the capacity to 'become': something whose justification rests in its potential futures, rather than its present. So, for instance, we might explain the 'development section' (bars 50–79) insofar as it either utilizes material from the preceding exposition or exposes possible re-imaginings of it through the kinds of processes Reicha lists. Our focus is on ways in which Mozart reveals the potential 'becomings' of the 'progenitor' theme (actually just the first two bars of the movement, since his development, seen from this perspective, uses only that thematic fragment and no other exposition material whatsoever). Specifically:

- *Developing the material* (Reicha's 'développer ses idées'): the opening theme (bars 1–2) reappears in its original disposition (in terms of intervallic shape, rhythm, length and texture) at the start of the development (bars 50–51), aligning itself now to the relative major key, C. The continuation beyond this point likewise maps retrospectively back to bars 3–4, though from bar 53 the tonality diverts towards an augmented sixth chord (C–E–G–A♯/B♭) extended by arpeggiated patterns unrelated to the main theme, functionally preparing for the resolution harmonically onto B major at bar 58 (a key structural dividing point in the development as a whole). This tonal diversion might also be read as one of Reicha's instances of 'producing novel and unexpected effects' ('produire des effets inattendus et nouveaux sur des idées connues d'avance'), although it emerges only indirectly from the progenitor theme.

- *Fragmentation* (Reicha's 'En tirer parti'): the extended central section of the development (bars 58–69) is founded wholly on the rhythmic aspect of the progenitor, which it sets in a new texture of fundamentally three-part counterpoint in the right hand over a decorated semiquaver pedal point. Only the first three beats of the progenitor (minus its grace note) remain intact here, and three-quarters of the length of each stage in a threefold harmonic progression underlying this passage is now devoted to imitative interplay of a dotted quaver–semiquaver pattern, probably inspired by bar 1 of the progenitor theme, though it now outlines a suspension chain. Successively, this fragmentation of the progenitor (bars 58–61, 62–5, 66–9) energizes a particular tonal series of 'circle of fifths', from B to E, E to A, and A to D minor. The novel textural and tonal setting amounts to Reicha's *presenting from different perspectives* ('les présenter sous différentes faces') in the sense that the dotted quaver–semiquaver aspect (alone) of the progenitor has been isolated and reconfigured according to a particular textural and tonal process. The third and final section of Mozart's development (bars 70–9) is thematically founded upon yet a further fragmentation of the progenitor: in bars 70–71 (whose pattern is replicated throughout the remainder of this passage) only the semiquaver–crotchet rhythm from beats 2–3 of the first bar of the movement remains, now surrounded laterally by a cadential trill figure and texturally by a continuation of the running left-hand semiquavers (now outlining a harmonic pace in regular minims). From bar 74, the texture is inverted, leading back through E to the recapitulation of the opening theme in the tonic at bar 80.

Understanding the development section in such terms has significant implications for performance. Should a player choose to shape the interpretation of these 30 bars accordingly, we might expect such an interpretation to highlight prominently the 'journey' of the progenitor motive, especially its rhythmic aspect. Since its dotted element is the principal feature that undergoes developmental treatment here, the player might focus on characterizing that element, slightly exaggerating its profile (over-dotting, perhaps), conveying perhaps something of a march-like character, or else exploiting Mozart's few dynamic markings for maximum effect, especially from bar 58 onwards, where the re-entry, *fortissimo* in A major and in high register, offers the opportunity to convey a frantic chase towards a climax. The textural balancing of this central circle of fifths would certainly favour the right hand dotted figures in counterpoint, underplaying slightly the whirling left hand semiquavers, except perhaps for the low octave repercussions on beats 1 and 3, in order to provide a relentless metronomic pulse against which to mark out a distortion of the dotted figures. Once the progenitor motive becomes utterly fragmented at bar 70, such a reading might convey that ultimate stage of the process by treating the dotted semiquaver value almost as a grace note, purposely overemphasizing its intervallic profile (springing upwards), especially once it has become an octave leap from the bass (bars 74–7). Whatever the precise interpretational choices, the effect of such a performance on the listener is clear: this section (and by extension, the movement of which it is a part) acquires a metaphorical dimension; it must be *representing something*, and grasping that something is the imaginative responsibility of the listener, who is impelled to respond (it is a mighty struggle of man against the elements, of the individual striving for expression of his inner angst; the brave hero – represented here by a virtuoso pianist – taming brute forces ...). Indeed, such a hypothetical reading might be rather appropriate (even historically so, and certainly attainable) when played on an Erard or Streicher pianoforte of Chopin's or Schumann's time, as if a recreation of Mozart performances in the 1820s or 1830s. The particular performance setting will, naturally, be crucial to the effect; a large, metallic modern concert grand positioned on a stage in a resonant concert hall seating thousands will naturally tend to favour the hypothetical account given above over a domestic rendition in front of a few friends played on a Stein or Walter fortepiano of Mozart's day. But my point here is not to denigrate some performance settings over others, for each obviously has its own advantages and disadvantages; nor is it to pontificate about the merits or demerits of a preference for Mozart on a Stein or Walter as opposed to a Steinway Model 'D'. The point is this: the situation of the performer and of the listener in the above hypothetical account demonstrates that the choice to apply Reicha's sonata-form model to this movement by Mozart is an *ethical* choice because *it resonates beyond the event of choosing*. It is insufficient to claim that ethics is irrelevant to such a choice, which is simply a private matter involving an individual, and has no consequence beyond his or her own purely private desire to understand Mozart's music. For even if that person's encounter with Reicha's theory and Mozart's music remained for ever entirely private, then that person's solitary playing of and/or listening to this music (perhaps just in the imagination) would still have been occasioned by the original choice, and would remain its disenfranchised and mute agencies.

If, as performers, we choose to be guided instead by the truly binary model of Koch in approaching this passage, contrasting possibilities present themselves. These too have ethical consequences.

As we saw earlier, Koch's description of the sonata form notes that '[t]he second section contains two main periods; the first [i.e. whatever immediately follows the central double bar, typically called the "development section"] is diverse in its structure.' Koch focuses strongly on the harmonic, rather than the melodic, aspects of the form in which a key is established and then departed from (part 1); that broad gesture is then counterbalanced by part 2, which restores the tonic. He makes no prescription as to how the 'diverse structures' opening part 2 of his conception might be organized, either melodically or harmonically, but it is clear that one of its roles is to contextualize the fact that by the end of part 1 the tonic key has been replaced by a contrasting and related key. This is done by exploring that new tonal space before establishing a return to the old tonic. Neither does Koch attempt to prescribe what the composer should do with the materials of part 1 in the first section of part 2, and in this respect, the range of developmental procedures outlined by Reicha in his *Traité* represents a substantial conceptual shift over the course of little more than a generation.

Koch, like Reicha, speaks indirectly to the performer. If his account is applied to the central section of K.310, there is no direction to attend primarily to the 'working-out' of thematic or motivic material (put another way, the player is not responsible above all else for representing that crucial constructive process in the performance – the section simply offers 'diverse structures'). This section is characterized by:

- Diversity of key, beginning with a restatement of the opening theme in the relative major, C, soon diverting to a chromatically altered form playing with the ambiguous tonal lie of an arpeggiation swinging back and forth in the treble before cascading downwards and resolving onto B major (dominant of the dominant). Bars 58–69, as explained above, traverse a three-stage sequence, leading to D minor (bar 70), from which point a further sequence is played out, resolving ultimately via a pivotal dominant preparation on E (from bar 74) to the tonic, A minor (bar 80), coordinated with the return of the opening theme.
- Diversity of texture, in which we are presented successively with theme and chordal accompaniment; rapid semiquaver arpeggiation; three-part counterpoint over a *moto perpetuo* bass; and ultimately textural inversion (bars 70–79) with thematic fragments above or below a running semiquaver bass.

These offer a range of possibilities to the performer, who might choose, for instance, to emphasize the fact that the diversity of harmonic progression and of texture are linked to some extent by the rate of chord change, which alternates subtly between the beat, the half-bar and the whole bar (and arguably, at bars 57–8, two bars) and between the regularly recurring and the unpredictably asymmetrical throughout. Such features could be portrayed in a variety of ways, for instance by seeking to bring out certain lines of the texture above the rest in a way that suggests medium-range and longer-range voice-leading within the counterpoint, and especially between treble and bass (for instance, in bars 70–78). One particularly challenging passage is bars 50–69, in which the right-hand voice-leading can be effectively conveyed within each four-bar phrase by a discreet *decrescendo* from the first to the second minim in each of the second, third and fourth bars (with a similar sense of *decrescendo* between each of the low left-hand notes on beats 1 and 3, the second sounding as an 'echo' of the first). But that leaves the longer-range progression through the whole passage (bars 50–69) to be managed so that dynamically it appears part of a broader trajectory, effectively a counterpointing of contrasting phrase-hierarchies.

Each of these approaches involves a clear ethical dimension for the performer. But beyond the individual cases lies a further ethical dilemma: the ethics of choice itself. Whichever model is chosen, effects flow and have an impact beyond the site of that choice: that is, we influence our own musical and technical responses to the material of K.310 at the keyboard. Moreover, we influence how the listener will respond to all this. These are consequences that resonate beyond that act of choosing. But even in the *act* of choosing, we act ethically, imparting a consequence further down the line. Choose to play K.310 in a manner that reflects the two-part sonata conception, and you play it in a way that is at least in accordance with *Formenlehre* of Mozart's own time rather than a later time. But that comes at a price, because in doing so, you are arguably denying a historical aspect of the work's identity. That is, you eliminate the element of reception that forms a part of the extended totality of the work.[16] On the other hand, by acknowledging that the historical 'afterlife' of K.310 is a vital ingredient in its identity, you may be lending it a quality that is 'inauthentic', namely a status as a 'Work Concept'. An ethical consequence of this is that you are playing it as a pianist in Vienna playing an 1830s Streicher piano might have done, namely as a work from the recent classical past recovered for the emergent romantic present and conceived and represented according to the stylistic agendas of that age, in which the solo sonata had become rather expanded both in length and in technical, musical and expressive demands on both player and listener, in which musical material was something to be moulded into a form that acquires near-physical stature, and which was authorized by new trends in published musical criticism and *Formenlehre*. Above all, your historically motivated choice means that you are, in effect, playing K.310 as a 'Work-with-a-capital-W' to be set alongside the benchmark of Beethoven's sonatas. That may be a perfectly defensible choice, but it is first and foremost a scholarly one. It could also be a scholarly choice to attempt to perform K.310 in accordance with *Formenlehre* of Mozart's own time, eliminating all later accretions. But it is worth pausing to reflect on which of these choices preserves more than it displaces. In a sense, playing K.310 'Mozart's way' (or 'Koch's way'), rather than 'Beethoven's way' (or Reicha's way'), becomes a scholarly choice only when set up as an alternative to the latter. What such a mode of performance would be displacing is an alternative historical context that arose in part as a consequence of concert performance traditions which cast new light on conceptions of genres such as the solo sonata and which emerged a generation after Mozart's death. Conversely, one would displace the original historical context, and the primary ethical consequence here involves squaring one's own conscience with the decision to reject a performance reflecting (as nearly as scholarship can bring us, at least) a conception of structure dating from the composer's own lifetime. One might, of course, play both contrasting interpretations *in succession* (one price to be paid for the primacy of performance is that one can perform

---

[16]   Indeed, retention of the ongoing reception afterlife of Mozart's sonatas, which includes, of course, their 'posthumous careers' on the nineteenth- and twentieth-century concert platform played on Steinways and Bechsteins as hors d'oeuvres before the main serving of Schumann, Liszt, Skryabin and Rachmaninov, might be the only justification still remaining today for performing Mozart on a modern grand piano.

only once at a time!). But that too has an ethical consequence and is this time, perhaps, unethical towards Mozart, since one would then be turning K.310 into an educational project, when it is actually something to *be performed*. Just as the Music is not the Score, Performance is not Education.

Indirectly, all analysis entails an ethical responsibility towards its intermediate and ultimate consumers. It is frequently thought of as a text-based activity and perhaps one that is historically decontextualized. But it is also has a historical dimension, whether in terms of its point of origin (in the case of Reicha's 'grand coupe binaire', as a theoretical model developed in the early nineteenth century in relation to certain repertoires and as an expression of a particular mindset integrating material and process) or in terms of the effects it subsequently produces when applied. It is not value-free. Nor does it operate in an ethical vacuum. We have a responsibility to remember that.

The same is true of pedagogy. Early in the nineteenth century, this same movement appeared in an institutional pedagogical context (to be introduced presently) that represents an important moment in the decline of local rhetorical gesture as a way of understanding the classical musical language (specifically here, Mozart's language) and its replacement by a uniformly legato style of playing. Legato had significant consequences for the representation of Mozart's highly articulated musical language in performance, but also conceptually, touching on the way we understand his scores analytically. Legato conceptions mean long phrases, seamlessly flowing as if no different in kind from the beautiful, vocally inspired themes of Chopin's nocturnes or Liszt's consolations. And long, seamless phrases suggest a bare minimum of subdivision into individual musical gestures. That in turn fosters a particular intellectual attitude, namely one in which the starting unit of division is relatively large (a phrase ending in a cadence; or a longer period mapping out a broader and usually symmetrical cadential plan and subdivided into two phrases; or a phrase subdivided into two clauses). By contrast, Mozart's musical language featured sharply profiled rhetorical gestures (virile, provocative, assertive, questioning, responsive – above all *articulate*). Legato playing undoubtedly has its place – but not especially in Mozart. It makes very good sense in relation to later pianistic repertoires conceived for later types of pianos. In fact, the piano was an instrument in considerable flux between c.1780 and c.1840, and developments to its machinery were responsible for developments in the language of piano music. That subject will be treated further in Chapter 6. For the present, suffice it to say that a legato model for representing (either on the page, in notation, or on the stage, in performance) is also an ethical choice resonating beyond the site of the activity itself.

Legato is a way of playing founded on a particular system of fingering; and when a system of fingering is applied to a piece of music, it leaves behind it an analytical trace. A fingering consists of two elements, an ordering sequence and a length. When a passage is fingered, notational symbols for sounds are passed through a 'grid' of physical possibilities for their production on a keyboard. For each passage there are clearly different fingering possibilities; a particular passage may be fingered in several different ways, and each of these potentially reflects different conceptions of how the passage is constructed in terms of its shape and length. In other words, a fingering reflects a conception of how a passage is broken down into its component parts in order to be physically managed in performance. Fingerings may be applied for at least two purposes: to enable the articulated projection of a musical surface and – more usually – to allow the passage to be played securely at the requisite speed. Professional training in conservatoires has typically focused on the installation of a reliable method of fingering, developed in scales and exercises that develop evenness and equality of touch in a systematic way, and sometimes the technical abstraction is extended to exemplary pieces of music. One such case is Louis Adam's *Méthode de piano du Conservatoire* (1805), the official instruction manual for pianists at the Paris Conservatoire in the early years of its foundation. As an appendix to the treatise itself is an anthology of works by J. S. Bach, Scarlatti, Handel, C. P. E. Bach, Mozart, Clementi and others. The first piece in Adam's 'Choix de morceaus dans les différens caractères et mouvemens' is the opening Allegro maestoso of Mozart's A minor Sonata K.310. Comparison of this text with Mozart's autograph (New York, Pierpoint Morgan Library, Robert Owen Lehman deposit) is instructive not only editorially, but insofar as Adam's edition represents (albeit consequentially as a demonstration of appropriate, institutionally authorized fingering) an early analytical conception. My claim is that the notation of fingering found here, particularly in conjunction with slurring, may actually be seen as a trace of an analytical perspective extending beyond performance indications in themselves.

In general terms, the 1805 *Méthode* has already travelled a long way in the direction of smooth, legato piano playing. This is obvious from Adam's chapter 7, 'De la liaison des sons et des trois manières de les détacher':

> Un des principaux points pour toucher du Forte Piano est de savoir bien lier les sons d'une touché à l'autre, et on n'y parvient que par un bon doigter, et en faisant raisonner les touches avec égalité … il ne faut jamais en abondonner une avant que le doigt ne soit place sur celle qui suit. Les sons doivent s'unir et se fonder les uns dans les autres, si l'on veut parvenir à imiter la tenue de la voix.

> [One of the main issues for playing the Fortepiano is to know how to connect the sounds in a good legato [as one moves from one key to the next], and one will not achieve that apart from a good method of fingering and in controlling the keys evenly … one [key] must never be released before the finger is in place on the next. The sounds must be connected and grounded one in another if one wishes to imitate a vocal line.]

Specifically, by 1805, if the choice of legato or staccato is left to the player, then 'il vaut mieux s'attacher au *legato* et réserver le *staccato* pour faire ressortir certains passages, et faire sentir, par un contraste amené avec art, les avantages du *legato*' ['it is better to hold to a *legato* manner of playing, reserving *staccato* for the highlighting of certain passages and to make us sense, by means of artful contrast, the advantages of *legato*'] (Adam's italics).

This approach extends also to the musical text that Adam presents of Mozart's K.310. By comparison with Mozart's autograph, the text is laden with slurs, often of a half-bar or a whole bar's duration. Examples include bars 3, 17, 19, 27, 30–33, 41–3 and 45–8 within the exposition, and analogous places in the recapitulation The articulations notated by Mozart are frequently eliminated or else replaced by slurs, for instance on the fourth-beat quaver pairs of bars 35, 36, 40 and 41. In addition, Adam greatly adds to the number of dynamic markings throughout the movement. Mozart's autograph is actually quite problematic in this respect, since it has so few dynamics. While it is not unusual for his piano sonata autographs to be bare in comparison to eventual first editions prepared under his supervision, the sparseness of dynamics in his autograph of K.310 is remarkable. There is no *forte* at the start, though it is apparent from the thematic, rhythmical and textural context; nor is *forte* marked at the recapitulation (bar 80). Dynamics sometimes last for extended stretches of time, despite obvious changes in the character of the music. As an extreme example, the last marking in the autograph of the Allegro maestoso is *piano* at bar 103; surely the movement is not intended to remain at that level literally until the end? And yet the same blanket *piano* applies to the equivalent passage in the exposition, and is not contradicted until bar 54; is the beginning of the development then intended to state the main theme *piano*, rather than *forte*? Probably not. Elsewhere the dynamics are applied with extreme precision. Bars 58–70 (developing the theme taken from bar 16) outline successively *fortissimo*, *pianissimo* and again *fortissimo*, each occurrence coinciding with the three presentations of the theme – surely a deliberate sequence. Here again, though, there is ambiguity: the *fortissimo* at bar 66 remains in force until contradicted by the *piano* at bar 84, that is, until the recapitulation is already underway. Does the recapitulation then begin *fortissimo*, or is Mozart's right-hand slur at bar 79 (the only slur in this entire passage) to be construed not simply as a shift in the type of finger articulation at this point but also as a *diminuendo* to the expected *forte* for the start of the recapitulation? Conversely, if the recapitulation is *fortissimo*, should the movement also start at that dynamic by analogy?

Adam's 1805 text applies and alters dynamics editorially according to his perception of the changing character of the music so that no such ambiguities arise. For instance, within the exposition, editorial dynamics occur at bars 34, 36, 38, 39, 40, 43, 44 and 45–7, imparting an ebb and flow that are by no means out of keeping with the musical content. Within the development, bars 58–70 are *fortissimo* throughout and at bar 79, Adam reduces the dynamic to *piano*, adding a *crescendo* through the slurred bar leading into the recapitulation, marked *forte*.

These contrasts between Adam's notation in 1805 and Mozart's in 1778 clearly have an impact on performance. By investigating one or two passages in more detail, I hope to show that there are also important, and latent, analytical implications besides.

Bars 23–6(right hand)

The continuous semiquaver pattern for each bar is divisible into two parts, each lasting a minim: part 1 consists of alternating rising step and rising third, whereas part 2 is always a rising step but is positioned along a descending scale moving in quavers, so that it seems to be an alternation of a rising step and a falling third each time. The alternating steps and thirds of part 1 are always of a quaver length; whereas the alternating step rise and falling third of part 2 cover just a semiquaver at each stage, so that in effect, there is a doubling of the pace of alternation from part 1 to part 2. (In terms of the harmonic pace it is ♩ ♫. In terms of pitches it is C – CBAG F – FEDC B – BAGF (E)). On the first half of beat 3 in each bar there is a degree of overlap between the pattern divisions, the rising step being at one and the same time the first component of both part 1 and part 2. The sense of a doubling of the pace of alternation from quaver to semiquaver may be represented by two contrasting fingering patterns, one lasting for the first minim of each bar and catering for the alternating step and third, the second catering for the more rapid rocking back and forth of the semiquavers on beats 3 and 4 (and quite possibly just involving two fingers all the way down the pattern[17]). That would create a distinction in the articulation of each half of each of these bars 23–6.

In the fingering given by Louis Adam in the *Méthode* that possibility is ruled out in favour of a more 'modern' sequential fingering pattern that ensures evenness and legato. The fingering (3424[3424]34231423) involves a mild shift of wrist position on beat 4 – not sufficient to produce an unwanted accent on that beat, but rather designed to allow the hand to move smoothly leftwards and deliver the thumb over the first note of each next bar a little ahead of time (the pattern 1423 on beat 4 ensures this). In fact, the use of the thumb is crucial to the fingering system, whose logic seems to be to deliver the thumb 'in advance' over keys so that the lateral wrist movements in successive changes of hand position are not jumpy and awkward, producing undesired accents to disrupt the flow. The principle is treated in chapter 4, 'Du doigter des gammes': 'L'usage du pouce est donc le seul régulateur pour tous les doigters possibles: il oblige à maintenir les autres doigts dans une position gracieuse et toujours légèrement recourbés afin qu'il puisse passer dessous librement.' ['The use of the thumb is thus the sole regulator for all fingering possibilities; it serves to keep the other fingers in a graceful position and always slightly curved so that it [the thumb] may pass beneath them freely [in moving from one hand position to the next].']

Clearly, Adam's fingering is motivated by an aesthetic aim: in order to achieve the desired smooth legato effect in the sound, a particular fingering pattern is applied involving a replicated succession of precise finger placements, each of

---

[17]   Though not, perhaps, the thumb and first finger in alternation, a characteristic Mozart derided in a letter to his father of 17 January 1778 (*Briefe*, 405: 86–8). Mozart is, however, referring there to right-hand fingering, so perhaps the question remains an open one.

a particular length. By applying this pattern, the student achieves a smooth and even result in playing. But the fingering is also a kind of analysis. In particular, the sequential fingering maps onto the music not only uniformity of sound, but uniformity of concept. All the semiquavers in each bar are in a sense neutralized in that they have had any implied internal contrasts of articulation (such as the doubling of the alternation rate hypothesized above) 'ironed out' by the application of the sequential fingering. Bar 24 and bar 25 are simply 'the same' as bar 23 conceptually insofar as they are each encoded as 3424[3424]34231423.

Bars 35–7 (right hand)

More telling in analytical impact is Adam's fingering for the right hand of bars 35–7, especially bar 37, where once again the aim is smooth lateral advancing of the thumb position to ensure a smooth scale descent. In fact, this pattern is a relative of bars 23–6, in that beats 2–4 of bars 35 and 36 are a straightforward transposition of the alternating shapes (rising step, rising third in quavers; then rising step, falling third in semiquavers at beats 1–3 of bars 23–6). In the autograph Mozart slurs all of bar 35 through to the first semiquaver of bar 36, but not the rest of bars 36 and 37, suggesting that the shift from quaver to semiquaver alternation patterns on beat 4 of bar 35 is not a prominent concern (i.e. it is a single gesture 'covered' by the slur in a specifically indicated legato), but that at the end of bar 36 it may be – the shift occurring on beat 4 and continuing as a distinct pattern through bar 37. Beat 4 of bar 36 would therefore be *generative of* the continuing semiquaver pattern, rather than *cadentially complementary* with beat 4 of bar 35. If so, then the implication is that beat 4 of bar 36 is conceptually different to beat 4 of bar 35 (and is to be treated differently in performance); Adam slurs each of these two bars, neutralizing this subtle possibility within an overall legato concept for the phrase as a whole. Similarly, Adam's fingering denies the possibility of a contrasting change of gear from beat 3 to beat 4 in bar 36, uniformly subsuming beats 2–4 in both bar 35 and bar 36 beneath an implied succession of 142434243423. Interestingly, when this pattern is transferred (extended) to the left hand at bar 40, Mozart retains the same slurring as for bars 35 ff. in the autograph; Adam's slurring is quite inconsistent here: he slurs beat 1 (only) of bar 40, then beats 2–4, followed by a slur from the second semiquaver of bar 41 through to the end of the bar, then in bar 42 a slur over beat 1, followed by another for beats 2–4, before concluding with a whole-bar slur in bar 43. The implication of his fingering for the end of bar 40 is the same as that just hypothesized for Mozart's notation (i.e. no articulation of the pattern shift). At the end of bar 41, however, Adam does imply a shift from one finger pattern to another at precisely the point where the alternation rate doubles from quavers to semiquavers, by placing the thumb on the last semiquaver of the bar (2131, instead of 2132 at the end of bar 40) and continuing in the first beat of bar 42 with 3131 (which by implication is replicated through the rest of the descending pattern until beat 4 of bar 43). Whether this was a deliberate intention may be doubted, though, since here (as at the end of bars 35, 36 and 40) it is masked by the slurring of the counterpointed cadential figure in the other hand (b″–g″–c″ quavers), which in Mozart's autograph is always staccato. Once more, the slurring and the fingering in Adam's text, when taken together, suggest a particular analytical stance towards the music, localized subtle contrasts of momentum within the figuration patterns being subsumed beneath a mindset privileging evenness and uniformity above the highlighting of contrasting cadential and generative features.

There may be a larger context for this observation. When this pattern recurs (transposed to the tonic) in the recapitulation (bars 116–17), Mozart's slurring is subtly different and may represent a subtle change of meaning. Each of these bars is slurred through to the first semiquaver of the next (whereas at bars 35–6 only the first is so notated), thus neutralizing the earlier possibility of a gear change from quaver-length to semiquaver-length alternations of steps and thirds within the pattern. Here, however, the continuation of the pattern is different, the alternating step rise and falling third semiquaver pattern of bar 37 being replaced by new figuration, which is chromatically diverted in the following bars 118–20. Mozart's different slurring of bars 116–17 arguably redefines the relationship between the last four semiquavers of each of these bars, the end of bar 117 now rhyming with that of bar 116, rather than initiating a new figurative beginning (as had been the case from bar 36, beat 4, to the end of bar 37). When the figure is transferred to the left hand in bars 121–5, the original slurring returns (i.e. just in bar 121, through to the first semiquaver of bar 122, with *no slur* in bar 122), the crucial difference here being that the continuation beyond these bars reinstates the original descending pattern analogous to that in bar 41, beat 4, to the end of bar 43. In this context, bars 121 and 122 behave differently from bars 116–17: bars 116–17 are *cadentially paired*, introducing a chromatic interruption in the following bars, while bars 121–2 are *generative*, as in the exposition, continuing towards a tonic cadence complementary to that in the exposition, but with its sense of closure this time more strongly reinforced as a result of the chromatic interruption introduced in bars 118–20. By contrast, bars 35–6 and 42–3 within the exposition were functionally paired, and were both generative. Arguably, then, Mozart's slurring at bars 116–17 hints at a strategic reinterpretation of that earlier function, enhancing the sense of closure at the end of the movement and thus being linked to considerations of large-scale structure. Adam's slurring of this passage simply replicates that of the exposition (except that the separate slurs on the first beats of bars 40 and 42 are removed in favour of whole-bar slurs at the analogous bars 121 and 123), so that – whether on a local or global level – there is no possible interpretive distinction between termination and beginning for this figure, depending on the positioning within the movement as a whole. The effect of the contrasting notations is perhaps marginal, but it extends beyond performance to analysis. Mozart's notation leaves open the possibility of contrasting interpretation for these moments (termination – beginning; cadential – generative), contrasts which impinge upon our appreciation of the sophistication with which Mozart could coordinate the precise manoeuvres of passagework with local and global structural signification within the classical musical language by 1778. The drift towards a uniformly legato performance style indicated by Adam's notation in 1805 does not. Something may have been lost as a result.

Issues of respective value are not the main concern here. Mozart's autograph and Adam's pedagogical text are sources of wholly different kinds, falling at different points along a path of historical development that led – depending on one's standpoint – away from the sonata as a domestic and primarily amateur form of music-making towards a professionalization of the genre in concert performance by virtuosos, or towards the privileging of virtuoso flim-flam over proper musical substance. My purpose here is to highlight the contrasting ways in which we may read such sources, not to place them in a hierarchy of value. The edition of K.310's Allegro maestoso presented in Adam's *Méthode* is clearly of a special kind. In promulgating a particular technical approach by means of fingering, phrasing and dynamics, certain features of Mozart's music are sacrificed in pursuit of an emerging aesthetic preference for uniformity and are, of course, institutional in origin. This is, after all, a treatise authorized by the Paris Conservatoire (a proudly national institution, then in its infancy) as a means of instruction for its student pianists, part of whose historical function would be to bring renown to the glorious institution of which they were products. Acquisition of a sound and reliable finger technique is the principal object of Adam's treatise, which commences with page after page of detailed illustrations of scales in all the keys, laid out in various patterns and with various fingerings. The *Méthode* specifically insists on evenness of touch as a virtue, all natural inequalities of strength and insufficiencies of mobility being rigorously addressed so that the aspiring pianist can tackle the demands of a growing virtuoso literature with confidence. Within such a project, it is unsurprising that Mozart's semiquaver passagework should be interpreted as if it were a specific scalic exercise, fingered in accordance with the general principles of the treatise (especially evenness in the lateral passage of the hand over the thumb, or thumb under the hand). What is surprising – and gratifying – is that the fingering turns out to have consequences for our understanding of Mozart's music.

This chapter has attempted to illuminate the Andante of K.533 and the Allegro maestoso of K.310 contextually, principally by locating them within an approach drawing upon Gadamer's interpretive strategy of a 'fusion of horizons'. Here, Mozart's sonata texts are understood in relation to historical, music-theoretical and pedagogic fields of view. In these encounters, his texts catalyse an understanding, and acquire their meanings differently and contextually each time. Meaning is produced (or constructed) outside the text, not essentially within it. The following chapter will consider Mozart's sonata texts from a different perspective, namely that of early editions.

Chapter 4
Editions

Most commonly, we encounter texts of Mozart's piano sonatas through editions. It is here that the disparity between the Work and the Score becomes most obvious. Different editions present different texts. Comparing two editions of the same sonata, even from Mozart's time, we find that slurs, staccatos and dynamics frequently appear in different places, or not at all. In what sense then does either of these editions *represent* the particular sonata? One school of thought is that the Work is found not exclusively in the Author, nor in the Score, nor in the Performance, but in a negotiation among these.[1] It might be objected that in this scenario the Work remains always beyond scrutiny since it 'floats' in a mental (and perhaps purely imaginary) space, inhabiting the cognitive collaboration between a composer long since dead, a typesetter also long since dead and a living performer for whom the particular edition presented by a published score is the nearest he or she can get to recovering an authorial intention (which is mysteriously distilled in that score). An additional complication is the contextual one treated earlier, according to which the assumption of an authorial intention rests on flimsy ground in any case. All in all, then, Ingarden's scenario of uncovering the Work by collaboration is not unproblematic, whether for Mozart or more generally.

Perhaps we are asking the wrong question here. Maybe we are asking too much of an edition of Mozart's sonatas to *represent* them to us? A more realistic way to approach editions may be to ask of them two sorts of question:

- What might they tell us about the habits of mind that the producers (or consumers) of early editions brought to an appreciation of Mozart's sonatas?
- What might they be telling us about ways in which the music might be represented in performance?

The first question touches on reception, the second on 'applied reading' (that is, how we assimilate the information contained in the score with the further intention to translate our understanding into a physical expression of it at the keyboard). The following section investigates these areas through a selection of case studies taken from early editions of Mozart's piano sonatas.

What might we understand about Mozart's sonatas from inspecting an early edition? First (or early) editions are felt to have a particular value, perhaps because

---

[1]   See Roman Ingarden, *The Work of Music and the Problem of its Identity*, trans. A. Czerniawski, ed. Jean G. Harell (Berkeley and Los Angeles, 1986), pp. 34–40.

we attach importance to their closeness in time and/or place to the composer himself, predating emergent nineteenth-century habits of mind according to which editors encoded their musical preferences for an even distribution of tone throughout a phrase, combined with an absence of beat-hierarchy, principally in the form of legato slurs covering substantial musical spans (examples of this tendency will be discussed later in this section). As we have already seen, the nature of whatever it is we find important here is not attributable (or at least not wholly so) to authorial intention. But early editions, in some cases produced in Vienna during Mozart's lifetime and possibly incorporating his direct input, do at least afford us some insight into the mindset of the time. A first edition such as *Trois sonates pour le claveçin ou pianoforte composées par W. A. Mozart, œuvre VI*, published by Artaria in Vienna in 1784 and containing K.330, 331 and 332, incorporates a record of deliberate choices made on several levels, all of which were nearly contemporary with the act of composition and made in the very city where the music was written, *viz.*:

- A choice by the composer to release these three sonatas into the public domain, subtly inflecting their generic origin as domestic, and perhaps pedagogic, music which acquired a large part of its meaning from the intimate circumstances of a private salon performance or a piano lesson.
- Possibly in consequence of this generic inflection, choices to do with the note-to-note continuity of the music in slow movements:
  - In the C major Sonata K.330, a short coda, which is not present in the autograph and derives from bars 36–40, is appended to the Andante cantabile (bars 60–64).
  - In the F major Sonata K.332, the reprise of the Adagio (bars 21–40) is substantially altered in the first edition, as compared with the autograph (in which Mozart simply marks a *da capo* for bar 21– bar 28, beat 3, continuing thereafter with a relatively literal tonic transposition of the original bars 8–19). The first edition presents a much more elaborate text of these bars (shown in small type in the *NMA* text, which treats the autograph as the primary source here) in which the right-hand part freely embellishes the original.[2] Moreover, the precise frequency, length and positioning of many of the slurs and dynamics are substantially different from those in the autograph.

What reasons might Mozart have had for the substantial alterations to the Adagio in Artaria's 1784 edition of K.332? Given that the *Trois sonates ... œuvre VI* were produced in Vienna by a publisher with whom Mozart developed something of a

---

[2]   Typically there is no actual alteration of the harmonic basis, though in bars 30–31 the left hand additionally doubles the right at the lower octave, and in bars 39–40 the slurring of the left-hand inner part is different from that in the autograph (at this point the right-hand part is identical in both sources).

relationship during the 1780s, and that the reprise (bars 21 ff.) in his autograph manuscript begins merely with a *da capo* indication, we are probably justified in assuming that Mozart had direct involvement in the text of the first edition. The appearance of this print might be read as a 'shop window' in which Mozart demonstrated to the Viennese public (primarily) his tasteful command of the subtle art of embellishment. Or perhaps Mozart included an embellished reprise because he felt that in its newly public context this movement required a more elaborate texture, following on, as it did, from a sonata (K.331) that specifically foregrounded textural elaboration in its first-movement variations – the set of three sonatas thus reading as a progression towards figurative complexity (which might go some way towards explaining why he chose *not* to embellish the reprise in the Andante cantabile of K.330, the first in the set[3]). On a practical level, of course, once this sonata had departed from what appears to have been an originally pedagogic context,[4] Mozart would no longer have been physically present (in a piano lesson) to suggest appropriate ways of embellishing its reprise, and thus needed to demonstrate how to do that in print. From both the historian's and the player's viewpoints, the fact that he did so is a valuable record of ways in which similar passages (including the reprise to the Andante cantabile of K.330, left unadorned in Artaria's edition) might be rendered in performance. As a consequence of Mozart's choice to exhibit what were fundamentally private domestic works in a public arena, we are afforded an important insight into his habits of melodic elaboration.

In the case of the first edition of the D major Sonata K.284 (composed for the young Baron Thaddeus von Dürnitz in spring 1775), a more radical choice seems to be at work. By the time Mozart had agreed its publication with Christoph Torricella in Vienna by July 1784, the sonata was almost a decade old and had previously undergone wholesale recasting even at the original compositional stage: a cancelled draft of 71 bars – extending well into the first-movement development section – appears in the main body of the autograph manuscript, and Mozart began again from scratch, completing the work in its now-familiar form. The occasion of its publication as the second item in *Trois sonates pour le claveçin ou pianoforte. La troisième est accomp: d'un violon obblig: composées par Mr. W. A. Mozart, dediées a son Excellence Comtesse Therese de Kobenzl ... œuvre VII* evidently prompted Mozart to yet further substantial rethinking. But in this case, the revision of the autograph text only occasionally involves melodic or rhythmic embellishment of the right-hand part (even in the most extreme departure, found in variation 11 of the finale). What preoccupied Mozart in the main was applying dynamics as an alternative means of shaping the continuity of phrases. In general, he seems to have approached dynamic gradation as a way of signalling movement towards or arrival at cadences, sometimes linked with melodic chromaticism, as

[3] The relevant passage is, like that in K.332's Adagio, simply marked *da capo*, and is not separately notated.

[4] A viewpoint supported by the fact that the right-hand staves are notated in soprano clef in the autograph.

in the *crescendo* and *piano* indications added to bars 26, 27 and 97–9 of the first movement[5]), and sometimes coordinated with accentual patterns, as in the opening phrase of the Rondeau en polonaise, in which *sf* markings are applied to the third beats of bars 1 and 3, with additional *sfp* marks to the demisemiquaver scale snippets in bars 5 and 6, the phrase concluding with a *crescendo* (from *piano*) through the second half of bar 7 (also incorporating mild chromatics) which dissolves back to *piano* at the very top of the phrase, marking its cadential descent. Later in this movement, at bars 29 and 65, subtle dynamic additions reveal a difference in local articulations as compared with the autograph: *forte–piano* alternations in paired semiquavers at bar 29 are recast in the first edition as 'one plus three' within each semiquaver group, the first *piano*, the second *sf* within a slur covering the whole four-note group. At bar 65 the pattern is managed slightly differently, in both the autograph and the first edition,[6] but in the edition, Mozart takes the altered pattern in bar 65 as his cue to enhance the role of dynamic contrast in the cadential extension that follows, replacing his original pattern of alternating *piano* and *forte* here with a graded descent from *piano* (bar 66) through *pianissimo* (bar 67), followed by a now more shocking and dramatic *forte* (bar 68), *piano* (bar 69) and *forte* (bars 70–71).

Mozart's most substantial recasting of dynamics occurs in the case of the finale variations. In variations 5, 7 and 10 he applies, in the Torricella print, carefully managed dynamic gradations somewhat as in the first movement, as a way of revealing the phrase-structure by highlighting moments of cadential arrival. Thus in variation 5, the succession of contrasting textural patterns is characterized by a *crescendo* (from *piano*) throughout the left-hand double thirds of bars 5 and 6 followed by an immediate *forte* where this texture is breached by the arrival of dotted rhythms at the cadence point (bars 7 and 8). Mozart adopts a different approach at the conclusion of variation 7 (bars 13–17). Originally, this phrase had been *forte* throughout, right up to the closing V–I resolution (*piano*); in the first edition the reprise of the opening figure in bar 13 starts *piano*, then has a *crescendo* to *forte* (bar 15, second half, timed precisely with the trill on the half-bar treble G) and a *sf* on the highest and syncopated note of this phrase, after which the original *piano* V–I resolution arrives as the conclusion of a much more eventful journey through the phrase and a worthy enhancement of this expressive *minore* variation. Bars 11–13 of variation 10 offer a *decrescendo* upwards through a chromatic patterns in broken octaves, articulating the mid-point of this section and replacing an original *piano* (bar 11–bar 12, beat 2) followed by *pianissimo*, and perhaps suggesting also a tailing-off of tempo as well as volume at this structural turning-point.

It is for variation 11, however, that Mozart reserves his most expressive application of dynamics. Once again, the autograph reveals its status as a composing manuscript, for Mozart's original sequence of phrases as he wrote this

---

[5]   These indications appear in small type in the *NMA* text.

[6]   The third beat is, by implication *forte–piano* in paired semiquavers in the autograph; *piano* throughout (in slurred pairs) in the first edition. See *NMA*.

variation across one and a half folios (fols 24–24v of the autograph) was from the opening to bar 8, beat 2; followed by bar 16, beat 3, to bar 25, beat 2 – each of these sections being marked for a repeat. That takes us to the end of staves 5 and 6 of fol. 24. At the beginning of the next pair of staves, he originally commenced variation 12 (complete with its new time-signature and extending as far as beat 2 of its second bar, though without its grace note); but before continuing further he decided on a different course, namely elaborate fully notated embellishments to each half of variation 11 in turn. He consequently cancelled the opening of variation 12 and wrote his more fully worked variation 11 on the rest of fol. 24 and the top half of fol. 24v, thereafter continuing to the bottom of that folio with the concluding variation 12, carefully marking in heavily inked roman numerals the correct continuous sequence of sections for variation 11.[7] All that was in the spring of 1775. For the Torricella print (summer 1784) Mozart embarked on a less drastic but expressively profound revision of his text of this variation, which up to that point contained not a single dynamic marking. In almost every bar of the Torricella edition Mozart creates a particular shaping of the local phrase by dynamic placement. Newly enabled, perhaps, by the purchase of his Anton Walter five-octave fortepiano in about 1782–3, which afforded him a hitherto unrivalled range of dynamic control, Mozart was able to graft onto the existing text an impressive array of *pp*, *p*, *f*, *sf*, *crescendo* and even *calando* indications that operate locally in the characterization of individual moments or phrases, but also on a broad structural level, creating correspondences across longer spans. In order to appreciate these fully, one ideally needs access both to the *NMA* text, which replicates both versions in a helpful vertical alignment,[8] and to a good copy of a Walter instrument. Assuming the latter to be impractical for most readers, a near-ideal substitute is the recording by Ronald Brautigam on a copy of a c.1795 Walter by Paul McNulty.[9]

Once again, we should remind ourselves that Mozart's dynamics here may best be regarded as indicative of possible approaches rather than constituting a final, definitive text superseding the original. So while the succession of dynamics found in bars 1–4, *p*, *crescendo*, *f*, *p*, *sf*, *crescendo*, *f*, *p*, *crescendo*, *f*, *calando* may be read as a series of *regulative* instructions determining the way the player moves through the musical space in these bars, highlighting in precise and contrasting ways (and

---

[7]   Thus the second half of bar 8 is marked 'II'; the second half of bar 16, 'III'; and the second half of bar 25, 'IV' in the autograph.

[8]   The text of the Torricella edition of 1784 is printed in small notation on the upper staves; following the *NMA* editorial policy, the autograph is generally taken as the primary source. The edition published by the Associated Board of the Royal Schools of Music, edited by Stanley Sadie and with performance notes by Denis Matthews (London, 1978), provides parallel texts of this variation (this time with the text of the autograph in small notation on the lower staves).

[9]   BIS-CD-836, recorded in 1996 and reissued as a boxed set of the complete piano music (BIS-CD-1633-36) in 2006.

in close succession) the management of an accumulation of treble turning-points as the phrase unfolds, they may also be read *indicatively*, expressing possibilities for how one might deploy dynamic shadings not only in playing this particular phrase, but in playing such phrases in general – a model for the dynamic management and representation of expressive content. Now contrast the dynamic indications found at the embellishment of the same phrase (bars 8–12). Mozart has already engineered a significant alteration of this phrase, remember, because he has notated a melodically and rhythmically more elaborate version. For this phrase's altered contours he applies a different sequence of dynamics, *p, crescendo, p, crescendo, f, p, crescendo, f, p*, tailored to the profile of the considerably busier treble line as it skirts its contrasting registers. While some features remain fundamentally unaltered (the half-bar upbeat commencement and bar 3; cf. bars 8 and 11), the dynamic layout of bars 9 and 10 is effectively reversed with respect to bars 1 and 2, suggesting a precise coordination between dynamic change and prominent register shifts in the second half of bar 9 and the beginning of bar 10: Mozart's breaking of the continuity here by an interrupting octave displacement is matched by a *crescendo* through the upper octave, then by *forte* for the continuation back at the lower register. Again, Mozart's dynamic markings here may either underscore a particular structural point ('this moment is a decoration of something previously heard'), or they may be interpreted as tokens of a type ('here is an example of what might be done in this kind of situation'). Perhaps the second (indicative) case offers a less stilted way of rendering bar 7 in performance, Mozart's alternating *forte* and *piano* marks on successive semiquavers being read not prescriptively, but instead as a call to rubato, giving enough space for the *forte* notes to appear melodic, not accentual (likewise in the analogous octave passage in bar 24)?[10] Whatever the particular solution or solutions adopted in performance, the clear impression given by Mozart's revised text of this variation is that its overtly expressive voice requires detailed characterization in performance in order to bring it to life. One way of doing that is to apply techniques of embellishment (here provided by the composer); another is to enhance that process further by the application of dynamic gradations and contrasts, having respect to the local contour on the one hand, and to a harmonically defined structural outline on the other.[11]

---

[10]   A literal rendering of Mozart's dynamics (should that be desired) is in any case somewhat easier to achieve on a fortepiano than on a modern grand, because of the much more immediate attack on the front of the sound and its much more rapid decay (compared with the modern grand, which speaks slowly, then rings on for a much longer time).

[11]   It should be noted that, in general, the Torricella print of 1784 purposefully adds dynamics where none existed in the autographs. This is certainly true of the B flat Sonata K.333 (the first item in the *Trois sonates*), whose autograph is conspicuously bare in terms of dynamics, especially in the second and third movements. In the Andante cantabile – all the tempo indications for this sonata come from the Torricella print, incidentally; none are given in the autograph, though they were added subsequently by Mozart in pencil to correspond with the print – the pervasive syncopated figure beginning with a falling step

It will by now be clear that my view is that we should not automatically assume that a specifically *published* text represents Mozart's final thoughts on the matter (a 'definitive' text; the composer's 'intention'). That would be far too simplistic a view. Rather, editions are agents in the process by which Mozart's sonatas have been represented and understood within an evolving historical context which has so far continued for well over 200 years. That agency has manifested itself in diverse arenas, including historical, analytical, pedagogical and performing ones. In the rest of this chapter some of these agencies and some of their consequences for understanding Mozart's sonatas are pursued, beginning with the C major Sonata K.330.

K.330

From the player's point of view, the contrasting texts of the C major Sonata K.330 offer a rich field of expressive possibilities. Between the autograph (Kraków, Jagiellonian Library) and the first edition produced by Artaria in 1784 (*Trois sonates pour le clavecin ou pianoforte ... œuvre VI*) there are frequent discrepancies of dynamic and especially slurring. In fact, the first edition, brought out by Artaria in 1784, went through three impressions, and there are some interesting variations to be found between the impressions.[12] For instance, in the first movement, bars 42–4, the right-hand slur extends over the barline and incorporates also the first treble semiquaver G (which has no staccato mark) in bars 42–3 and 43–4 in the third impression, whereas in both the autograph and the first impression the slur is contained within the bar (covering the groups of demisemiquavers). The shape of the figure is consequently altered, the first treble G in bars 42 and 43 having considerably less weight and coming right at the end of the slur, whereas in the alternative, the first treble G lends more impetus to the continuation. Moreover, the extension of the slur to cover the first treble G creates continuity with the notated

---

and first heard in bar 9 is often emphasized by a *sf* or *sfp* marking (for instance through bars 44–7). In the finale, Allegretto grazioso, dynamic contrasts are frequently applied to mark contrast between ritornellos and episodes (for instance, beginning at bar 20) or else between registers (as at bars 133–8), or in order to make some special harmonic excursion (as at bars 177–98). In the case of the Violin Sonata in B flat K.454 (No. 3 in the Torricella print) the dynamic discrepancies between autograph and print are less one-sided, though there is a general tendency for *sf* marks to appear in the print and not in the autograph. For a recent critical edition, see *Mozart: Violin Sonatas:/ Violinsonaten*, vol. 3: *K.454, K.481, K.526, K.547. Variations / Variationen K.359 & K.360*, ed. Cliff Eisen (London, Frankfurt am Main, Leipzig and New York, 2006).

[12] For an edition based in part on the reading of a supposed first impression of Artaria's 1784 edition, see *Mozart: Sonatas for the Pianoforte*, ed. Stanley Sadie and Denis Matthews (London, 1979). Recent unpublished research by Rupert Ridgwell, to whom I am grateful for communicating this point, shows that, in fact, this particular copy is a second, or probably, third impression after all.

shape of the following figure (bars 44–5, in which the slurring extends to the first of two repeated treble Gs); the notations of the autograph and first impression offer contrasting scansions here, with 'retakes' on the downbeats of bars 43 and 44, followed by slurring across the beat in bars 44–5.

The right-hand slurring of bars 129–32 and bars 135–7 towards the end of the first movement offers a bewildering variety of choices to the player:

- Autograph: bar 129, demisemiquavers slurred in a single sweep to the end of the bar; bar 130, each separate group of demisemiquavers individually slurred; bar 135, first two groups of demisemiquavers slurred together, but the third group slurred separately and continuing over the barline to include the first of the two repeated treble Cs in bar 136 (and likewise in bars 136–7).
- First edition, first impression: bar 129 as in the autograph; bars 130, 135 and 136 all as in bar 129.
- First edition, third impression: bar 129, no slur; bar 130, demisemiquavers slurred in a single sweep to the end of the bar (i.e. as in the first impression); bar 135, each separate group of demisemiquavers individually slurred, except that the first (trilled) note of the demisemiquaver groups is not contained within the slur, which covers just the second, third and fourth notes of each group (and likewise in bar 136).

Interestingly, in Artaria's third impression the notation of staccato does seem to distinguish purposely between dots and strokes, and this may be indicative of a particular (and contrasting) approach to articulation in performance. Throughout the first movement, only strokes are used, whereas in the central Andante, only dots are used. Frequently the Andante employs a three-quaver upbeat figure repeating the same note (at the opening, for instance), and this is usually notated with a combination of a slur and staccato dots, perhaps suggesting a light and unaccented touch. But even when no slurs are present (the descending semiquaver scale in bar 6, for instance), dots, not strokes, are used. The consistency of this and the consistency of contrast with the first movement suggest that in performance lightness and gracefulness of expression are called for, and these in turn will affect the choice of tempo. In particular, the fact that there is no indication of a heavier attack for the staccatos in the central minor-key section (compare especially bars 36–40 and bars 60–64, added as an afterthought for publication – these bars do not appear in the autograph) may suggest that no radical exaggeration of expressive contrast with the major-key *da capo* is required in performing this Andante.

A different situation occurs in a later edition of K.330, published in Leipzig in 1803 by Hoffmeister and Kühnel.[13] Here there is considerable variety within the

---

[13]   *Sonate pour le forte-piano composé par W. A. MOZART.* Copy consulted: London, British Library, Hirsch IV. 28. The same plates (147) were reused for an edition of 1815 issued by C. F. Peters (Leipzig).

Andante between staccato dots and strokes for the player to ponder. The three-quaver upbeat figures are still notated with dots, but the semiquaver scales in bars 6 and 36 are given with strokes, as are the final right-hand quavers of bars 9 and 31 and the *forte* chords in bar 34. Dots and strokes coexist also in the outer movements in this source, strokes being especially associated with figures such as the rising arpeggios in bars 5 and 6 (also bars 92–3) of the first movement. Yet they do not apparently mean that such figures should be associated necessarily with a sharper attack, since strokes also appear within *piano* phrases such as the lead-in to the recapitulation (bars 86–8, which in the autograph, as also in both impressions of the Artaria first edition, is given as staccato *dots*). Especially notable in the Hoffmeister and Kühnel print is the appearance of *crescendo* and *decrescendo* signs not found in earlier sources. A brief list:

- Bar 46 *decrescendo* from *forte*; bar 52 *decrescendo* from *forte*.
- Bar 85 *crescendo* to *forte* (at the beginning of bar 86, and replacing a *forte* mark in the autograph and first edition).
- Bar 87 *crescendo* from *piano* to *mezzo-forte*.
- Bars 133, 139 *decrescendo* from *forte*.

Within the Andante cantabile, *crescendo* marks frequently enhance the three-quaver upbeat figure (for instance at bars 4, 5, 44, 45 and 52), sometimes leading, as in bars 45 and 46, to *sfp* marks on the ensuing downbeat, and, in the final coda, to an expressive *pianissimo* (bars 62–3). Perhaps by 1803 an emerging tendency in performance of works such as this was to maximize fine gradations of dynamic rise and fall on the local level for expressive effect? Finally, the left-hand slurring in Hoffmeister and Kühnel's print departs markedly from that found in the autograph and first edition (even where those sources agree among themselves). This is especially the case in the finale. In the section beginning at bar 33, the autograph and first edition agree at first with two-bar slurs for bars 33–4 and 35–6, though the third impression switches to single-bar slurs for bars 35–6. Hoffmeister and Kühnel give bars 33–4 with single-bar slurs and bars 35–6 with no slur (possibly implying that its alternating C♯–D and C♮–D figure be foregrounded as an element within a dialogue rather than simply a background accompaniment at this point); thereafter the accompaniment is slurred in whole bars (bars 37–8), then in single *beats* (bars 39–43), a whole bar (bar 44 – an engraving mistake?) and single beats once more (bars 45–6); bars 39–46 in the autograph and both of Artaria's divergent impressions lack slurring altogether. Certainly, the incursion of single-beat slurring in Hoffmeister and Kühnel gives the player a cue to mark out the descending bass line, which carries the forward harmonic momentum at this point, emphasizing the prevailing harmonic pace and suggesting a deliberate change of gear at bar 39, as if the previous six bars should retrospectively be regarded as three relatively relaxed two-bar units giving way to something more energetic. Whether this is a deliberate intention is difficult to ascertain. At the analogous moment in the recapitulation of this sonata-form movement, the slurring in Hoffmeister and Kühnel is subtly different:

- Bars 132–3: single-bar slurs.
- Bars 134–5: slurred across the two bars from the second semiquaver of bar 134 until the fifth semiquaver of bar 135.
- Bars 136–7 and 138–9: single-bar slurs.
- Bars 140–44: single-*beat* slurs.
- Bar 145: single-bar slur.

Nevertheless, the overall effect of a change of impetus from the bar to the beat level is clear in both passages as represented by Hoffmeister and Kühnel; it simply arrives one bar later in the recapitulation than in the exposition. (In the autograph and both Artaria impressions the same slurring obtains here as formerly.) For the player the choice is between a reading that gives overall prominence to the treble line, allowing this to float over a relatively unarticulated flow of accompanimental semiquavers; and a reading that features explicit changes *en route* to the articulation of the harmonic underpinning, creating a much more engaged dialogue between the hands.

K.333

In addition to the autograph of the B flat Sonata K.333 (Staatsbibliothek zu Berlin) and the wellknown first edition published by Christoph Torricella and including also the D major Sonata K.284 and the Violin Sonata in B flat K.454 (*Trois sonates pour le clavecin ou pianoforte. La troisième est accomp: d'un violon obblig: ... œuvre VII* (Vienna, 1784)), Artaria brought out a text of K.333 in 1787: *Due sonate per il clavicembalo o forte piano ... opera 7*. Artaria's edition bears the same plate number (118) as Torricella's and is identical in all respects.[14] The autograph texts to both the piano sonatas (K.333 and 284) were revised for publication (significantly so – as we have already seen – in the case of K.284), evidently by the composer, whose pencilled tempo markings for the second and third movements added into the autograph of K.333 were taken over in the first edition. There are numerous variants to the slurring between autograph and first edition, and these open up several contrasting dimensions for expressive performance. I shall examine two here, one from the central Andante cantabile and one from the rondo finale (Allegretto grazioso).

First, melodic expression. Mozart's notation of the right hand in bar 56 of the Andante has a slur extending through the first three syncopated notes (B♭–A–A♭), and a further slur covering the four final semiquavers in the bar (i.e. starting on the tied A♭ semiquaver). Artaria notates this slightly differently:

14 Copy consulted: London, British Library, e.5.m.(8.).

the first B♭ quaver is separate; a slur joins the syncopated A–A♭; and a slur joins just the final three semiquavers of the bar. Mozart's notation suggests a degree of melodic relaxation through the first three right-hand notes; Artaria, by contrast, points up far more the offbeat A♮, beginning the slur at that point. The effect is a subtle reconfiguring of the placement of dissonance within the bar: Mozart highlights the downbeat dissonance at the beginning of the bar (B♭ over F in the bass); Artaria highlights the fact that the A♮ (slightly stressed by virtue of its slur) becomes dissonant against the moving bass line on beat 2, and then proceeds on the quaver beat to a stronger dissonance still. There is also a contrasting accentual quality about Artaria's slurring, for additional weight is given not only to the crotchet A♮, but also to the semiquaver G from which his three-note slur commences within beat 3. So whereas Mozart's notation of the melody is relatively smooth here, Artaria's slurring imports a degree of accentual intervention at two points, and counterpoints this against an added harmonic prominence for the left hand on beat 2.

At the close of the finale, one might imagine a situation in which local slurring has much broader ramifications – namely for how one manages the important task of closing the sonata in performance. A possible structural implication for local use of slurring is found towards the close of the finale (from bar 215). In the first appearance of Mozart's subdominant-inflected cadential figure (bars 215–17) the slurring of the left-hand quavers is in whole-bar lengths in all sources. But whereas the autograph continues thus in the decorated repeat (bars 219–21), Artaria breaks the whole-bar slurs found in the autograph into beat-unit slurs, by implication emphasizing the inner contrapuntal strand moving F–A♭G–(D)–E♭ over the dominant pedal. Assuming for the moment that the whole-bar slurring in bars 215–17 implies a less prominent emphasis on this inner-part feature (remember that it was normal practice in the eighteenth century for slurs also to imply a steady *diminuendo* through the phrase), the transition between the two meanings if one were to perform from Artaria's text as opposed to Mozart's autograph reading amounts to a textural shift from 'theme and accompaniment' (bars 215–17) to a three-part contrapuntal texture (bars 219–21), timed precisely with an embellishment to the leading treble line. It simultaneously draws attention to harmonic motion on the minim-beat unit as the close approaches, and the player might adopt a deliberately more 'measured' quality to the playing at this point as an expressive device in order to signal closure. Interestingly, in Artaria bars 217 and 221 invert their respective slurring: in bar 217, the right hand has beat-length slurs, giving two four-quaver groups (over a whole-bar slur in the left hand); whereas in bar 221, the right-hand quavers all lie under a single slur, but the left-hand alternations of C and B♭ are divided into minim beat-lengths. In the former case, the implication for the player is a subtle melodic emphasis on the fifth right-hand quaver, and in the latter a similar emphasis on the fifth left-hand quaver – in context, therefore, a shift from the foregrounding of melodic gesture in favour of harmonic gesture emphasis as the sonata draws to its close.

Cipriani Potter's 1848 Edition

Mozart. / An Entirely New, and / Complete Edition / of the / Piano Forte Works, / with and without Accompts. / of this / Celebrated Composer, / Humbly Dedicated by express permission to / Her Most Gracious Majesty, / The Queen. / Edited by / Cipriani Potter. / London, / Coventry, 71 Dean Street, Soho Square.[15]

Thus the English pianist and composer Cipriani Potter (1792–1871) announced his 1848 edition of Mozart's piano works. Potter was a child prodigy, memorizing the whole of J. S. Bach's *Das wohltemperirte Clavier* in his teens. He enjoyed considerable acclaim as a pianist, having studied with Beethoven and Aloys Förster in Vienna in his mid-twenties. At its foundation in 1822, Potter was appointed the first piano teacher for the male division of the Royal Academy of Music, becoming Director of Orchestral Practice five years later and, in 1832, Principal, a post he retained until 1859. From the mid-1830s Potter appeared frequently as a soloist in concerts of the Philharmonic Society; he gave the English premières of many of Mozart's piano concertos (notable for his embellishment of the solo parts) and was especially associated with the Third and Fourth Piano Concertos of Beethoven. He was, by all accounts, a brilliant player.[16] Seen against this backdrop, his edition of Mozart's piano sonatas, published around the mid-point of his tenure as Principal of the Royal Academy of Music, might be felt to carry some pedagogic authority.

Potter's 'New and Complete Edition' appeared in nine volumes, *viz.*:

> Volume 1: Variations
> Volume 2: Rondos and miscellaneous works
> Volume 3: Duets
> Volume 4: Piano sonatas
> Volume 5: Piano sonatas
> Volume 6: Violin sonatas
> Volume 7: Violin sonatas
> Volume 8: Trios with piano
> Volume 9: Quartets with piano

It was an expansion of his 1836 *Chefs d'oeuvre de Mozart, a New and Correct Edition of the Piano Forte Works. (with & without Accpts.) of this Celebrated Composer*, as Potter explained in the preface to the 1848 set:

---

[15]   Copy consulted: London, British Library, R.M.11.g.1.

[16]   See P. H. Peter, '*The Life and Work of Cipriani Potter (1792–1871)*' (dissertation, Northwestern University, 1972); C. B. Oldman, 'Cipriani Potter's Edition of Mozart's Pianoforte Works', in Walter Gerstenberg, Jan La Rue and Wolfgang Rehm (eds), *Festschrift Otto Erich Deutsch* (Kassel, 1963), pp. 120–27.

From the increased taste for Classical Music the Editor has been induced at the suggestion of the Publishers to present to the admirers of Mozart, a correct Edition of the Piano Forte Works of this Celebrated Composer.

The original intention was to offer to the Public the Chefs d'Oeuvre of Mozart only, but from the great demand for each number as it appeared, and the universal desire expressed for the whole of the Piano Forte Works of this great Master, the Editor and Publisher decided on completing the Edition.

Independent of the usual inaccuracies of the Music Engraver, there exists sometimes a deficiency of marks of expression, though Modern Composers are frequently too exuberant on this point, nevertheless the correct notation is absolutely necessary to enable a performer to give the true effect to works of this magnitude.

The solo piano sonatas appear in volumes 4 and 5 (each entitled *Mozart. Sonatas, for the Piano Forte*). Volume 4 contains K.475 and 457, K.533 and 494, K.331 (with separate accompaniments for violin and cello: "Sonata, with Violin & Violoncello Accts. (ad lib.)"), K.333, K.280, K.284, K.310, K.332 and K.282. Volume 5 contains K.281, K.279, K.309, K.330, K.547a,[17] K.311 and K.283.[18]

Potter's edition has two remarkable features. Firstly, he gives composition dates for each individual piece (where he knew it). Secondly, he gives metronome marks for each movement, as follows:

Volume 4

Fantasia K475
Adagio: ♪ = 56; Allegro: ♩ = 120; Andantino: ♪ = 56; Più Allegro: ♪ = 144; Primo Tempo: ♪ = 56

Sonata K.457
I: ♩ = 96; II: ♪ = 63; III: ♩ = 72 (featuring quite extreme variations of fast and slow as one progresses through the sonata)

---

[17] K.547a in F was then regarded as a solo piano sonata (the first of its two movements derives from the Violin and Piano Sonata in F K.547, while the second is a transposition to F of the finale of K.545).

[18] It will immediately be noticed that K.545, K.570 and K.576 are absent. K.570 was then regarded as a violin and piano sonata, despite Mozart's annotation to the entry for this work in his thematic catalogue that it was for keyboard alone. It is found in vol. 7 of Potter's edition as a 'Sonata with Violin accc.t'. K.545 and K.576 are nowhere to be found. The last item in vol. 5 is the A major Piano Concerto K.488 in an arrangement for solo piano and with a cadenza to the first movement by Potter requiring a six-octave keyboard for its performance. He does not adapt the overall range of Mozart's sonatas beyond the five octaves of Mozart's original conception.

K.533 and 494
I: ♩= 120; II: ♪= 100; III: ♩ = 132 (a very deliberate pacing of the first movement)

K.331
I: ♪ = 96 (within which variation 5 has ♪= 88, and variation 6 has ♪= 112); II: Menuetto ♩ = 104; III: 'Allegrino alla Turca' ♩ = 126 (variation 5 and the Menuetto both quite slow)

K.333
I: ♩ = 120; II: ♪= 104; III: ♩ = 112 (finale quite slow)

K.280
I: ♩ = 138; II: ♪= 84: III: ♩ = 96

K.284
I: ♩ = 126; II: ♪= 144; III: ♩ = 126 (within which variation 12 has ♩ = 108)

K.310
I: ♩ = 112; II: ♪ = 92; III:♪ = 72 (outer movements quite steady, particularly the Presto finale; Andante rather quicker than Potter's other metronome indications for this tempo, in K.309, for instance)

K.332
I: ♩= 138; II: ♪= 92; III: ♩ [*recte* ♩.]=96 (but given the somewhat slow pace indicated for other finales, one wonders if Potter's ♩ = 96 was indeed his intention here)

K.282
I: ♪=96; II: ♩ = 120; III: ♩ = 112

Volume 5

K.281
I: ♪= 138; II: ♪= 72; III: ♩ = 152 (showing how slow an 'Andante amoroso' had become by the mid-nineteenth century)

K.279
I: ♩ = 120; II: ♩ = 50; III: ♩ = 120

K.309
I: ♩ = 112; II: ♪= 63; III: ♪= 132 (first movement anything but 'con spirito'; Andante *molto* adagio)

K.330

I: ♪= 138; II: ♪= 96; III: ♩ [*recte* ♪] = 144 (finale surprisingly steady; unplayable at ♩ = 144)

K.311
I: ♩ = 100; II: ♪= 112; III: ♩ = 58 (all three movements remarkably steady, the Andante con espressione similar in its pace to that of K.309 in Potter's rendering, presumably inspired by Mozart's explicit 'con espressione' marking)

K.283
I: ♩ =108; II: ♪= 84; III: ♩ [*recte* ♩.]=108 (the opening movement paced similarly to Potter's minuets – that of K.282, for instance – and suggestive that he regarded K.283 as beginning with a movement of this type; as in the case of K.332, one wonders if, given the somewhat slow pace indicated for other finales, Potter's ♩ = 108 was indeed his intention here.)

(Volume 7: Music for Violin and Piano)

K.570
I: ♩ = 120; II: ♪= 84; III: ♩ = 72 (first and last movements surprisingly steady)

There seems no obvious reason for the noticeably steady tempos indicated for some of the outer movements (and selectively highlighted in the above listing). Potter's frequent choice of the quaver subdivision of the beat as the pulse perhaps suggests of a *bel canto*-inspired approach, savouring each legato connection between melodic intervals throughout a phrase within the Andantes and Adagios. Alternatively, his choice may indicate the need to leave space for virtuosic embellishments (such as he is supposed to have improvised in his public performances of Mozart's piano concertos) in much smaller note-values than any indicated in the actual score, though Potter nowhere notates such embellishments. A further, more practical, possibility is that since English pianos of the 1840s had become rather heavier and deeper of touch than their predecessors, in order to render Mozart's quicksilver passages satisfactorily a slower overall pace was needed. Whatever the actual reason, the finales rarely come across as sparkling culminations to the sonatas if Potter's tempos are adopted.[19]

Potter frequently adds expression marks to Mozart's texts, suggesting an overtly emotional approach to their performance. Thus the 'Andante cantabile' heading of

---

[19]   Not that such a trajectory for Mozart's sonatas as whole works (or should that be Works?) is a necessary criterion of excellence in performance, or that the absence of such a trajectory renders Potter's metronome markings suspect or his edition as inferior or uncharacteristic. A taste for sparkling finales is simply something for which Potter does not specifically cater in his edition of 1848.

the second movement of K.310 is extended to 'con espressione',[20] while the Presto finale is marked 'agitato'; the Allegro assai finale of the C minor Sonata K.457 has 'con spirito' at bar 17, 'con forza' at bar 21 and 'agitato' at bar 74.[21] To the 'Andante' heading of K.533 is added 'Molto espressivo e legato' (there could be no more apt a benchmark for Potter's entire rationale for his Mozart edition, in fact). Example 4.1a, showing bars 28–46 of the Andante, -typifies Potter's interventions, with its *sf* marks, left-hand arpeggiations,[22] *fp* marks and *crescendo* and *decrescendo* hairpins. Accents are regularly applied to indicate how to shape Mozart's phrases for the audiences of the 1840s (see Example 4.1). That they were not exclusively percussive in intention is shown by their somewhat deliberate, weighted quality within the metronome marking given to the Presto finale of K.310 ($\bullet$ = 72); accents frequently mark out the phrase-shapes here, for instance at bars 37, 38, 39, 45, 46, 47; 52, 56, 60 and 61, at the first reprise (bars 111, 112, 113, 119, 123, 124) and at the *majore* theme (bars 144, 145, 147, 148, 149, 152, 153, 154). Example 4.2 shows the role of accents in defining melodic profile within the opening bars of K.282 in E flat.

The tendency of nineteenth-century editors of Mozart's sonatas to smother them beneath legato slurs, thus habilitating them within the prevailing cantabile pianism borrowed from *bel canto* opera, is epitomized by Potter's texts. While it would be unfair to claim that he entirely supplants Mozart's originally very precise and articulate local slurring with long phrase-slurs, this is the general approach to his presentation of the leading melodic lines. His rendering of the opening of K.309's Andante un poco adagio, which Mozart so carefully marked for his pupil Rosina Cannabich in the autumn of 1777, is a case in point (Example 4.3). Whereas Mozart marks the articulations very precisely on the level of the beat and sub-beat,[23] Potter phrases in whole bars or groups of bars. His legato and cantabile conception is especially prominent in the second main theme (bars 33–6).

---

[20]   An amplification which is also found in the 1792 Artaria print of this work: *Sonate pour le clavéçin ou piano-forte composé par W. A. Mozart oeuvre 20 a Vienne chez Artaria et comp.*, with which Potter's text shares a number of identical readings in respect of slurring and articulation (though not sufficient to suggest that the Artaria print served him as a copy text – Potter's copy texts for his 'New and Correct' edition remain elusive).

[21]   'Agitato' is not appended to the tempo heading, however. In the 'dedication copy' of K.457 (Jerusalem, Jewish National and University Library) presented to Mozart's pupil Thérèse von Trattner (1758–93), the composer added 'agitato' to the tempo heading.

[22]   Arpeggiated chords for expressive effect are rife among Potter's texts. Some examples: K.280, arpeggiated chords to left and right hands at the beginnings of bars 2, 3, 8, 34, 36, 38, 39; K.310, arpeggiations to first beats in the closing cadential bars 31 and 86; K.311, arpeggiations on first beats at bar 15 (each left-hand crotchet), 39 (right hand), 41 (left and right hands), 45 (left and right hands, 49 and 51 (left hand), 57, 58 (left and right hands), 77 (each left-hand crotchet), 111 (left hand, both minims), 112 first beat (left and right hand).

[23]   Further on Mozart's indications to this movement and their performance implications, see below, pp. 108–16.

Example 4.1a   Sonata in F K.533/ii, bars 28–46

Example 4.1b   Sonata in F K.533/ii, bars 101–14

Example 4.2   Sonata in E flat K.282/i, bars 1–12

Example 4.3   Sonata in C K.309/ii, bars 1–8

Two features related to slurring stand out from Potter's edition:

- His long slurs sometimes end with a staccato stroke (wedge) to the final note. Instances may be clearly seen in Example 4.2 above and in bar 11 of Example 4.4, showing the opening phrase of the F major Sonata K.332.[24] Two perhaps interconnected explanations for this suggest themselves. First, by 1848 the habit of realizing slurs as also *diminuendi* towards the last note of the group (as recommended in eighteenth-century performance

---

[24]   Their length contrasts markedly with those found in Mozart's autograph, in which the slurring is in individual bars or beats. Potter's slurring of the left hand (a single slur covers all of bars 1–4) buries Mozart's suggestion that bars 1–2 (with subdominant inflection) constitute a single harmonic unit, followed by two one-bar units – a very characteristic momentum.

practice treatises, including that of Leopold Mozart) and in which the last note was also somewhat shortened had perhaps been forgotten, as part of a trend in which an articulate mode of musical speech focusing on the characterization of local gesture was replaced by the long-line *vocalise*. Perhaps Potter felt that the performer therefore needed reminding of this convention. Secondly, if the performer were playing Potter's edition of Mozart's sonatas on, say, a quite recent English-action piano by Broadwood or Wornum, on which the sound decay of the notes is not so rapid as on a Viennese-action instrument of c.1800 (or later models by Graf or Fritz with which Potter may have become familiar during his Viennese sojourn from 1817),then the player would need actively to impart a sense of physical shortening to these phrase terminations in order to round them off smartly – exactly as Potter notates with his staccato wedges.

Example 4.4   Sonata in F K.332/i, bars 1–12

- Phrase-slurs to the bass line. These regularly appear in Potter's texts, typically underlining cadential approaches, and they imply a recommendation to think harmonically in one's playing; illustrations of such harmonic representation may be seen in Example 4.3, from K.309, above (for instance, bars 6–7, 7–8, 14–15). More broadly, Potter's bass slurring tends to show phrasing and perhaps offers further evidence of the longer units of thought characteristic of his own performances of Mozart's sonatas by the mid-nineteenth century. Example 4.5 shows Potter's phrase-slurs to bars 1–16 in the finale of K.457. Interestingly his bass slurs sometimes diverge on recapitulation later in a

Example 4.5   Sonata in C minor K.457/iii, bars 1–16

movement. Compare, for instance, Example 4.1b showing bars 101–14 of and Andante of K.533 with Example 4.1a showing bars 33–46 earlier in the movement. The fact that the precise application of dynamic marks in these parallel passages also diverges suggests that the later appearance of bass slurs is not an example of 'the usual inaccuracies of the Music Engraver' but a deliberate underscoring of the sense of tonic arrival towards the end of the movement.

Johann Baptist Cramer and K.310

An instructive historical context for the A minor Sonata K.310 is provided by an edition published in about 1860 as *Sonate sentimentale pour le piano-forte ... revisé par J[ohann] B[aptist] Cramer* (London: Cramer & Co.).[25] Johann Baptist Cramer (1771–1858) was generally regarded as one of the finest pianists of his generation. His solo piano works, and especially his instruction manual, *Studio per il pianoforte*, published in 1804 and 1810, contributed significantly to the development of an idiomatic piano style during the early nineteenth century. Beethoven apparently regarded the *Studio* as the ideal technical preparation for performances of his

---

[25]   It appears as No. 7 in Cramer's series 'Morceaux characteristiques et brillantes' and is preceded by a two-page Adagio introduction to Mozart's sonata consisting of rhapsodic arpeggios composed by Cramer himself. Copy consulted: London, British Library, h.321. rr.(4).

own piano sonatas. Cramer's noted command of the legato touch was to become something of a stylistic benchmark for performances of Bach, Haydn and Mozart in the early nineteenth century; indeed, Ignaz Moscheles commented particularly on the vocal quality of Cramer's performances of Mozart. Following the very successful example of his teacher, Clementi, Cramer established himself, from about 1805, as a music publisher (the publishing house still survives). His edition of Mozart's K.310 repays careful study.

Cramer's slurring of the Allegro maestoso's secondary theme beginning at the upbeat to bar 23 perhaps represents his view of how he understood the internal unfolding of its phrase-patterns. He begins with three whole-bar slurs (bars 23–5); bar 26 splits into two half-bar slurs; bars 27–30 each return to whole-bar slurs; bar 31 reverts to two half-bar slurs; bar 32 proceeds in a succession of four *beat*-length (crotchet) slurs; bar 33 consists of a half-bar slur (beats 1 and 2), followed by two beat-length slurs; finally the cadential bar 34 is split as a half-bar slur followed by the minim trill and resolution into bar 35. Representing Cramer's notated succession in performance implies that the regaining of the higher octave register in bar 26 will be shown quite overtly by marking the third beat somehow (possibly with a slight *tenuto* on the first semiquaver of the group, C); that is, it evidently proceeds as a two-stage ascent to treble G rather than as a seamless flow. As the cadence is approached (bars 32–5), Cramer's implied pattern of emphases – crotchet–crotchet–crotchet–crotchet; **minim**, crotchet–crotchet; **minim**; **minim** – suggests a relatively fractured, accentual interpretation in contrast to a steady and generally uniform flow in whole- and half-bar units that characterizes the first part of this secondary theme. A subtly different pattern of phrase-slurs appears at the analogous point in the recapitulation. There is still an overall trend from relatively smooth and uniform at the start towards a more angular approach as the cadence looms, but bars 113–15 (equivalent to bars 32–5 of the exposition) are now structured crotchet–crotchet **minim**; crotchet–crotchet–crotchet–crotchet; **minim**; **minim** – possibly indicating a conception of cadential impetus different in the minor key (the music is cadencing into the tonic, A minor, at this point) as compared with the major (the exposition cadenced into the relative major key of C in bar 35). Such distinctions are perhaps to be expected in a piece whose *Affekt* was specifically represented as 'sentimentale'. Certainly Cramer's habit seems to be to highlight chromatic harmonies – especially in opposition to diatonic ones – by distinguishing the slurring. At the structurally pivotal bars 56–7 within the development section (an augmented sixth chord preparing for the series of pedal points over B, E and A leading to the dramatic departure from the main theme at bar 70, in D minor), Cramer notates the arpeggio descents from treble B♭ to A♯ two octaves lower as a succession of *beat*-length slurs, in contrast to the whole-bar slurs that have preceded this moment. The intended effect is evidently to give accentual prominence to the augmented sixth, highlighting its structural harmonic function. Likewise, at the close of this movement bars 126 and 127, outlining two different diminished seventh chords in close succession, are treated to *beat*-length (crotchet) slurs throughout, in contrast to half-bar (minim) slurs following from this point until the end of the movement, which proceeds harmonically as a series of dominant–tonic chord alternations.

Finally, a point about Cramer's dynamics. Generally he does not interfere in a movement that is remarkably sparse in its dynamic indications. On the third beat of bar 46 he notates *fortissimo* (no dynamic occurs here in either the autograph or first edition[26]), and on the second beat of bar 78 he gives *dim[inuendo]*, which appears in no other source. Interestingly, the next dynamic in Cramer's text is *piano* at bar 84 (the three-quaver upbeat figure); is the implication that the *diminuendo* is a rapid one, lasting only until the E major chord at the start of bar 79 (preceding the chromatic scale-run which leads into the recapitulation of the main theme, to be played – by implication – *forte*), or is this a long-range *diminuendo* lasting until bar 84, in which case the recapitulation of the main theme takes place in the context of a steady dissolving of energy built up during the development? Such a strategy would indeed highlight the supposed 'sentimentale' quality.[27]

---

[26]   The last effective dynamic in either of these sources is actually *piano* (from bar 23). An edition from 1792 published by Artaria (*Sonate pour le claveçin ou piano-forte composé par W. A. Mozart oeuvre 20*) gives *forte* mid-way through bar 46 (copy consulted: London, British Library, Hirsch IV.25).

[27]   Arguably a gradual decay of sound at least until the return of the theme itself is reinforced by Cramer's slurring pattern here: bar 78 proceeds from two *beat*-length (crotchet) slurs to a half-bar (minim) slur; bar 79 has two half-bar slurs. Overall the pattern suggests a progressive dissolution of tension.

Chapter 5
Approaching the Texts

The Rhetoric of Continuity

In an earlier study of Mozart's piano sonatas, I attempted to demonstrate possible rhetorical frameworks for their appreciation, drawing in detail on models from ancient Greece and Rome and their reinterpretation by eighteenth-century writers.[1] My intention here is not to revisit that linguistically inspired approach to narrative continuity but to complement it by reference to broad rhetorical readings that may inflect our understanding of Mozart's texts, either conceptually or else in performance.

Concepts underlie performances, of course, and let us begin with perhaps the most closely dissected of Mozart's piano sonata movements from the rhetorical point of view, the first Allegro of the F major K.332. Notable for the mobility of its surface continuity at the opening (each four-bar phrase seems to set out on a new tack), it has attracted the attention of critics whose perspective is influenced by Topics (*topoi*).[2] After beginning with a minuet-like phrase, Mozart diverts at bar 5 to a flowing texture in two-part counterpoint, then (bar 12) to a hunting motive, a cadential close returning to the world of the minuet, perhaps (bars 19–22), and a sudden lurch into the world of *Sturm und Drang* (bars 22–40). Each of these successions operates by association (with the minuet, with the worlds of 'learned counterpoint', the hunt, the wild and dramatic *Sturm und Drang*), and suggests that the perception of narrative continuity may – if we know how to read the signs – be influenced by factors external to the originally domestic environment of the solo keyboard sonata. Topical reference as a guide to the understanding presupposes that the frame of reference is a broad one and no respecter of generic identity. To put it the other way round, perhaps topical perception suggests that genre is but an artificial construction for delimiting works in the classical period and that *Sturm und Drang*, for instance, makes just as much sense in the context of a solo sonata

---

[1]   John Irving, *Mozart's Piano Sonatas: Contexts, Sources, Style* (Cambridge, 1997), part III.

[2]   Among them Wye J. Allanbrook, 'Two Threads through the Labyrinth: Topic and Process in the First Movements of K.322 and K.333', in Wye J. Allanbrook, Janet M. Levy and William P. Mahrt (eds), *Convention in Eighteenth- and Nineteenth-Century Music. Essays in Honor of Leonard G. Ratner* (Stuyvesant, NY, 1992), pp. 125–71; John Irving, 'Deconstructing Topics: Tracing their Status in the Allegro of Mozart's Piano Sonata, KV332', *Mozart Studien*, 15 (2006): 269–76; Leonard G. Ratner, 'Topical Content in Mozart's Piano Sonatas', *Early Music*, 19 (1991): 615–19.

as in a symphony. Assuming that topical migration underlies our appreciation of this opening, are we subsequently to regard the secondary theme (entering at bar 41) as relatively stable in kind? Its lack of migration to competing associative dimensions for a whole 16 bars is contextually quite interesting: only the *Sturm und Drang* episode retained its identity for longer (18 bars), and that was a *transitional* section, not a thematic statement. In bar 58, it does give way to something else, though this introspective and syncopated passage (eventually animated by dynamic oppositions of *forte* and *piano*) holds the stage for almost as long. What follows until the triumphant cadence arrives marking the end of the exposition is likewise remarkable, when measured against the opening *embarrassement de richesses*, for its calm and steady poise. Topical association prompts two kinds of understanding here: firstly, it translates Mozart's rather crowded opening in K.332 into four *spaces for action* (yet another external reference point suggests itself here: the operatic stage on which these four contrasting characters enter in hurried succession, each presenting its credentials with varying degrees of success); and secondly, by drawing our attention to such a crowded environment, it suggests a broader, rhetorical space for this exposition, namely that of an opening fizzing with energy which gives way to calm poise once the dominant key is reached and yet more characters are allowed to claim our attention, but this time for longer. Seeing the broad design this way may – it is to be hoped – discourage the interpretation of Mozart's *forte–piano* alternations in bars 60–65 as an excuse for *sforzando* accents. Surely, the *fortes* are enhancements of the harmonic colour at this point, melodic dissonances lasting a full crotchet to be teased out of the texture, perhaps with the application of a little rubato (especially in bars 64 and 65) rather than a trail of brutal stabbings, after which the theme announced in bar 71 sounds ludicrous.[3]

The idea of a rhetorical dimension for continuity in Mozart's sonatas offers us a variety of perspectives for understanding them. We might read the first movement of the C minor Sonata K.457 for instance, as a structure feeding on the rhetoric of dramatic interruption. That notion extends not just to the wholesale silencing of phrases (for instance at the opening, or bars 45 and 50, or bars 83–99), but likewise to the smaller local scale (the breathlessness of bars 13–19, bars 27–8, bars 30–32, bars 59–61 and so forth), and to the shocking contrasts of dynamic, register, articulation and texture which pervade the whole movement. Perhaps another way of configuring this rhetoric is 'invasion'. There is no space inhabited by any of the material in this movement that is not ultimately threatened by the invasion of something else within it. Examples (not an exclusive list):

- The rapid evolution of the transitional E flat theme commencing in bar 23 allows it no real time to assert itself before it changes into a variant (bars

---

[3]   Try playing this passage (including the continuation beyond bar 71) on a clavichord and you will appreciate both that Mozart's *fortes* are not *sforzando* accents and that there is an underlying conformity of the musical characters all the way through the second part of this exposition, in contrast to the opening section.

27–8) which is immediately cast aside by the chromatically side-slipping chords in bars 30–34.

- The secondary theme (in E flat, at bar 36) is disturbed by a wild chromatic outbreak (bars 44–5 – threatening also in terms of registral breach); no sooner has that breach been repeated than a mighty cascade of triplets sweeps back and forth through almost the entire range of the keyboard.
- By the end of the exposition, even the opening theme (but is it an opening theme? – it is used here as a conclusion) is competing with itself for space, entering now in close stretto.
- Stretto invades the opening theme yet more closely at bars 118–20 (in the recapitulation), and again in the coda, where even a diversion to A flat cannot shake off this spectre of itself before the whole movement ends quietly with a troubling lack of resolution.

Either way, Mozart seems to have acknowledged that this is a movement in which extremes are made to cohabit uneasily; for instance, he changed the tempo designation from a simple 'Allegro', which he appended to the so-called 'Dedication Copy'[4] of K.457, to 'Molto Allegro' in the first edition, which Artaria produced in Vienna in 1785, evidently appeared under the composer's supervision. Perhaps we should read it – and play it – in this spirit.

Returning to the rhetoric of generic association beyond the sonata's domestic frame, we might notice prominent *orchestral* simulations in the first movements of K.309 in C and K.311 in D, both written at the end of 1777 in Mannheim. where Mozart was exposed to perhaps the finest orchestra of his day. Both sonatas open with strong *unisono* figures reminiscent of the 'call to attention' that was such a feature of orchestral music of the time, and it is tempting to read the succession of textures against an imagined orchestral palette of scorings featuring strings alone, perhaps a solo flute or oboe doubling here and there (K.309, bars 39–42 of the first movement, for instance; K.311, first movement, bars 20–24) and blazing tutti outbursts (K.309, bar 43; bar 50; K.311, bar 48; bar 66). Read this way, both movements call for an interpretive expressive scale beyond the normal frame of domestic reference.[5]

---

[4]   This is a fair copy, not in Mozart's hand, made for the sonata's dedicatee, Maria Theresia von Trattner (1758–93), one of his piano pupils. It is today held in the Jewish National and University Library, Jerusalem. Artaria's first edition of December 1785 (*Fantaisie et sonate pour le forte-piano ... oeuvre XI*) combines the sonata with the subsequently composed *Fantaisie* in the same key, K.475. For the *Fantaisie* and its possibly rhetorical function as *exordium* (introduction), see Irving, *Mozart's Piano Sonatas*, pp. 73–82 and 147–50; also Eugene K. Wolf, 'The Rediscovered Autograph of Mozart's Fantasy and Sonata in C minor, K.475/457', *The Journal of Musicology*, 10 (1992): 3–47.

[5]   Quasi-orchestral textures in these two sonatas are not restricted to first movements. Outbursts such as are found at bars 58, 69, 111, 162 and 173 of the finale of K.309, and

The contrasting rhetorics of freedom and constraint repeatedly suggest themselves across the pages of Mozart's sonatas. At one extreme we might imagine the opening of Mozart's first surviving sonata, that in C major K.279. As Robert Levin has perceptively observed, its opening is built from figures that are the stock-in-trade of the brilliant improviser, flitting to and fro among patterns falling first this way, then that – effectively a notation 'after the facts' of something that started life not conceptually as 'conceptual composition', but as a series of physical gestures emerging spontaneously under the composer's fingers at the keyboard.[6] Examples of the spontaneous, improvisational quality of this movement include the surprising subdominant-coloured offbeat accent in bars 12 and 13 and the loose succession of textures and gestures (for instance, in bars 25–31, and the expansion of the figure sounded at bars 16–20 subsequently at bars 70–74, which betrays the improviser's fingers at work exploring the keyboard range while opening out new harmonic areas). There is a mobility to the surface of this Allegro that belongs in the physical, rather than the mental, exploration of space. Above all, perhaps, is the sensation of semiquavers overflowing, effortlessly and almost impolitely.

Such an insight might, for instance, encourage us to view this opening not from the rational perspective of assumed order lying within the conception, to be uncovered by systematic analysis of thematic and harmonic procedures, but instead from a curiosity about ideas in play. There is order here, to be sure, for Mozart's melodic gestures are no amorphous scramble of notes chaotically riding the waves of his imagination. They relate to the underlying harmonic scheme. There is a scheme, and it is a logical one, non–negotiable and with a tonal trajectory headed for a definite outcome; the precise material content at any moment within that harmonic route map (whether melodic, figurative, textural, registral ...) is there for the taking. It could go in any one of several directions. It so happens that Mozart chose to notate in one such way. Play the exposition repeat, and you may decide that some of this material content might change; that you might take a different course; that you become involved on the compositional level, liberating yourself from the detail of the score (and from a mindset that regards the actual provision of the notes as 'not the performer's business'). Or you may not; you may play in exactly the same way all over again. Quite a lot is at stake here, namely the fundamental relation of the player to Mozart's text, which in turn bears on what we believe that text to mean – did Mozart have an express *intention*, for instance? There may ultimately be no correct answer to that question, but reading the opening pages of K.279 as a texted version of something spontaneous is a good start.

---

bars 33, 56, 127, 168, 229 and 266 in the finale of K.311 seem to call forth similar external associations. Orchestral gesture as a trait in K.309 is examined in greater detail in Chapter 6.

[6]   See Robert D. Levin, 'Mozart's Solo Piano Music', in Robert L. Marshall (ed.), *Eighteenth-Century Keyboard Music* (New York, 1994), pp. 308–49 (at pp. 308–9 and 314).

At the other extreme is the very last sonata of Mozart's to survive: K.576 in D. Here freedom is disciplined by counterpoint. The carefully crafted harmonic trajectory is given an extra rigour by the presence of exposed two-part contrapuntal textures that at once characterize and precisely shape the moment-to-moment continuity. Mozart uses imitative counterpoint in a regulative way. That regulative power may be seen on the local level, as bars 8–16, whose direction, both thematically and harmonically, is very precisely controlled by a particular stretto imitation of the opening theme two quavers apart. But it also operates structurally, for Mozart inserts strettos at important moments in the outlining of the form, using contrapuntal process as a series of marker posts. For example, within the exposition, a stretto on the opening theme at just one quaver's distance singles out the passage between bar 27 and bar 41 as a reinforcement of the dominant key (attained already, but weakly, in bar 27), preparing for the arrival of a contrasting secondary idea in bar 41. Again, stretto, now at one bar's distance, maps out strikingly remote tonal space (starting from B flat) within the central development. Within the recapitulation, stretto serves to draw out attention to Mozart's recasting of the thematic ordering: the original bars 27–41 are repositioned within the unfolding sequence so as to follow the contrasting main secondary theme, highlighting the potential of classical phrase-construction to be understood as a linear succession of modules capable of arrangement into several equally satisfying shapes. Reading the notes on the page encourages us towards a particular view of continuity.

Yet there is a contrasting, rhetorical, kind of continuity here too: the strict, regulative aspect of stretto which we might read off the page is itself 'counterpointed' against a playful curiosity with stretto possibilities. Once again, there is an almost physical dimension to this experience. Passages such as that beginning at bar 27 arguably leave a trace of Mozart's curiosity as an improviser at the keyboard ('so what happens if I imitate the theme after just one quaver?'). The notated text records not just a presumed fixed compositional 'intention', but exploration in action. The same is true of bars 62–72, where the stretto overlap is much looser and is repeated with the hands swapped round; and yet again, at bars 137–44 – a sequential extension of bars 27–34. The recurrence of this last passage is significantly delayed within the recapitulation, perhaps because of the use of stretto within the central development (it should have returned after the dominant cadence in bar 121). Mozart plays not only with the ordering of themes, but also with the relation between function and place. The cadence just referred to in bar 121 follows a stretto on a different theme, growing out of the semiquaver suffix at bar 108. From bar 108 until bar 118 Mozart develops the potential of this suffix to combine with itself in order to effect a satisfying tonal transition to the cadence in bar 121. The function here, then, is transitional modulation; but the mechanism is thematic development of the kind seen within the development 'proper' (most especially bars 59–82, which similarly deploys stretto overlap of a different suffix to define a precisely modulating tonal space). The relation of theme and mechanism has become a game in which material identity is in turn confirmed and questioned by being transplanted out of its expected locale. Tracing its journey across the pages of Mozart's score in K.576 recovers the fingerprints (literally) of Mozart the skilful improviser.[7]

The Whole Picture

What of Mozart's sonatas as three-movement wholes? We tend to value Mozart's handling of sonata form as a touchstone of compositional skill within the classic period generally,[8] and that encourages us to concentrate, understandably enough, on first movements. Much of the discussion of how we might understand form in this book has to do with first movements also. But what of the slow movements and finales?

It would be a misrepresentation of Mozart's sonatas to regard them, by and large, as tracing a path away from the conventional expectation of a relatively weighty first movement to which two further movements are merely appended just for the sake of it. That would be to devalue – for instance – the slow movements and finales of K.279, 280 and 281. Indeed, in the case of the F major Sonata K.280 (spring 1775), we find an early example of a slow movement with real emotional depth. It is particularly notable for the combination, following the central double bar, of chromaticism with dramatic hiatus for expressive effect. Yet it cannot truly be regarded as the emotional 'heart' of K.280 as a whole. Nor in the first two sonatas do the relatively lightweight rondo finales counterbalance the first movements. That of K.280 comes quite close, with a genuinely developmental section after the central double bar leading to a dramatic breaking-off, *forte*, on A major (the dominant of the relative minor key) in bar 106, before the *piano* return of the main theme at the end of the next bar.[9] In the case of K.281, Mozart's finale, an extended rondo with

---

[7]   That persona may be glimpsed also in the finale of K.576, which likewise indulges in the imaginative possibilities of stretto combination of the opening theme against itself at bars 34–40, 103–8 and 125–31. The sheer variety of counterthemes against the main theme in this movement (for instance bars 9–12; 26–34, inverted in bars 95–8; 99–102) is at once a compositional *tour de force* and the echo of the brilliant improviser's mind and fingers in creative action.

    [8]   A recent demonstration of that tendency is James Hepokoski and Warren Darcy, *Elements of Sonata Theory: Norms, Types and Deformations in the Late-Eighteenth-Century Sonata Form* (Oxford, 2006).

    [9]   Although Robert Levin takes the opportunity to introduce an improvised cadenza at this point when the second half is repeated (*Mozart: Piano Sonatas K.279, K.280 & K.281 on Fortepiano*, vol. 1, Sony BMG Music Entertainment/Deutsche Harmonia Mundi, 2006 [82876 84237 2], track 6), bridging the silence and raising the interesting question of whether, even at this early stage, Mozart's solo sonata texts contain notated and (as at this moment) un-notated clues to their realization in performance that would tend to make them stray beyond the domestic frame and into the realm of public concert representation in a manner similar, generically, to his contemporary piano concertos such as K.238 and K.246.

some elements of tonal organization borrowed from sonata form (though not quite a sonata-rondo), is the genuine equal of the first movement. Partly, this has to do with the tonal identity of the opening theme, which begins surreptitiously with a sequential cadential progression easing into the tonic, B flat, from the dominant of C minor, which, though delicate and graceful in its melodic contours, suggests through its underlying harmonies a broader frame of reference that obtained in either of the finales to K.279 and 280. It has, moreover, two prominent middle episodes, in C minor (bars 52–70) and E flat (bars 90–114). The first is notable especially for its chromatic inflections of melody and harmony and also for bold gestures involving texture inversion; the second exploits colouristic effect, principally the upper register of the keyboard, and also dramatic dynamic and textural contrasts (bars 101–5). Their combination of registral, textural and dynamic effects influences the way in which Mozart brings back the main rondo theme in bar 114, a curtailed reprise beginning beneath a protracted trill (with the hands subsequently inverted). The lack of separation between the episode and the opening theme's return is striking. It is as if the reprise is spoken by the voices inhabiting the middle of the movement: in effect, a continuation of the business of gesture and colour that characterized that portion, rather than a strong return to different protocols. That breaching of conventional expectations of how the different sections of a rondo will behave is partly what lends this particular finale an independence, worthily complementing the tersely argued narrative of the first movement.

The remaining sonatas of this earliest group balance their three movements in contrasting ways. K.282 in E flat begins with a slow movement, but in a fully developed sonata form, against which the subsequent minuet and trio and 2/4 finale represent a progressive acceleration of tempo over the course of the whole work. In K.283 the first movement retrospectively sounds lightweight compared with the expansive rhetoric of the Andante (note especially the expressive use of silence in bar 13, of chromatically inflected melody after the double bar and of thematic development allied to contrast of register and texture for colouristic effect in bars 16–23). But the real climax comes in the finale, which is longer and with a wider range and variety of themes and phrase-lengths than K.279, 280 and 282, and with a genuine sonata-form development. As in K.282, the impression overall is of a journey leading towards a culmination in the finale, though it is achieved by different means and in differing proportions. The D major Sonata K.284 takes

---

There are certainly reports of Mozart performing his early sonatas and concertos in what seem to be public concert settings in Augsburg and elsewhere in 1777, sometimes side by side in the same concert. See Otto E. Deutsch, *Mozart: A Documentary Biography*, trans Eric Blom, Peter Branscombe and Jeremy Noble (London: Barrie & Rockliffe, 1965, repr. 1990), pp. 165–8. If we feel that there is some discomfort in navigating across the generic boundaries of sonata and concerto, then that may be the result of subsequent (nineteenth- and twentieth-century) constructions of their respective roles in a predominantly civic concert culture, and of our expectations of these genres, rather than Mozart's views on the matter.

the question of complementarity further still. Here a weighty, orchestrally inspired sonata-form first movement is more than adequately balanced by an extended set of variations (the only variation finale found among Mozart's piano sonatas). K.284's outer movements make their serious points in radically contrasting formal ways (the tersely argued logic of the sonata[10] versus the open-ended variations re-tracing the same thematic and harmonic ground in successive statements, each of the same length and proportion[11]), a tension nicely separated by the intervening minuet and trio, which perhaps function as a 'neutral' area within the work as a whole.

Working through the chronology of Mozart's sonatas, we find no shortage of examples where the central movement exerts a strong gravitational pull on the work as a whole. K.280 and K.283 have already been mentioned; others include K.310, K.333, K.457, K.533 and K.576. In each of these sonatas the central slow movement arguably becomes the site of a subjective foil to the outer movements: more personally narrative in kind than the broader, block-like statements found there. The significance for the whole sonata of this reversion in slow movements to a more introspective stance is of no small importance. In part, it has to do – in varying proportions, according to the particular case – with the quantity and diversity of material they contain; contrasting characters; journeys to remote tonalities; developmental writing (in the sense later meant by Reicha, with fragmentation and reorderings of thematic elements); contrasting textures, dynamics and registers. Sometimes, as in K.576, the appearance of introspection may be put down to a shift to the minor mode (unusually for Mozart, this section is in F sharp minor, and perhaps evocative in a loosely intertextual way of the slow movement of the Piano Concerto K.488, completed some three years earlier). But the modality does not explain the whole effect, which hangs also on the intervallic patterning (those diminished thirds, fourths and fifths in bars 17–18), which creates local tensions against the underlying one-chord-to-a-bar harmonies, and on the register changes (which speak more colourfully on a fortepiano of Mozart's day than on a modern grand).

In K.457 the sheer density of musical material in the Adagio is overwhelming (with written-out embellishments of the reprises[12]) and extends beyond thematic variety to rhythmic complexity, giving a spaciousness to this movement that

---

[10]   Mozart abandoned an extensive draft of the first movement in his composing manuscript, replacing it with the version we know today. It is possible that the reason for his second thoughts had to do with the way in which he wished to integrate thematic content with developmental procedures; see William Kinderman, *Mozart's Piano Music* (Oxford and New York, 2006), pp.117–27, which starts from a refutation of László Somfai, 'Mozart's First Thoughts: the Two Versions of Mozart's Sonata in D major, K.284', *Early Music*, 19 (1991): 601–13.

[11]   Though Mozart significantly recast the bar-to-bar sequence of variation 11 in his manuscript at some point before publication of the first edition.

[12]   Others, long lost and different from those printed in the first edition, survive in Mozart's autograph, recovered in 1990. See Irving, *Mozart's Piano Sonatas*, pp. 80–82.

is certainly the equal of its surrounding movements. Syncopation becomes a characteristic feature (bar 19), as do extreme register contrast (bar 29), chromaticism (bars 5–6 and 30–31) and precision of dynamic contrast (bars 34–8). Tonal disruption and return provide a broader perspective for such details (the contrasting central theme first sounded at bar 24 in the subdominant, A flat, returns at bar 32 in G flat, after which sequential ascents serve the dual and simultaneous purpose thereafter of tonal restoration and subjective utterance).

One way in which we may interpret the effect of this Adagio's impassioned style of speech within the C minor sonata as a whole is to read it as a departure from the 'public' mode of discourse found in the preceding Molto allegro. There, Mozart's thematic and textural materials (principally), while characteristic and memorable in themselves, are directed towards mapping out broad tonal schemes, the internal design of phrases being teleological rather than locally expressive in function. For instance, the opposition of a loud opening gesture in octaves with a soft, sighing, pleading gesture featuring slurred falling fifths and sixths in a harmonized context and moving I–V, followed by a balancing repeat of this pairing returning V–I and continuing with a dominant pedal, might plausibly be regarded as a *functional deployment* of these materials just as much as a *statement* of those materials, staking out the ground for this sonata-form movement. Compared with this mode of discourse, that of the Adagio might be read instead as a 'private' world of localized expression in which individual gesture is 'of the moment', a present-tense utterance of an individual voice, rather than a blueprint functionally directed towards the service of a structure. Thus the thrice-repeated right-hand chromatic gesture of bars 30–31, with its diminished thirds, C♭–A♮, circling around the pitch B♭ and declaimed within a precisely order scheme of dynamics, makes its point purely for its own sake, rather than as part of a broader structural purpose; and the fact that it occurs three times in succession is perhaps a marker of some kind: pleading or insistent? At any rate, this gesture commands attention locally and now, for what it is being in the act of its declaiming.

Or does it? We might instead notice that there is a material level of function here after all. The picking out of the pitch B♭ is a preparation for an unexpected tonal diversion to G flat at bar 32 (B♭ is reconfigured across the barline as the major third of the G flat triad), and thus a participant in a broad tonal scheme, cross-referring thematically back to bar 24. Alternatively, we might even point to the similar picking-out of the same pitch, B♭, in bars 30–34 of the Molto allegro (once more supported by chromatic sidesteps involving a C♭), functionally preparing the arrival of a secondary theme at bar 36 (albeit in the expected relative major, rather than the remote flattened mediant major). Are these two moments, then, cross-references between movements, suggestive of a whiff of cyclic connection? That is perhaps stretching a point. The broader issue here is of ambiguity. We can make this moment mean two different things in our interpretive interventions. An interpretation celebrating retreat into a subjective world of introspective utterance, departing the public frame of conversation for the private thought (perhaps even soliloquy), before returning to the fray in the Allegro assai finale, seems to fit the character of Mozart's Adagio best. But whatever our interpretive perspective, this Adagio is nothing if not rhetorical, and it opens up with great success an expressive, personal, subjective space of its own between the outer movements. As a result, the C minor Sonata as a whole is a richly characteristic work (perhaps, even, Work), which, unsurprisingly, was inspirational to Beethoven in his own early sonatas in that key Op. 10 No. 1 and Op. 13 (whose slow movement opens thematically and tonally in strikingly similar vein to Mozart's countertheme at bar 24).

In the later sonatas, Mozart seems to have taken the view that finales should effectively counterbalance the opening movements. This he achieved in a variety of ways. In K.332 virtuosity as a rhetorical topic is the key, though the sheer exuberance of the sextuplet figuration regularly scaling the upper limits of the fortepiano's range is an important factor too. In K.533 and K.576 Mozart's finales are not only complementary in function; they point to a cyclic view of the work as a whole, not in thematic terms but procedurally, for he pointedly returns in each case to the regulative role of counterpoint that has been so strong an underlying feature of both first movements. In the case of K.533, completed and noted in Mozart's *Verzeichnüss* on 3 January 1788, the finale is a contrapuntally refashioned version of the Rondo in F K.494 (1786) and was previously published as an independent piece by Philipp Heinrich Bossler in Speyer in 1787. The three-movement sonata was published by Hoffmeister in Vienna in 1788. Mozart's revision of the rondo for this publication inserts a new section (bars 143–69), the latter part of which (beginning at bar 152) incorporates a stretto fugato, giving retrospective context to earlier contrapuntal textures such as bars 95–9, which are subsequently treated in partial inversion at bars 109–12. It is as if Mozart is consciously *making* the material of the revised finale return to the world of the first movement, in which figurative flamboyance shares the stage with a more contrapuntally disciplined neighbour.

Individual Case-Studies

K.330 Allegro: Dynamics and Thematics

Among Mozart's sonatas for which both the autograph and a first edition from his lifetime survive, none shows greater divergence in respect of dynamics than the C major K.330. Whereas Mozart's autograph text of K.330 has scarcely any dynamic indications in the first movement, Allegro moderato, the printed text issued in 1784 by Artaria as the first of *Trois sonates pour le clavecin ou pianoforte composées par W. A. Mozart, œuvre VI* is abundant in its application of especially *forte* and *piano* markings. This can be conveniently observed in the *NMA* text, which is based on the reading of the Artaria edition: dynamic indications in small roman type come from the Artaria print; those in large type from Mozart's autograph (restricted to bars 31, 34, 38, 54–57, 62, 63, 118, 121, 124, 141–8); those in italics are editorial. As can readily be seen from Artaria's text, the published dynamic markings cover almost every bar of the movement. While this is not systematic, the strong tendency is to apply *forte* and *piano* either in alternate bars or in alternating two-bar groups, reminding us that one way of reading Mozart's narrative is as an unfolding series of localized statements and decorations of right-hand melody over a simple and simply textured harmonic pattern. In such a dynamically profiled alternating structure, the contrasting gestures and characters of the material, as well as their functional setting within the phrase as beginnings, middles or ends, are thrown into the sharpest relief, aiding the comprehensibility of the second subject group (bars 19–58) in particular. This richly polythematic section gains in comprehensibility when seen in a context of ongoing dynamic contrast. In particular, its prolific thematic invention is rescued from the likely appearance of diffuseness by the fact that such frequent and short-range dynamic contrast has the effect of limiting our expectations of thematic significance to the purely local and immediate site.[13]

Take, as an example, bars 19–34 (the start of the second subject group). Beginning *piano*, the phrase is answered *mezzo forte* in a higher register (suggesting a progression of the narrative beyond the initial statement) and falls again to *piano* for the embellished restatement (a reminder of the starting-point) before moving decisively by means of a *forte* flourish to the point of arrival in bar 25. Such alternations of dynamics effectively highlight localized thematic contrasts and returns, alternations of register and diverse rhythmic profiles to clarify the bar-to-bar narrative. They also spark off an element of play. Note that although there is a change in texture at bar 26 (introducing broken-chord triplet semiquavers in the accompaniment) there is no change of dynamic, which, as in the analogous bar 22, remains *forte*. Is bar 27 (*piano*) a new beginning or an answer to bar 26? Texturally it is an answer, a responding element within a texture introduced just beforehand. But dynamically the *piano* of bar 27 leads off on a new track, to which bar 28 (*forte*, and rising, not falling) responds. And if bar 27 is a beginning, then bar 30 should be a response to bar 29, which it is dynamically – but not texturally, for the triplets cease in the previous bar. There is a delightful counterpoint of dynamic and textural phrase profiles, therefore: bars 26–7 and 28–9 form a textural

---

[13]   Which is not to say that the lack of dynamics in the autograph means that Mozart did not originally imagine such possibilities at the time of composition. Coupled with the fact that the autograph places the right-hand part in the soprano clef, the key, character and technical diversity of the movement suggests that it may have been conceived as teaching material (see also Irving, *Mozart's Piano Sonatas*, pp.66–72), and its 'clean' text may have had a deliberate purpose, namely to allow, in the teaching process, a variety of possible dynamic alternations for his pupils. The published text of 1784 – addressed like other sonatas printed in Mozart's lifetime to a growing market of fortepiano-owning amateurs and no longer pedagogic in an immediate sense – needed to specify appropriate dynamic contrasts on a touch-sensitive keyboard. In fact, there is good reason to believe that Mozart was intimately involved in the production or the Artaria edition: the brief coda at the end of the Andante cantabile – absent from the autograph and based on an afterthought linking the central episode to the *da capo* – is surely Mozart's own work rather than that of an in-house editor.

scheme, and bars [25–6], 26–7, 28–29 [and 30–34] a dynamic one, the elision of
the two occurring in bar 26. Without the bar-by-bar alternations of dynamic level
this subtle point might go unnoticed. Mozart's dynamic contrasts and gradations
may play a part also in shaping the continuity of the development section, being
carefully placed in relation to:

- The introduction of the new figure in bar 66 (*piano*).
- Its extension as a syncopated phrase in higher register leading into A minor
  (bars 69–71).
- The expressive reinterpretation of bars 71–2 (*piano*) in bars 73–4 (*cresc
  … forte*).
- The sequential fragments and embellishments of bars 75–8.
- The extended dominant pedal (bars 79–87) preparing for the tonic return at
  the recapitulation, especially the final fragmentation at bars 83–7.[14]

If we view analysis as something involving a symbiotic relationship between a
conceptual object (i.e. a notated musical text) representing the work 'as such' and
an enlightening theoretical methodology justified by that conceptual object – or
perhaps justifying it – then the view of K.330's first movement offered above
may seem rather too empirical to count as analysis at all. A different and perhaps
more rigorous-seeming picture of this movement is suggested by a reading derived
from more familiar analytical ground, namely motivic construction. Without a
doubt, we may justifiably claim a major role for motivic organization within the
Allegro moderato. Apart from its fundamental reliance upon thematic statement
and embellishment for continuity (for instance, bars 9 and 10 in relation to bars
5 and 6), it demonstrates a tendency towards generative motivic usage. Examples
include:

- The influence exerted by short, descending scale fragments (ultimately
  derived from bar 1 of the opening theme) over much of the content of
  bars 1–18. As well as the obvious evolution of bars 13 and 15 from bar
  11 by decoration, it is possible to interpret the cadential steps in bars 7–8
  as decoration of a more fundamental stepwise descent, g″–f″–e″, traceable
  back to the first three notes of bar 1. Such a view would, incidentally, be a
  claim that intervallic shape consisting of a particular sequence of ordered
  events (adjacent falling scale-steps), pitch identity (g″–f″–e″ in each case)
  and length (just three adjacent scale steps in each case) operate on different
  hierarchical levels, being expressed either in the form of a local melodic

---

[14] Neither in the autograph nor in the Artaria print does a forte dynamic occur at
the return of the main theme in bar 88 (the autograph has no dynamic; the print has forte
in bar 90). The piano at bar 4 of the print (again, the autograph has no dynamic marking)
suggests that the movement opens forte, in which case the recapitulation should perhaps
do likewise.

statement (bar 1 – a gesture of commencement) or else as a cadential process dividing up the structure (in this case at bars 7–8) into meaningful portions. Alternatively, the conceptual stepwise succession g″–f″–e″–d″–c″ underlying bars 1–2 of the opening theme might also be claimed as an underlying pitch framework for the repeated descents g″–c″ in bars 11–15. Or perhaps by a reverse process of reasoning the falling single step a′–g′ suggested by bars 5–6 and 9–10 (which are less a melodic than a harmonic gesture outlining the chord progression IVc–I) generate the striking melodic exclamation a″–g″ at the start of bar 11. Such potential interconnections abound in this section.

- The evolution of bars 23–34 in stages from the material of bar 19. Bar 23 decorates bar 19, especially its second half, which may relate to bar 25, concluding with a new suffix analogous to that of bar 22, but with a contrasting, rather 'martial' profile that seems to generate the succeeding phrase leading up to the cadence at bar 34 (containing references en route to the second half of bar 19 and its embellished form at bar 23).

- More closely knit are bars 42–6, which begin with repetition followed by obvious fragmentation of the end of the figure in bars 44–45, before this is extended in a continuous scale ascent to d‴.

- The 'development' section: although wholly unrelated to material from the exposition, bars 59–87 are far from episodic in character and in fact lend themselves well to a motivic approach to form building.[15] Bars 60–61 are sequential with bars 59–60, as in turn are bars 61–2. Bars 62 and 63 fragment and repeat one feature from this figure, veering briefly towards the minor mode before cadencing in bar 66. Thereafter a new figure is introduced, sequentially exploited and extended in bars 69–70. Following yet another new idea in bars 71–2 and their transformation in bars 73–4, completing a stepwise fourth descent by way of register transfer (c″–b♭′– a″–g″), there is more sequence, chromatic embellishment and segmentation of bar 74's cadential fall before a change of direction heralding the arrival of the recapitulation in bar 88.

---

[15] Mozart brings back the material of bars 59–63 to conclude the movement casually and *piano*. Whether this ending is truly a coda is a question worth posing. By following the decisive cadential material of bars 144–5 with a return to the material that opened the development, Mozart throws bars 59–63 once more into the spotlight, most especially if his indication to repeat from bar 59 is followed. What is their status? Are they truly the beginning of a development, or an afterthought to the exposition, linking through to the new idea at bar 66? Alternatively, are bars 59–63 a dominant-key response, rather than a beginning or a link, to the tonic statement in bars 145–50, if the repeat is included? At any rate, the fact that the section from the central double bar (following the decisive arrival in the dominant G major) to the end of the movement is framed by this ambiguous material arguably strengthens a binary view of the movement over a ternary one (exposition– development–recapitulation).

The point here is not to set up a relative scale of values for these two contrasting analytical approaches. They are simply different in kind, each pursuing its own agenda. A motivic view illuminates certain possibilities for internal organizational relationships predicated upon a belief in the power of intervallic shapes to sustain patterns of repetition and deformation that together form a referential network capable of exerting a degree of structural logic, even control. By contrast, the empirical analysis deriving from the placement of dynamics in the first edition of K.330 promotes a 'surface' view of its continuity that derives not so much from notation *as notation*, but rather from notation as a symbol for sound. While dynamic is something that primarily inhabits performance, the scheme of its notation in Artaria's print serves as an analytical tool as well, and consequently as an influence on our understanding of musical structure in this movement (involving the relation of separate thematic statements and embellishments to a strictly localized context of sonority). Analysing the movement in this light is, moreover, a practice with a particular *historical* origin, namely one deriving from Mozart's decision to make the work a public document in 1784 and to present its text in a particular way. Its identity has somehow changed in the process leading from autograph text to published text. More important than that is the fact that neither text is more than a provisional record. If we regard the Artaria text as 'definitive' then that is our construction of the facts, not Mozart's, and derives from an agenda of a particular type – and possibly in this case an anachronistic type – linked to the idea of the 'Work Concept' so convincingly elucidated by Lydia Goehr,[16] which deems the achievement of such a definitive state as a historical necessity. That necessity is a socially constructed one, presupposing an author who is the creator of a work which fixes a concept in the form of a cultural object to be represented publicly (in performance, but also as an object for intellectual understanding, expressed in prose) and, finally, carrying an afterlife whose value projects beyond its own time into future imagined cultures in which to be represented afresh. Any analytical practice, whether empirical or systematic, is embedded in this social construction. Realizing that fact is significant both for analytical practice and its musical object.

K.545 in C First Movement: A Question of Content

This is perhaps the most familiar of all Mozart's piano sonata movements. He entered it in his *Verzeichnüss* with a date of 26 June 1788, describing it as 'Eine kleine klavier Sonate für Anfänger' ('a little piano sonata for beginners'). That epithet was corrupted somewhat in the first edition of February 1805, published by the Bureau d'Arts et d'Industrie in Vienna, on the title-page of which it was advertised as 'Sonate facile'. No autograph survives, regrettably, so we shall never know if Mozart equated 'beginner' so readily with 'easy'. The fact that

---

[16]   Lydia Goehr, *The Imaginary Museum of Musical Works: An Essay on the Philosophy of Music* (Oxford, 1992).

no dynamic markings are to be found in the first edition may suggest that its text was drawn from a manuscript that was used by Mozart for teaching purposes and was deliberately plain, so that a variety of expressive approaches might be demonstrated in lessons. Or it may not; Mozart's normal habit was to elaborate manuscript texts on publication, providing detailed dynamic indications for the use of those beyond his direct tutelage and approaching his compositions now as public documents, rather than the subject of private conversations between master and pupil. Still, we should not forget that no source of K.545 dates from Mozart's lifetime; perhaps the piece was never really intended for public consumption.

Perhaps the most remarkable feature of the opening movement[17] is that its material content is extremely focused on classical music's 'mechanical' building-blocks of scale and arpeggio patterns. While these are fundamental to the content of Mozart's music, they almost always divert rapidly and creatively from one suggestion of a scale or arpeggio fragment to another and in their total effect never appear to be 'mere passagework', but retain instead a vocal agility whose quality rarely dips below the exceptional. Indeed, the diversity of migration among and between hints of this or that scalic succession is one of the key contributions to the development of the classical idiom found in Mozart's music in any genre. Yet in the first Allegro of K.545 we find – at least in its visual appearance on the page – succession after mechanical succession of scales (for instance, bars 5–9, 35–41, 46–54) or arpeggios (bars 18–22 63–7). Is this perhaps to be explained by an intended didactic purpose? Mozart does not say in his *Verzeichnüss* in what discipline the 'beginners' are beginning (piano-playing, or composition?), and it is possible that the unrelieved, un-nuanced scale and arpeggio successions are there to provide demonstrations of material design: skeletons on which alternative divisions of the same harmonic successions might be subsequently improvised by the novice composer, perhaps.[18] Underlying it all is a regularity of harmonic pace that is also atypical for the mature Mozart, and possibly a hint of a didactic origin.

Interestingly, on further inspection, the movement does not appear so mechanical after all. Both the tonic-key opening theme and the contrasting dominant-key theme (bars 14–17) are 'thematic'; only their transitional continuations are founded on, respectively, scales and arpeggios (namely, the device of the scale and that of the arpeggio as resources for narrative continuation are kept separate – another strategy well suited to *demonstration*). Mozart deals with these contrasting typologies further in the central development. He first shows how a cadential figure used to close one passage (bars 26–7) may alternatively be used to open another (bars 29–30); and he immediately places that contextually in two-bar alternations with scalic material perhaps derived from the transitional scales first heard at bar 5, now

---

[17] The 'Allegro' tempo marking is absent from the first edition, but is shown thus in André's edition from the same year: *Sonate facile pour piano-forte composée par W. A. Mozart a Vienne au mois de juin 1788* (Offenbach am Main, 1805).

[18] Or, for the really bold, a skeleton on which alternative divisions might be improvised in performance of the repeats.

coupled with its inversion (bars 31–2), drawing together representative samples of two quite different regions of the exposition in close conflict and exploring new harmonic territory starting out from the dominant minor. This alternation is not quite exactly replicated in bars 33–6, for the scale-plus-inversion portion is itself subjected to textural inversion in bars 35–6), beyond which point the alternation is superseded by half-bar dialogues of just the inverted (descending) fragment, hurrying through a circle of fifths and leading to the much-famed subdominant recapitulation of the Allegro's opening theme (bar 42).[19] Starting out from this base, one might imagine that Mozart would simply replicate the opening I–V trajectory of bars 1–12, ending on a half-cadence in C major and continuing in that same key as tonic to the end of the movement. He doesn't.[20] Instead a longer transition is composed to prepare the tonic more convincingly and reinstate the transitional scale mechanics once again in the form of texture inversion, which now borrows at least a part of its meaning from the experience of the central development. The ensuing arpeggios arising out of the secondary theme take on a renewed meaning too, for they are memorably coloured by an entirely unnecessary upward transposition (bars 65–6) linking these by now not-so-mechanical 'patterns' to the nuances of keyboard colour (on the fortepiano, the separation of the registers is far more pronounced than on a modern piano, where the subtlety of Mozart's effect is lost). Finally, when considering 'mere' passagework, we might take the harmonic aspect closely into account. When Mozart inverts the scalic texture of bars 46–9 in bars 50–54 he is not exactly replicating these bars. On the fourth beats of the inverted texture, the right hand's crotchet chords are now temporarily dissonant against the flowing semiquavers beneath (or, depending on one's viewpoint, the

---

[19]   Why the subdominant recapitulation? It is a natural question to ask, but we should be wary of expecting a revelatory answer along the lines of 'by doing so-and-so, Mozart enables such-and-such'. He may have intended to counterpoint a surprise of tonal process with the apparent predictability of his scale and arpeggio material. He may have intended it simply as a joke (leading those 'in the know' to expect that this was a false recapitulation of the opening theme (which would surely turn up in C major eventually – but then it never does); or he may simply have liked the fact that, by pitching the theme in this tessitura and in F major, he could sound the highest note on his fortepiano at the end of bar 43. Any and all of these explanations are plausible. None, however, is as impertinent as the assumption that there must be a reason for the subdominant recapitulation (to be divined and explained theoretically, for instance).

[20]   The curious reader is invited to try this out. It looks perfectly acceptable on the page (and even just fits the strict five-octave compass of Mozart's 1782 Walter piano without requiring reshaping of the pattern), but there is something awkward and unsatisfying about the necessary tritone leap from C to F♯ moving from the cadence into the secondary theme's preparation (analogous to bars 12–13). Interestingly, the G–C♯ tritone of bars 12–13 does not jar; there must be something about the tonal context (moving away from the tonic, as opposed to reinforcing the tonic after a journey outside it boundaries) that creates the difference in perception.

first semiquaver of each fourth-beat group in the left hand becomes an accented passing note); that is not the same as before. Subtleties count in this movement.

K.576 Finale

Bars 1–16 of the Allegretto finale of the D major Sonata K.576 may be understood according to the organizational plan shown in Figure 5.1 Such a model stresses two aspects in particular: the hierarchical ranking of organizational layers; and the symmetry that each of these layers exhibits, both internally (along the horizontal aspect of the plan) and relationally (vertically within the plan). It may be read as a succession of subdivisions. The complete paragraph (level I, at the top) is explained as comprising on the next level down two balancing periods each of eight bars; *and simultaneously as* four phrases each of four bars (level III); *and simultaneously as* eight two-bar clauses (level IV). And of course, levels II and III are each themselves explicable in terms of the next lowest level(s). That feature which level II most prominently articulates is the recurrence at bar 9 of

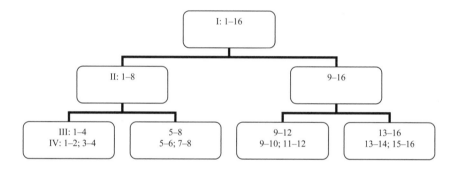

Figure 5.1   Diagrammatic representation of nested phrase-structures in K.576 finale

the opening material, now in a contrapuntal setting which firmly stresses the downbeats (by contrast with the opening chordal accompaniment). Additionally, the open cadence in the dominant (bar 8) is balanced at the end by a strong V–I progression in the tonic, D major. Level III focuses on contrast across four-bar successions, the material of bars 9–12 and 13–16 gaining meaning (i) locally, as answering phrases to the main theme and its repetition (in the case of bars 13–16, the lively triplet figuration unfolds as an extension of the left-hand counterpoint to the main theme, in fact; (ii) structurally, in terms of their internal sequential design; and (iii) architecturally, in relation to each other as phrases whose quality is 'responsorial', leading to particular types of cadential closure after four bars. In level IV local sequential relationships are perhaps the dominant feature, whether between two-bar successions (as in bars 1–2, 3–4) or within single groups (bars

5–6); notice that the left-hand triplet accompaniment from bar 9 adds a sequential component not present originally.

To such a model might be appended a fuller account of the tonal unfolding on the level of the phrase or clause and a description of the harmonic rhythm, noting particularly:

- The subtle distinction to be drawn between the one-chord-per-bar of bars 1–4 and the passing-note motion within different positions of the same chord in bars 5 and 6 before the onset of cadential motion in crotchet beat units (bars 7 and 8).
- The contrasting harmonic rhythm of bars 9–13 in relation to the opening with far more in the way of dissonant passing-note motion characterizing the contrapuntal texture.
- Chord *changes* on the crotchet unit in bars 13–14, in contrast to the passing-note motion of the analogous bars 5 and 6.
- The quaver-beat chord changes at the closing cadence, occurring for the first time arguably to mark out this important architectural moment.

Interesting though such an organizational representation is, it should be stressed that if we choose to understand the music in this way, our understanding is a conditional one, and does not represent the way the music necessarily 'is'. Such approaches as the one above are tools for the understanding. They condition our attention according to certain fundamental structures of knowing. In this case, the organizational matrix combines pattern recognition (most obviously concerning thematic and harmonic shapes, but also unit lengths) with the identification of repetition and contrast in order to construct the design. In other words, these fundamental structures are the site of our understanding, not Mozart's music. While a hierarchical system is a perfectly reasonable, workable and useful design, it is not the only possible interpretation of this paragraph. Another way might be to regard bars 1–8 as 'introductory' to the more virtuosic statement underpinned by running triplet semiquavers beginning in bar 9 (a perspective not dictated so much by thematic patterning and an awareness of cadential rhyme-schemes as by sensitivity to the expressive partnership of texture and register); or again, the brash arrival of C♮ in the left hand in bar 13 might be thought a (structural) harmonic outcome of the gentle chromatic dissonances in the right hand in bars 2 and 4. Both of these alternatives are perhaps sited in the act of playing, rather than in the reading of a notated score.

K.333 Allegro: Analysis and Ideology: A Cautionary Tale

Consider the first movement of the B flat Sonata K.333. The 63 bars of its exposition divide neatly into primary and secondary material, the primary material being of a monothematic nature already incorporating, at bars 14–18, developmental tendencies, whereas the secondary material (bars 23–63) is rather more varied with supplementary thematic ideas at bars 39, 43, 50 and 59. Nevertheless, the two sections share processes in common. Both rely on restatement and partial transformation as a mode of narrative progress (compare bars 10, 31, 40 and 54, each of which is a repetition of material just previously heard). Both the primary theme and the main secondary theme (first heard at bar 23) feature syncopation, though in contrasted ways strongly marked by the notated articulations. In bar 1 the dotted crotchet b♭′ is lightly separated from the preceding slurred quaver pair and merges seamlessly into what follows. By contrast in bar 2's 'answer' to this opening gesture, the e♭″ on the second beat is slurred off the first-beat f″, a pattern repeated at the start of bar 3, where the slurring of the three remaining quavers a′–b♭′–c″ retrospectively shades the emphasis of the syncopation on the dotted crotchet a′. So in each of these three bars of the opening theme the 'pointing' of the syncopation is subtly different – an evolving rather than static rhythmic feature. During the restatement of this theme in bars 10–18 further transformations occur: bar 11 merges the slurring of bars 1 and 3 and bar 12 that of bar 2, though the continuation soars skywards in a single sweep until beat 2 of bar 14.[21] This moment may be seen as developmental in relation to the opening: whereas the extension of the quaver pairs of bar 1, beat 1 (c″– b♭′) into crotchets (f″– e♭″) in bar 2 is a purely motivic relation, at bars 11–12 the progression from c′– b♭ quavers to f′– e′ crotchets generates a further continuation that breaks out of the motivic mould established thus far into florid figuration, migrating between two different expressive characteristics (an observation which may guide the performer here, for instance). Thereafter, the character returns firmly to the motivic, the tendency being to negate the syncopation (absent in bar 15, diminished to half its value, straddling beats 1 and 2 in bar 16) while isolating just the original falling quaver pair (bar 17). Retrospectively, the whole of this opening paragraph seems to indulge in a playful fascination with length in relation to intervallic definition, a feature which is visible in the score (if one looks for it) but which makes its impact most clearly in performance, provided that Mozart's articulations are observed.

Yet Mozart is not quite finished with the syncopation. In bar 24 (belonging to the main secondary idea) it returns, this time neatly separated by the slurring both from the preceding quaver pair (rising this time) and from a balancing stepwise pair at the end of the bar, continuing with quaver–crotchet–quaver syncopations in each half of bar 25 (the degree of syncopation is enhanced a little more in the restatement at bars 32–3).[22] And yet a further pattern evolves over the dominant pedal, F, in bars 50–51 and bars 54–5 (this time as a quaver and a dotted crotchet in each half of the bar, the dotted crotchet's worth comprising straight semiquavers – a pattern not obvious notationally, but clear in performance by virtue of Mozart's

---

[21] A similar flourish occurs in the secondary group, bars 35–8, similarly growing out of a thematic restatement.

[22] For a contrasting view of the relation of this secondary idea to the main theme, see Hepokoski and Darcy, *Elements of Sonata Theory*, p. 136.

accentual staccato wedge on the first quaver, separating this from the rest of the pattern, which is editorially slurred in the text of the *NMA*).[23]

Viewing the exposition in this way perhaps sets up the development for a particular kind of attention. Since there is evidence of rather close motivic working within the exposition (indeed there is more 'developmental' writing to come subsequently in the recapitulation, at bars 107–10 and 142–51), we may approach the development section proper in the expectation of actual development for once, rather than of Mozart's habitual episodic writing. To begin with, that is exactly what happens. Commencing with a statement of the opening theme, Mozart promptly reconfigures it by diluting the sense of syncopation in the second bar (bar 65), now consisting of a new descending triad of dotted quaver, semiquaver and crotchet decorated with a grace note. The original sense of a narrative progress through varying shades of syncopation is wholly lost in bars 66–7, which form a near-exact melodic and rhythmic sequence with the preceding phrase. Thereafter the grace-note-plus-descending-triad component is isolated at bars 68–9, all the time racking up the harmonic tension through diminished sevenths, then relaxing onto the temporary tonic, F (deflected to the minor mode) in bar 71. From this point the material ceases to relate to the exposition at all closely, though the surreptitious reinstatement of the falling scale step in slurred crotchets from bar 87 (animating a dominant preparation for the return of B flat major) is quite masterly – even incorporating syncopation, this time in the accompaniment of bars 91–2 – and making the recapitulation of the opening theme (with the original quaver step fall) at bar 93 seem casual and inevitable at the same time (in performance at least, if Mozart's slurring is observed).

The foregoing account draws primarily upon performance considerations. Avoiding any particular analytic methodology or theoretical modelling of sonata form, in which systematic thematic and/or harmonic functions are classified, it has no pretensions at completeness but moves from the simple observation that there is a relatedness between certain melodic and rhythmic features of this movement of K.333, towards an interpretive strategy that seeks to establish an organizational procedure (that is, one imputed – not claimed as the composer's 'intention').[24] We might instead read this movement in terms of Schenkerian voice-leadings,

---

[23]   It has to be admitted here that Mozart's notation distinguishes between bars 50–51 and 54–5. In the latter, the syncopation seems intentional since the left-hand quavers are slurred in threes; in bars 50–51 the texture and octave register are slightly different and the accompaniment consists of just a pair of slurred quavers on the off-beats.

[24]   Incidentally, it subconsciously occasions the use of terminology such as 'exposition', 'development' and 'recapitulation', as if this were a movement that conformed already to the models advanced in the wake of Beethoven's sonata practices in the early nineteenth century (for instance, the understanding of its 'development section' stemmed fundamentally from the presence of motivic development relating to the exposition material, contrasting with free episodic material and a stealthy final hint once more at the motivic before the onset of the recapitulation).

prolongations and structural hierarchies of dissonance.²⁵ Or we might think of the adapted re-entry of the opening theme at bars 10–12 as a thematic remodelling necessitated by a transitional tonal function in the following bars, classifying that intervallic deformation as a fingerprint both of Mozart's conformity to a certain formal and tonal procedure and simultaneously of a type of theoretical understanding of that process. Each of those practices is a kind of investigative behaviour that presumes within Mozart's music an underlying logic to be revealed, and the application of each practice signals the presence (or at least the potential) of valuable structures of conceptual thought engaging in a relationship with Mozart's creative thought. And of course, each practice will offer different perspectives when applied to the Allegro²⁶ of K.333.

A reasonable question that flows from this is whether analysis (from whichever perspective) actually reveals 'what is there'. Or does K.333 *appear to be* that way, when considered analytically, because the mental structures we tend to apply in analysis are innate to us, and because as a consequence what we perceive when acting analytically is simply what our perceiving apparatus permits us to perceive when perceiving? That is a dilemma which was faced in full measure by Immanuel Kant during Mozart's lifetime, and it is a debate to which musical analysis belongs. Kant's discussion of the aesthetic consequences of our ways of interacting with our world, expressed in judgements of beauty, first appeared in print in 1790.²⁷ In such an encounter, the object that we find beautiful may not exist as a material form that directly induces our recognition of its beauty. Instead, that object is adapted to the *a priori* conditions governing the operation of the human mind when it perceives, and it is through that omnipresent apparatus that we do in fact perceive. That, according to Kant, is analogous to the *a priori* conditions of his earlier *Critique of Pure Reason* (1781; to do with how we have knowledge) and *Critique of Practical Reason* (1788; to do with how we apply that knowledge in a moral context), in both of which the conclusion is that categories such as time, space, quantity, quality and relation are not absolutes (not essences of the world 'out there') but rather part of our apparatus for interacting with our world (which is why we see things that way). We perceive phenomena, not their actualities. By extension, in an aesthetic encounter, such as that which we might have with K.333's Allegro, our perception

²⁵ See, for instance, Allen Forte and Stephen Gilbert, *Introduction to Schenkerian Analysis* (New York and London, 1982), pp. 143 and 145–6, which explores the concept of prolongation in the opening phrase.
²⁶ The tempo marking appeared first in the first edition published in Vienna in 1784 by Torricella: *Trois sonates pour le clavecin ou piano forte. La troisième est accomp d'un violon obblig:composées par W. A. Mozart, dediées a son Excellence Comtesse Therese de Kobenzl ... œuvre* VII (the other works being K.284 and the Sonata for Piano and Violin K.454). Subsequently 'Allegro' was pencilled into the autograph, along with tempo markings for the other two movements also taken from the first edition.
²⁷ Immanuel Kant, *Kritik der Urteilskraft* (Berlin, 1790). The fullest modern English translation is that of Werner S. Pluhar, *Critique of Judgment* (Indianapolis, 1987).

of its attributes (including the possibility that we may be experiencing a quality that we call beauty) is not a perception of any attributes the sonata may have in and of itself. Rather, its outward form provokes an engagement of our mental faculties of imagination and understanding, and it is in this involuntary response that we consequentially take our pleasure, provided that we remain objectively detached from the experience in respect of any quantitative or qualitative or relational properties of the thing we perceive. In that brief moment we may indeed know the work 'as such'. But the moment we categorize our experience of that moment – that is, the moment we *analyse* – we lose the encounter in a network of rational operations which substitute themselves as an impression of the supposed object.

An alternative approach to this issue of ontology is the concept of *difference* introduced by Jacques Derrida.[28] Derrida's argument is that *différance* is an all-constituting property lying at the origin of our process of conceptualization, a way of distributing, spatially and temporally, into categories both 'differed' (spatially) and 'deferred' (temporally) what he describes as an 'originary state', whose characteristics are beyond our powers of perception and even conception. *Différance* is a perpetual 'differing' and 'deferring' of an actual encounter with the Object of our perception (namely its full, authoritative presence within an encounter), denying us resolution in the form of a certain and stable answer, of the presently separate strands of uncertainty. All we can ever achieve is a *way of knowing*, not actually knowing.

As analysts of music, then, we face the possibility that those quantitative material characteristics through which we define the organization of musical structure are likewise an effect of *différance*. Not only is the material content of a composition just a spatially and temporally distributed mode of expression by means of which the work (or a section of it) is presented to our perception as analysts; that holds true also for the composer, for the moment the thoughts solidify in his mind into notes bearing apparent individual properties and relationships among themselves, he is already experiencing an effect of *différance*, namely the distribution of that which generated those particular notes into those inescapable *ways of knowing by means of quantitative characteristics*. Thus what we analyse as quantitative or relational characteristics within a piece such as Mozart's K.333 are conceptually constructed features (for him originally, as well as for us centuries later), not essences residing in that material with which we grapple.

As an object for analysis, then, Mozart's sonata movement becomes the site of that rather uncomfortable admission that we are not sure of the fixity of what we perceive: that neither is the object under our scrutiny of a concrete form capable of holding together and of existing in a relationship with the perceiver nor do our perceiving habits serve us true. We sincerely attempt a relationship with an object of our analytical concern, but are not sure that what we think we have is authentic.

---

[28]   Jacques Derrida, *Writing and Difference* (Chicago, 1983), Christopher Norris, *Derrida* (London, 1987) and Stuart Sim, *Derrida and the End of History* (Cambridge, 1999).

In the absence of such authenticity, attention focuses instead on usage. Analysis might still underpin structures of historical knowing and help to place this work stylistically in the overall progress of Mozart's oeuvre. The usage here is as a tool enabling the historical, and given that the autograph of K.333 is undated, it falls to analysis to help position this closely argued musical organism in a convincing chronology. That is precisely what Théodore de Wyzewa and Georges de Saint-Foix attempted in their magisterial *Wolfgang-Amédée Mozart: sa vie musicale et son oeuvre.*[29] On stylistic grounds, they confidently assigned K.333 to the Paris journey of 1778, specifically between July and September that year.[30] All editions of the Köchel catalogue to date give either 1778 or 1779. Wyzewa and Saint-Foix's stylistic opinion is founded on quite precise observations of material content that (deliberately) influenced my account above. K.333 falls into Wyzewa and Saint-Foix's 26th and 27th style periods for Mozart. These are characterized by a greater precision in the expression and narrative than is evident in Mozart's previous works and even incorporate the pathetic ('L'expression deviant plus precise, plus "parlant" et volontiers, plus "pathétique"'). In adapting his musical language to the requirements of French taste during the Parisian visit, Mozart sacrificed an element of virtuosity that had been characteristic of the recent Mannheim compositions (for instance, the C major and D major Sonatas K.309 and 311) in favour of longer works in a more learned idiom focusing on rigorous thematic treatment ('Ses morceaux redeviennent à la fois plus longs et plus savants, avec une sérieuse élaboration thématique se substituant au goût de virtuosité rapporté naguère de Mannheim'). Possibly 'élaboration' means intensification and/or amplification and/or embellishment rather than *motivic development* as such (for which the term would perhaps have been 'développement'). Nevertheless, for Wyzewa and Saint-Foix, Mozart's working with the thematic material in K.333 stands as an alternative to the virtuosity that they note as a style-feature of the Mannheim sonatas. In comparison with K.309 and K.311, there might well seem to be a broadening of the expressive range, especially in the use of melodic and harmonic chromaticism. The profile of the secondary idea in K.333 (beginning in bar 23) blends together a world of intervallic and rhythmic suppleness – underpinned by a tightly controlled network of motive forms – unimagined in K.309's sturdy and exciting exposition, for instance. This observation, empirically extracted from painstaking study of a broad range of Mozart's piano works, does indeed suggest a state of belonging for K.333 somewhat apart from K.309 and K.311.

But Wyzewa and Saint-Foix's comparative context (virtuosity replaced by motivic coherence and thoroughness) risks becoming allied to an agenda of progress and valuation: the interpretation of material characteristics emerging from analytical contemplation somewhat loses its purity when it becomes merely the first term in a progression: analysis → interpretive judgement → historical

---

[29]   5 vols (Paris, 1912–46).

[30]   Vol. 2, pp.405–6. A slightly later date (January–March 1779, after Mozart had returned to Salzburg), was suggested in vol. 3, authored by Saint-Foix alone.

ideology. That is not quite what Wyzewa and Saint-Foix were doing, for theirs was not an agenda of historical progress; rather there was the assumption that the adaptation of Mozart's style at this stage in his musical development (those 26th and 27th style periods) coincided precisely with his arrival in Paris and his exposure to French taste. They refer specifically to the abandonment in works such as K.333 of a recent Mannheim style in this latest stylistic guise, to the quitting of a 'taste' for virtuosity in favour of thematic concentration ('une sérieuse élaboration thématique se substituant au goût de virtuosité'). Perhaps that refers, subconsciously, to a particular 'way of listening' in 1770s Paris, within which virtuosity fulfilled only a relatively shallow and sensuous purpose. Perhaps cogency of thematic argument (that 'sérieuse élaboration thématique') satisfied deeper intellectual needs of at least some Parisian listeners. It is true that Mozart accommodated himself specifically to the Parisian taste during his visit, as we know from two letters to his father of 12 June and 3 July 1778 regarding the 'Paris' Symphony K.297. From these letters we learn that Mozart had observed and absorbed local symphonic preferences: 'I have been careful not to neglect the *premier coup d'archet*', he writes on 12 June,[31] though to judge by his sarcastic tone he regarded that famous device as a pretty tired formula, and he recast it significantly, including also a 'dernier coup d'archet' and other effects that played with audience expectations. Although Mozart talks of effects in these letters, rather than compositional technicalities or a sense of stylistic evolution expressed in motivic logic, there is undeniably a sense in which he acknowledges that the accommodation of his style to a particular place and a particular taste is crucial in establishing his credentials. Perhaps it is one responsibility of analysis to concretize that: to demonstrate something conclusive, based on a fixed text, working forensically towards proof of a case, and in K.333 we do indeed have a particular collection of material attributes whose defining characteristics and inter-relations, expressed by analysis, lay a secure foundation upon which to draw testable conclusions, in this case coming to the aid of history where documentary facts are lacking.

Incidentally, K.333 was not composed in Paris at all, and not in 1778 or 1779. As Alan Tyson convincingly showed, it is on a rather unusual paper-type which Mozart probably purchased in or near Linz in October–November 1783.[32] We should beware enmeshing analysis within ideology.

---

[31]   *Briefe*, 453: 115–16 and 121–5.

[32]   Alan Tyson, 'The Date of Mozart's Piano Sonata in B flat, K.333/315c: The "Linz" Sonata?', in M. Bente (ed.), *Musik – Edition – Interpretation: Gedankschrift Günther Henle* (Munich, 1980), pp. 447–54; reprinted in Alan Tyson, *Mozart: Studies of the Autograph Scores* (Harvard and London, 1987), pp. 73–81. The watermark is no. 69 in Alan Tyson (ed.), *Wolfgang Amadeus Mozarts Werke: Wasserzeichen-Katalog*, 2 vols, *NMA*, supplementary vols X/33/2 (Salzburg, 1996).

K.457 Allegro: Genre, History and Valuation

A rather lame question to ask of Mozart's piano sonatas – but one with revealing consequences – is 'which is the best one?' Perhaps that question hides within it a presumption that among the hierarchy of genres, the sonatas come some way down the list, below Mozart's concertos, and also below Beethoven's sonatas, which seem like mighty symphonic arguments by comparison with Mozart's 'trifles'. With one exception: K.457. Probably this is the most often performed and recorded of the sonatas, one likely reason for that being that in its material, treatment and form, it seems to prefigure the 'serious' sonata as subsequently established within the emergent realm of professionalized concert pianism by Beethoven. It is also in C minor, like Beethoven's Op. 10 No. 1 and the 'Pathétique' Op. 13.[33] Seen from a historical vantage-point (and possibly invoking also a rather special status as a cultural object that claimed the attention of Beethoven as a source of influence), K.457 is a characteristic piece going beyond the frame of a domestic genre. The material is of a narrative, even dramatic kind. This is evident from the very beginning, which presents a dialogue suggestive of two radically conflicting characters, juxtaposing (i) a staccato arpeggiated rising figure covering an octave and a minor third, *forte* and with markedly downbeat scansion, breaking off provocatively on the second crotchet of the bar, against (ii) a milder figure, slurred and legato, in a higher register but more limited in range, *piano* and featuring a prominent upbeat. While not actually telling a story or representing an image, K.457's material is of an overtly communicative nature, which cannot do other than provoke a response from the performer (and listener). For instance, following those sharply contrasting profiles in the first eight bars, Mozart introduces a dominant pedal – unusually early for such a device which typically occurs in a structural context of preparation (for instance, at the end of a development section ahead of the tonic return), rather than as here, starting out from a second-inversion chord and prolonging the sense of tonal instability at the opening. While the tonic, C minor, does indeed return in bar 19, it is immediately (and with a jolt) diverted to E flat. In other words, the material Mozart works with may be read as being about destabilizing an environment early on so as to justify its familiarization later. The language is of a sort abstracted from *Affektenlehre* and typically employed as a basis for dramatic expression in opera. That in turn suggests a special kind of listening environment, namely a public setting in which the sonata is presented to the attention of listeners gathered for the specific purpose of engaging with

---

[33] K.457's opening phrase is similar to that of Beethoven's Op. 10 No. 1, while the broken octave pedal in the left hand at bar 9 is similar to the accompaniment underlying the main theme of the Allegro of Beethoven's Op. 13 (the right-hand contrapuntal texture and the chromaticism at this point in each work are likewise similar).

such music, rather than as a pleasant background to their knitting, drawing or card games in the context of a fashionable salon.[34]

Generically, then – and rather like his symphonies and concertos – K.457 borrows the language of opera and its public setting. It is within that communicative framework that the sense of a narrative works. That includes rather severe demands on the listener to *follow it through*, whether simply as presentation (and there is rather a lot of material to be absorbed, for instance between bars 23 and 74 of the first movement) or as process: for instance, the harmonic path from bar 19 to bar 23; the more complex one from bar 44 to bar 59; and most especially bars 75–99, which also requires the identification of bars 79–82 in a new context of modulating link rather than, as originally, a contrasting 'secondary' theme, and also the derivation of the triplets (bars 77–78 and 85–94) from bars 21–2 and their new textural situation in dialogue. All in all, that is quite a challenging set of expectations for a composer to pose. Perhaps they can be satisfactorily met only in analysis, quietly and reflectively after the event, but my point here is that Mozart's material absolutely requires a degree of engagement in the context of listening: that is, the listener is part of the experience. The performer is part of that experience too, for K.457 is technically difficult. A talented amateur could certainly play it, but Mozart begins to stretch the boundaries of the sonata beyond that level, pointing towards the professionalization of the sonata genre. K.457 is not simply about playing the notes. It cannot satisfactorily be 'played through'; it requires careful practice to master not simply its technical challenges (not just the notes, but also the dynamics and articulations in consort, for instance at bars 23–30), but also to manage the transition between the different *Affekten*, for instance from bars 34–43 (cantabile and diatonic, paying careful attention to evenness of register in the hand-crossing) to the strident and chromatic bars 44–5, then back and forth more rapidly between the two types (bars 46–50) before yet another *Affekt* intervenes at bar 51, linking to the delicate resolution of bars 57–9. In an important sense here, a struggle with the material, to mould it into a coherent and – in the context of public communication – convincing form is paramount. K.457 requires a *reading* from the performer, an interpretation. And that fails (or is insufficient) outside a specific environment requiring the focused attention of a listener. K.457 might be said to acquire a cultural value from such an environment. Indeed, we might justifiably claim it as another early manifestation of Lydia Goehr's 'Work Concept'.[35]

But let us reconsider the ontology of all this. Is the impression outlined above one that emanates from within K.457, triggering in its course the contextual

---

[34]   Just such a setting is described by Mozart in a letter of 1 May 1778 from Paris (*Briefe* 447: 39–42), where he visited the Duchesse de Chabot in order to play the clavier at her salon; he complains that the Duchess and her companions never for a moment troubled to interrupt their drawing in order to listen to him play. Further on the salon, see Volkmar Braunbehrens, *Mozart in Vienna*, trans. Timothy Bell (Oxford, 1991), pp. 142–72, and Irving, *Mozart's Piano Sonatas*, pp. 11–13.

[35]   Goehr, *The Imaginary Museum of Musical Works*

historical reading described above? Or is it a reading whose origin actually is the historical context, seen in relation to the development of sonata-form theory from Koch to Marx, or the transformation wrought by Beethoven on the sonata genre, or the impact of developments in fortepiano construction (a Stein is arguably insufficiently light in touch and tone for K.457; ideally, a Walter is required to realize its power effectively), concert presentation and the cult of the virtuoso – all of which circumstances retrospectively generate a particular way of considering the materials and processes of K.457 (whose text is therefore an analytical construction)? In other words, this reading may actually be a historically produced one, imprinted on the text of K.457 and willing us to read it that way, emanating not from Mozart but from socially situated inter-related practices of musical scholarship, along with its perpetuating literature and its various readerships. Dramatic-seeming though K.457 undoubtedly is, to read and categorize the elements of its musical language and its processes analytically in terms that presuppose an identity presaging the era of Jan Ladislav Dussek, Johann Baptist Cramer, Schubert and above all, Beethoven is to locate analysis firmly in the controlling grip of history.

Part II
Playing Texts

Chapter 6
Instruments

About 1782, Mozart bought a piano by Gabriel Anton Walter (1752–1826). Mozart's piano, on which the majority of his mature keyboard works were composed and performed, still survives today, and may be seen in the Mozart Geburtshaus in Getreidegasse 9, Salzburg. Most recordings and performances of Mozart's sonatas on period pianos are on modern copies of Walter instruments.[1] Mozart's own piano was made by Walter shortly after 1780 and is one of the majority of that maker's surviving instruments with no identifying name-plate on the front fallboard. Walter's were durable instruments, able to accommodate the developing fashion for thicker keyboard textures, generally louder playing and virtuosic showmanship that emerged towards 1800 in, for instance, Beethoven's trios and sonatas Opp. 1, 2, 5 and 12. A Walter piano is considered by many present-day fortepianists to be the ideal instrument upon which to play Mozart's keyboard works. Compared with a modern grand piano, it has a light touch allowing great rapidity in scale work without the need for artificial finger staccato playing; the hammers are covered with strips of leather (graded in thickness from bottom to top across the five-octave range of the keyboard); its soundboard, strings, hammer striking-points, thin case and all-wooden construction contribute to produce a lively, clear and direct sound that greatly clarifies the textures of Mozart's music, whether within solo piano works, or in, say, the piano and violin sonatas, the 'Kegelstatt' Trio K.498, the piano quartets or the Piano and Winds Quintet K.452. Walter effectively standardized what is known as the 'Viennese piano action' at the end of the eighteenth century, with the hammers that strike the strings mounted directly on the far ends of the keys.[2] This gives the player astonishingly immediate physical control of dynamic nuance and articulation and is ideally suited to conveying the lightness and clarity of Mozart's piano music. By contrast, the modern piano makes a far more shrill and metallic sound rich in overtones, a tendency which developed steadily during the century or so following Mozart's death in order to express a sound world wholly different from that through which his musical thought was conveyed.[3]

---

[1] For instance, all but one of the recordings discussed in Chapter 7 are on modern copies of Walters.

[2] The so-called *Prellmechanik* action, as opposed to the *Stossmechanik*, in which the hammers are mounted on a rail separate from the keys. Walter actually manufactured both types. For details, see Michael Latcham, 'Mozart and the Pianos of Gabriel Anton Walter', *Early Music*, 25 (1997): 382–400.

[3] Remarkably, the argument is still sometimes encountered that Mozart would have preferred the sound and technical capabilities of a modern grand piano and would have

Partly, the very different sound stems from the fact that the modern concert grand has a good two octaves' extra range, requiring the use of a cast metal frame to bear the vastly increased tension of extra and much thicker strings, heavily overwound with copper. Also the hammers are felt-covered, much larger and much denser than those of Walter's instruments, and activate the strings in a more percussive, initially unpitched way at first, eventually blooming, after a brief delay, into a bell-like, rounded tone of considerable resonance and beauty, sufficient to penetrate a large concert hall – which during the course of the nineteenth and twentieth centuries became the normative acoustic for the public representation of music, and by means of which, reflectively, 'music' became instead 'concert music'.[4] By virtue of the mechanics of sound-production on the modern instrument, the textures of Mozart's (domestically conceived) sonatas therefore sound thicker, and the harmonics of the immensely powerful lower strings enhance (or sometimes obscure) the music in the treble register played by the right hand. Finally, the touch of a modern instrument is significantly heavier: its depth of key travel (the 'key dip') is roughly three times that of a Walter instrument; moreover, the weight needed to depress the key to sounding point on a modern grand is between three and four times that needed on a Walter (several lead weights are incorporated into modern piano keys deliberately in order to provide resistance). Taken together, these two factors mean that rapid passagework is considerably easier to play on an early instrument than on a modern concert grand. Mozart's piano music of his Viennese years is best regarded as the unique imaginative response of a genius to the particular physical characteristics of the pianos of his day and their sound-world – something utterly contemporary.

What the Walter fortepiano strikingly offers in Mozart's music is clarity of texture. In particular, each register of the instrument has its own markedly distinct tone quality, making the music speak in a much more colourful and characteristic way than on the modern grand. Within such an environment, the textures of Mozart's music gain in clarity compared with what is possible on the modern instrument. Distinctions between strands of counterpoint are enhanced by tonal contrasts produced by the instrument itself, rather than their having to be forced out

---

written for such an instrument should he have had the chance. Presumably, Michelangelo would likewise have preferred to work with a digital camera rather than a *camera obscura*, or fibreglass rather than marble. The fact is, had Mozart lived at a time when the mechanical possibilities of a modern grand piano were available, he would have been writing music in a rather different style anyway. The claim that he would have preferred to use the modern instrument for music within the stylistic parameters of his own time dismisses the fact that mechanical and musical developments are agents which interact in an unfolding *social* setting – in other words, aspects of the *history* of music. This is not to say that Mozart *should not* be played on a modern instrument, of course.

[4]   This is certainly not the place for a detailed account of the construction and mechanics of the modern concert grand. For an introduction to this, see David Rowland (ed.), *The Cambridge Companion to the Piano* (Cambridge, 1998).

of a uniform tonal landscape. All in all, a Walter fortepiano exhibits a relatively dry and sparkly tone in its upper register; a warmer, more singing quality in its middle register and a dark yet always clear bass – qualities noted by the contemporary Viennese commentator Johann Ferdinand von Schönfeld in 1796.[5] Passages such as bars 51–5 in the first movement of the C minor Sonata K.457 (and also its coda, bars 168–85), bars 152–62 in the finale of K.533 and 494 and bars 27–34 or bars 81–96 in K.576's opening Allegro benefit significantly from these fundamental tonal characteristics (as, indeed, does the coda of the latter movement). The straight stringing, in which the thin strings – brass in the bottom octave or so, iron from there to the top – run parallel to the grain of the soundboard, rather than the bass strings running diagonally across and above the higher strings (as on the modern grand), enhance this lucidity. From the bottom of the keyboard up to about B or B♭ above middle C, the instrument is double strung; thereafter it is triple strung. Taken together, all these factors mean that there is rarely any need to overproduce the treble lines on the fortepiano, since the tone quality of the lower registers never overpowers that of the treble.[6]

Walter's pianos would seem, therefore, to be the ideal instruments for performing Mozart's piano sonatas. Or are they? Mozart's piano has been much inspected in recent years, and internal evidence of the construction confirms that the instrument in the Mozart Geburtshaus, which is still occasionally used for recordings and concerts, does not any longer sound as Mozart would have heard it, since it was substantially overhauled by Walter himself in c.1800, on the instructions of Mozart's widow.[7] Among other interventions made by Walter at that stage, were (i) conversion of the original *Stossmechanik* action, in which the hammers were mounted on a rail at the back of the keys, to a *Prellmechanik*, in which the hammers are mounted directly on the keys (namely the 'Viennese action' mentioned above); and (ii) the radical alteration of the sustaining mechanism by the addition of knee-levers beneath the keyboard, replacing the earlier hand-stops (which activated the split damper rail). This latter point is crucial for the

---

[5]   Johann Ferdinand von Schönfeld, *Jahrbuch der Tonkunst von Wien und Prag* (1796), facsimile, ed. Otto Biba (Munich, 1976), pp. 89–9.

[6]   Fundamental studies of the construction and mechanics of the fortepiano include Katalin Komlós, *Fortepianos and their Music: Germany, Austria and England, 1760–1800* (Oxford, 1995); Richard Maunder, 'Mozart's Keyboard Instruments', *Early Music*, 20 (1992): 207–19; Richard Maunder, *Keyboard Instruments in Eighteenth–Century Vienna* (Oxford, 1995); Richard Maunder and David Rowland, 'Mozart's Pedal Piano', *Early Music*, 23 (1995): 287–96 and David Rowland (ed.), *The Cambridge Companion to the Piano* (Cambridge, 1998). By far the most comprehensive account of the relation between instrumental design and performance practice in this regard is Sandra P. Rosenblum, *Performance Practices in Classic Piano Music: Their Principles and Applications* (Bloomington and Indianapolis, 1988), specifically chapter 2.

[7]   For a comprehensive survey of this instrument, and of Walter's developing technique as a builder, see Latcham, 'Mozart and the Pianos of Gabriel Anton Walter'.

performance of Mozart's keyboard sonatas. While it is not expressly necessary to use a sustaining device (Mozart does not notate any 'pedal marks' in his sonatas)[8] the question necessarily arises as to how one was supposed to manipulate the hand-stop sustain while actually playing. With knee-levers, of course, one is free to raise the damper-rail as seldom or as often as desired, even if both hands are playing. Might the original state of Mozart's Walter piano (as he knew it during his lifetime) be a hint suggesting only infrequent use of the sustain device?[9] Would Mozart typically have achieved the illusion of undamped resonance by so-called 'finger pedalling', much applied by harpsichordists? He clearly was aware of knee-lever sustains at least as early as 1777 when he first encountered the fortepianos of the Augsburg maker Johann Anton Stein (see the following section). It does seem odd that he did not have this flexible device available on his Walter instrument. The separate pedal-board that Mozart subsequently had made for it would have added further dimensions to the tonal depth and perhaps compensated for the relatively basic mutation possibilities offered by Walter's hand-stops (and would in any case have kept his feet and legs too much occupied to manipulate knee-levers).[10]

K.309 and the Fortepianos of Johann Andreas Stein: The Search for Expression

Performance decisions are sometimes bound up closely with the expressive capabilities or potentials of specific keyboard instruments, and this relationship provides an important layer of contextual understanding. In the following section I shall explore this in relation to Mozart's C major Sonata K.309 (October–November 1777).

In October 1777 Mozart visited his father's home town of Augsburg. Among his first ports of call was the bureau of the instrument maker Johann Andreas Stein

[8] Strictly speaking 'pedal' marks would be an anachronism for Mozart anyway, since Viennese fortepianos with which he was familiar did not possess foot-operated sustain devices during his lifetime.

[9] A most rewarding practical demonstration of the contrasting possibilities of Mozart's Walter piano, in both its original and its reordered state, has recently been attempted by Tom Beghin and the builder Chris Maene: *Wolfgang Amadeus Mozart: Sonatas K.331 Alla Turca, K.570, Fantasia K.397, Adagio K.540* Klara Et'cetera, 2005 [KTC4015]. Beghin shows that it is indeed possible to apply the hand-stop sustain mechanism effectively, sometimes by setting it at the start of a piece; sometimes taking advantage of rests for one hand, or of general fermatas to apply or disengage the sustain during a piece; and sometimes by positioning the stop only slightly 'on/off', creating an appealing thin 'halo' of sound. Beghin shows us that the hand-stop sustain was certainly not an-all or-nothing device.

[10] See Maunder and Rowland, 'Mozart's Pedal Piano'.

(1728–1792).[11] It was an encounter that would change the composer's life, for from that moment flowed a realization that a truly expressive style of keyboard playing now lay within his grasp, a realization that was to bear rich fruit in a torrent of keyboard sonatas and also concertos that flowed from his pen almost continuously from this point until the end of his life. Mozart's encounter with Stein's fortepianos effectively maps onto the idiomatic style of keyboard writing found in the C major Sonata K.309, which he wrote during the next three weeks for his pupil Rosina Cannabich in Mannheim.[12] So powerful was this circumstance that Mozart was compelled to document it in a succession of letters to his father in the weeks immediately following. These letters underpin a quite remarkable synchrony between Mozart's keyboard idiom and the mechanical capabilities of the instrument.

In contrast with Mozart's previous experience of fortepianos, which were uneven in touch, whose keys jammed and jangled and whose dampers did not work reliably, Stein's much more reliable and responsive instruments suited his ideal playing style completely. Mozart lost no time in translating these mechanical properties into previously unimagined technical and expressive resources within K.309. The story begins in a letter from Mozart to his father of 17 October 1777 from Augsburg:

> Now I'll start straightaway with Stein's pianos. Before I had come across any of Stein's work, I had always preferred Spath's claviers. But now I have to give first place to Stein's because they damp so much better than the Regensburg instruments. When I strike [the key] hard, I can either keep my finger on the note or lift it off, but either way, the sound ceases the moment I have produced it. However I touch the keys, the tone is always even. It never judders, it is never louder or softer or missing altogether [in different registers]; in short, it is always

---

[11] Stein was one of the most inspired and renowned manufacturers of keyboard instruments in the eighteenth century. His firm continued to produce instruments until 1896, his fame living on after his death through his daughter, Maria-Anna (Nannette) Stein (1769–1833), a close friend of Beethoven whose appreciation of her pianos is attested in his letters. In 1794 Nanette Stein married the composer Johann Anton Streicher. Her piano company was founded in 1802, the instruments bearing the designation 'Nanette Streicher née Stein'. Their son Johann Baptist Streicher (1796–1871) further developed the Viennese action in instruments built during the 1830s and 1840s, and his pianos were much admired by Brahms. Stein's technical innovations contributed greatly to the early development of the piano. See M. R. Latcham, 'The Pianos of Johann Andreas Stein', *The Galpin Society Journal*, 51 (1998): 114–53.

[12] Rosina was the eldest daughter of Christian Cannabich (1731–98), Konzertmeister of the Mannheim orchestra from 1759 and director of instrumental music from 1774. Rosina was evidently quite a talented keyboard player, as Mozart's remarks suggest. On 13 February 1778, she performed Mozart's B flat major Concerto K.238 in a concert at her father's house, aged just 14; see Otto E. Deutsch, *Mozart: A Documentary Biography*, trans. Eric Blom, Peter Branscombe and Jeremy Noble (London, 1965, repr. 1990), pp. 172–3.

even. Admittedly, he does not sell one of these pianos for under 300 gulden, but the skill and effort that Stein puts into the making of it is beyond price. His instruments have a special advantage over other makes in that they have an escapement action. Only one in a hundred makers takes the trouble to do that. But without an escapement you simply can't avoid juddering and shuddering of the hammers after playing the keys. Stein's hammers fall back in an instant once they have struck the strings, whether you hold they keys down or let go of them.[13] Stein told me himself that, once he has finished making one of these claviers, he tries out all sorts of running and jumping passages on it, and he then trims and works on it [the action] until it can do anything.[14]

Later in the same letter, Mozart noted that his D major Sonata K.284 sounded exquisite on Stein's instrument, remarking that the knee-lever (operating the damper-rail – the equivalent of the later pedal) 'is superior on his instruments, compared with others; I only have to touch it and it works perfectly; and whenever you move your knee, even just a fraction, there's not the slightest squeak [from the action].' K.284 in D major, to which Mozart refers here, was composed in February–March 1775 in Munich for Baron Thaddeus von Dürnitz and provides a useful context for appreciating the symbiosis of style and instrument found in K.309. It is the last of a set of six solo keyboard sonatas (K.279–84) written in winter–spring 1774–5. The autograph – as so often, Mozart's composing score, rather than a fair copy – contains a large number of dynamic markings as well as very precise indications for the articulation, and obviously sounds to best effect on a touch-sensitive fortepiano, rather than a harpsichord.[15] There are many places in

---

[13]   The escapement action went through subtle developments in Stein's instruments. The most developed, further adapted as the 'Viennese action' in due course by the rival maker Anton Walther from c.1785, is seen only in surviving Stein instruments dating from 1781. This may mean that the version that so impressed Mozart in 1777 was an earlier prototype. For detailed information, see Latcham, 'The Pianos of Johann Andreas Stein' and his liner notes to the recent recording *Mozart am Stein Vis-à--Vis*, played by Andreas Staier and Christina Schornsheim (Harmonia Mundi Records, 2007 [HMC 901941]. A detailed organological examination of the state of development of Stein's fortepianos at the time Mozart encountered them in 1777 is given in Latcham's forthcoming paper 'Johann Andreas Stein and the Search for the Expressive *Clavier*'. I am grateful to Michael Latcham for sharing this work with me before publication.

[14]   Original in *Briefe*, 352:1–19.

[15]   Kraków, Uniwersytet Jagiellonska, MS V, 5, inw. no. 5995. The autograph of the six sonatas K.279, 280, 281, 282, 283, and 284 contains all but the first movement of the first sonata in C. For that movement, the text of the *NMA* (ed. W. Plath and W. Rehm) is taken substantially from an 1841 edition issued by the firm of Johann Anton André (Offenbach am Main), which they claim to have been closely modelled on the (now lost) autograph. One enigma regarding these sonatas is the fact that, at the time of their composition, Mozart is not known to have encountered the fortepiano. In Munich in the winter of 1774–5 he may have played on a fortepiano, and, compared with Ignaz von

K.284 where the attack of a harpsichord, in which the strings are plucked and the player has no possibility of controlling the dynamic, minimizes the opportunity for contrasts of articulation, register, texture and idiom – all essential to the character of this music. Obvious examples from the first movement include the entry of the secondary theme in bar 22 and the intervention of the delicate *piano* phrase at bars 34–40, sandwiched between *forte* passages and strongly suggestive of an orchestral layout contrasting upper strings with the full tutti. A more subtle illustration is the two-bar *piano* insertion, bars 46–7; the second bar repeats the material of this first a little higher and with a slight harmonic intensification (a diminished seventh chord), leading towards the climactic re-entry of the (implied) tutti for the cadence. While no dynamic differentiation between bar 46 and 47 is notated, the slightly higher register and slightly more intense harmony of bar 47 can be effectively conveyed by a subtle gradation of the degree of piano from bar to bar, as well as by 'voicing' the texture (that is, making a minuscule *crescendo* in the right hand, proceeding from bar 46 to bar 47, while retaining exactly the same dynamic level for the left-hand chords at the beginning of each bar, the effect being to enhance the degree of separation between the two strands of the texture in bar 47 relative to bar 46). The musical reason for such a strategy is to avoid making bar 47 seem to be merely an echo of the preceding bar, of lesser intensity, after which the *forte* of bar 48 arrives as a jarring shock. Clearly Mozart had dynamic contrast between this two-bar *piano* insertion and the following cadential climax; but the register and harmony of bar 47 are clues that he envisaged bar 47 as being at least equal in intensity to bar 46, and in order not to give the opposite effect (of tailing-off) in performance, some sort of creative intervention by the player is required. A touch-sensitive instrument allows the player to capture what Mozart's notation does not explicitly convey without having to adapt other aspects of the narrative (for instance, the articulation, as would be necessary on a harpsichord). Perhaps it was passages such as these that sounded 'exquisite' to Mozart when he played on Stein's instruments and which he could render far more suitably than had previously been possible for him on harpsichords or on other fortepianos (including those of Spath). In all the respects he lists in his letter (sensitivity and evenness of touch, effective escapement action and dampers, operated by a responsive and mercifully silent knee-lever), Stein's fortepianos would have allowed him to render passages such as bars 34–43 exactly as notated

---

Beecke, appeared to one commentator to have been rather inexperienced on the instrument. See John Irving, *Mozart's Piano Sonatas: Contexts, Sources, Style* (Cambridge, 1997), p. 56 for further details. Evidently between 1775 and 1777 he gained in experience to the point where he could make a detailed qualitative comparison of the characteristics of a Spath *versus* a Stein. Nevertheless, the precise notation of dynamics throughout K.279–84 is a little puzzling. The Mozarts had a five-octave clavichord at home, and the sonatas may have been conceived on that instrument. In a letter of 24 October 1777 (*Briefe*, 355), Mozart implies that on 19 October he had played one of these sonatas on a clavichord (possibly one made by Stein) in Augsburg.

(including, no doubt, 'voicing' of bars 34–6 in such a way as to make a subtle dynamic distinction between the repeated e′ quavers and the inner melodic line in the left hand)[16] and thereby to achieve a carefully designed expressive effect, not just locally, but in the context of the surrounding textures.

What Stein's instruments made possible for Mozart was the full realization of a truly expressive style of keyboard playing which – to judge from the notation of the six sonatas K.279–84 – he had aspired towards since at least late 1774–5, but which he could only imperfectly grasp on fortepianos by Spath and others because of mechanical inadequacies. If Mozart's own testimony is to be believed, it would seem that he recognized an advance in his own fortepiano playing at this time. In his letter of 24 October 1777, he explains to his father that:

> [Whereas Stein] was previously besotted with Beecke's playing,[17] he now sees and hears that I play better, that I don't make grimaces when I play, and yet play with such expression that, to his knowledge, no-one has ever played his instruments so well up to now. The fact that I play strictly in time astonished everyone. They don't realize that in tempo rubato in an Adagio, the left hand should keep to strict time. With them, the left hand wanders [in time with the right]. Count Wolfegg and numerous of Beecke's passionate followers, confessed publicly the other day that I beat him hands down. Indeed, the Count was running around the hall saying 'I have never heard anything like that in my life'. And he said to me: 'I must say, I have never heard you play so well as you did today.[18]

Mozart's first reference to K.309 appears in a letter to his father of 4 November from Mannheim, his next port of call:

> I am at Cannabich's house each day … He has taken quite a liking to me. He has a daughter [Rosina] who plays the clavier quite well; and, so as to cement our friendship, I am writing a sonata for his daughter, which is nearly finished except for the Rondeau finale. Once I had written the opening Allegro and the Andante, I took those along and played them, and Papa cannot imagine the reception which this sonata had.[19]

Subsequent references to this sonata appear in Mozart's letters of 8 November (*Briefe*, 366: 41–2), 13 November (*Briefe*, 370: 79–80), 14 November (*Briefe*, 373: 33–51), 29 November (*Briefe*, 381: 87–91, 95–8), 3 December (*Briefe*, 383: 47–8,

---

[16]   Voicing of the *piano* chords at the end of bars 40 and 43 so as to maintain the treble line's thirds in adequate focus above the left-hand octaves is another textural subtlety that can be rendered effectively only on a touch-sensitive keyboard.

[17]   Ignaz von Beecke (1733–1803), Kapellmeister at the Oettigen-Wallerstein court and a fine keyboard player.

[18]   Original in *Briefe*, 355: 83–101.

[19]   Original in *Briefe*, 363: 10–17.

92–5) and 6 December 1777 (*Briefe*, 386: 27–40). By early December, a complete text of K.309 had arrived in Salzburg, and both Leopold and Nannerl Mozart had perused it thoroughly. Nannerl wrote to her brother on 8 December: 'Thanks for the first movement and Andante of your sonata; I have already played [these] through. The Andante certainly needs keen concentration and accuracy. I like it very much. It is clear that you composed it in Mannheim.'[20] Leopold noted its peculiar style in a letter written to his son three days later: 'Nannerl plays the whole of your sonata excellently and with great expression … The sonata is unusual, isn't it? It contains something of the artificial Mannheim taste, but not so much as to spoil your own good style.'[21] Not possessing a fortepiano at home (and certainly not one by Stein), Leopold and his daughter could only have imagined the sound-world that Wolfgang now had literally at his fingertips in the autumn of 1777.

In what ways do Stein's mechanically unrivalled fortepianos leave their fingerprint within the pages of K.309? We may usefully approach this question under three headings, 'Technique', 'Expression' and 'Sound'.

Technique

Repeated Notes

- Themes: Allegro con spirito, subsidiary themes at bars 18–19, 27–8, 110–11. Rondeau finale, opening theme (specifically bars 1–2, 3–4, 5–6, 6–7). Accompaniments: repeated chords (Allegro con spirito, bars 21–6, 50, 116–21, 144).
- Virtuosity: extended rapid tremolando octaves (Rondeau, bars 55–61, 69–74, 111–14, 162–5, 173–8, 221–7).
- Decoration: embellished restatements of themes (Allegro con spirito, bars 65, 69. Andante un poco adagio, bars 17–19, 36–7, 37–8, 56–7, 57–8, 72–4. Finale, bars 32–5, 55,108–9, 159, 197, 199).
- More subtle melodic or rhythmic repercussions (Allegro con spirito, bars 60–61, 87–8, 91–2. Rondeau, bars 42–3, 46–7, 149–50, 153–4, 250–51).

Evenness of Touch

- Semiquaver or demisemiquaver passagework (Allegro con spirito, bars 43–7, 56–8, 84–5, 137–41, 150–51, 153–6. Rondeau, bars 40–52, 116–31, 143–57, 179–86, 204–10).
- Decoration (Andante un poco adagio, bars 27–30, 53–6, 60–62, 67–8).

---

[20]   Original in *Briefe*, 387: 106–10.
[21]   Original in *Briefe*, 389: 8–18.

Effective Damping

- Cleanness in exposed intervallic patternings (Allegro con spirito, bars 21–32, 43–7, 103–7, 116–26, 137–41. Andante un poco adagio, bars 33–6. Rondeau, bars 139–43, 207–10, 228–32).
- Clarity in melody-and-accompaniment textures (Allegro con spirito, bars 33–42, 127–36) and in contrapuntal textures (Andante un poco adagio, bars 40–44, 60–64).
- Rapid, usually chromatic, melody or chord shifts (Allegro con spirito, bars 103–8. Andante un poco adagio, bars 64; 69–71. Rondeau, bars 225–7).

Expression

The following is not a comprehensive list, but cites examples where the expressive quality of the music depends wholly upon the ability reliably to control and shade dynamics:

Dynamic Contrast

Allegro con spirito, bars 1–2, 3–7, 8–9, 10–14, 48–9, 54–6, 56–8, 59–62, 67–72, 82–93, 101–7, 142–3, 148 – end. This feature is essential to the entire Andante un poco adagio, and may be observed on both local and general levels. A small selection:

- Local: the opening theme, bars 1–4; the first paragraph more generally, bars 1–16; the secondary theme, bars 33–6; its continuation, bars 36–40; the coda, bars 76 – end.
- General: compare the subtly different dynamic placements of the analogous bar 4 (upbeat) – bar 8 and bar 20 (upbeat) – bar 24; bar 14 (upbeat) – bar 16 and bar 30 (upbeat) – bar 32; and bar 49 (upbeat) – bar 52 and bar 72 (upbeat) – bar 76. In each case, the second phrase is an embellishment of the first, retaining the harmonic and phrase outlines, yet expressively different because of the contrasting dynamics.

Rondeau, bars 37–48, 66–9, 85–93, 131–5, 142–57, 170–73, 179–87, 213–17, 244 – end.

Dynamic Gradations

Allegro con spirito, bars 33–4, 108–9, 127–8. Andante un poco adagio, bars 15, 50–51. Rondeau, bars 55–7, 159–60, 210–12, 228–30.

Chord and Texture Balance

- Allegro con spirito, bars 54–6, 59–62, 82–4, 86–93, 129–32, 148–50. Once again, the whole of the Andante un poco adagio depends on the ability to manage subtle dynamic shadings so as to give the effect of balance, or 'voicing', of the chords or textures. Frequently, the hands are wide enough apart for this quality to manage itself simply by dint of register contrast, but careful gradation by the player is certainly needed to clarify the textures at just about every cadence point, and also at bars 5–6, 21–2, bar 36 (upbeat) – bar 44, bar 56 (upbeat) – bar 64. Rondeau, bars 42–3, 46–7, 53–6, 66–9, 131–7, 145–6, 149–50, 153–4, 157–61, 170–72, 244 – end.

Articulation

Articulations (principally staccatos and slurs) are a vital aspect of this sonata's expressive impact in performance. All three movements apply them precisely (representative examples include bars 103–9 of the Allegro con spirito and bars 131–6 of the Rondeau). In the Andante un poco adagio, Mozart employs these articulations with especial refinement.[22]

Sound

Could Mozart have been inspired, by the mechanical possibilities of Stein's instruments, to attempt to capture an 'orchestral' sound in his keyboard writing, given that he was in Mannheim and exposed to the sound-world of the famous Mannheim orchestra? Its textures are quasi-orchestral, especially in the first movement, Allegro con spirito, with its opening 'Mannheim rocket' figure, its driving chordal accompaniment textures featuring repeated chords in the left hand and its 'busy' Alberti bass patterns. Also the textures are quite varied in the Allegro con spirito. The secondary theme (bar 35) is suggestive perhaps of a reduction, in orchestral terms, to upper strings; the opening of the development (which in this case actually *is* a development, rather than an episode) is perhaps a dialogue between tutti (bars 59–60) and a pair of flutes or oboes (bars 61–2). Dialogue textures animate this movement to quite an extent, in fact, most obviously in the *forte–piano* disposition of the opening theme, but also in bars 73–93, at first tutti (to bar 81) and thereafter alternating between brief *piano* or *pianissimo* phrases (wind pairs or upper strings) and *forte* tutti interjections. Dialogue textures play an important role in this movement, most obviously providing a kind of 'counterpoint' to the tonal course of this section and the ongoing process of thematic development, which involves fragmentation of the opening theme (bars 61–2) along with intervallic adaptation of the entire opening phrase and sequential repetition (bars

---

[22] These are explored further in Chapter 7; see pp. 126–31.

73 ff.). The return of the dialogue texture of bars 59–62 at bars 86–93 creates a peculiar sense of reprise within the development and simultaneously reinforces the (temporary) sense of tonal arrival at A minor (bar 86). Arguably, the dialogue texture also has the effect of setting up rather well the actual recapitulation of the opening theme in bar 94, making its entry (on C) seem a climactic point of arrival after two successive upward steps, A (bar 86), B (bar 90) and C, a stature it might not naturally enjoy coming after such a turbulent textural and harmonic passage as bars 73–82.

Perhaps there is no straightforward answer to the question of which fortepiano suits Mozart's sonatas 'best'. Taking a 'historically informed' view, we might opt for a Stein for K.279–84 (for some of which pieces there is evidence of performances by the composer in or around Augsburg on Stein's instruments in late 1777[23]), and also for K.309 and K.311, both of which works were composed then – remembering all the time that Stein's principles of manufacture were in a state of rapid flux during the 1770s and 1780s and that none of the surviving instruments from which modern copies have been made may represent the precise design that Mozart had encountered in 1777. But what about K.310, written in Paris the following year? We know nothing very precise of the fortepianos he played there, save that the instrument he played in freezing conditions for the Duchesse de Chabot and her inattentive guests in April 1778 was of poor quality.[24] For the remaining sonatas, all composed after his removal to Vienna, perhaps we may reasonably opt for a Walter, given Mozart's ownership of one of his instruments from 1782 or thereabouts. But we should remember that Walter's fortepianos were then no more standard in their action design than were Stein's, and that they were felt by his contemporaries to be ideally suited to the forceful style of playing characteristic of the emerging virtuoso tradition of pianism[25] – which is not truly where Mozart's sonatas belong.

---

[23]   See Irving, *Mozart's Piano Sonatas*, pp. 53–4.

[24]   *Briefe*, 447: 39.

[25]   See von Schönfeld, *Jahrbuch der Tonkunst von Wien und Prag* (1976), pp. 89–9.

Chapter 7
Embellishing Mozart's Texts

Should We Do It?

As players of Mozart's sonatas, we may choose to embellish his notated texts. Indeed, some of us have already chosen – not just on the level of the individual performance, but as a defining characteristic of our professional practice when we play Mozart – to intervene creatively (to varying degrees) when we engage with his texts. Our practice expresses a belief that to play Mozart's notated texts 'straight', as if they were anything other than provisional, is not (for us) a historically defensible or sustainable position to adopt.[1] Wherever we may be along that particular path of intervening within Mozart's texts, we do need benchmarks for questioning our own practice (and it is much to be hoped that we ask some questions, rather than none). We may begin to approach the issue of whether, where and to what extent to introduce embellishments into our performances of Mozart's sonatas by considering these few contexts:

- Quantz retains the Italianate view that florid embellishment should be the norm in repetitions of phrases and sections, starting from the presumption that generally speaking, wider intervals need to be artfully filled-in and structural melodic notes rendered more expressive by the judicious addition of dissonant grace notes. Thus the performer must always pay attention to the harmonic underpinning of a melody, not just to the melodic shape in itself. Quantz makes the point that the embellishment should improve the original; that it should respect the *Affekt* of the original (no lively

---

[1]   The alternative, namely, to regard Mozart's notation as capturing exactly his (by implication single, once-and-for-all) *intention* and consequently as being strictly regulative of the performer's behaviour when reproducing the text in performance, is a characteristic of conservatoire traditions of professional education extending at least throughout the twentieth century. Leaving aside the question of whether or not such an objectification of Mozart's notation was actually *Mozart's* notation, or that of a nineteenth-century editor adapting Mozart to modern taste, instruments or performance settings, it should be acknowledged that this is a perfectly respectable and responsible approach with which to align oneself as a player, provided that the historical context for this behaviour is also acknowledged (mostly it is not – either by players or critics). Playing Mozart 'straight' is rendering him as broadly conceived within a particular tradition – the conservatoire. Such performances are socially produced meanings for Mozart's sonatas (as, indeed, are historically informed performances). Both approaches are products of ages later than and different from Mozart's own; but that is about as much as they have in common.

embellishments in a melancholy piece, for instance); and that it should only really be added where an absence of embellishment would result in a boring piece. Effectively, Quantz is discussing the application of *diminutions* to existing notation.[2]

- C. P. E. Bach[3] and Leopold Mozart take a stricter view on the application of embellishments. C. P. E. Bach felt that these were not infrequently excessive and inappropriate and considered them to be matters of taste in the application of commonly understood grace-note patterns, rather than grammatical necessity. In his father's music, embellishments were generally already written out into the score. In C. P. E. Bach, one gets the sense that the art of diminutions was regarded as something no longer current or appropriate. Varied repeats were something else. In his *Sechs Sonaten für Klavier mit veränderten Reprisen* (Berlin, 1760) he offers extended examples of the art of recomposing an original upon the repeat. The patterns found are generally not formulaic fragmentations of the original melody into smaller note-values, but a significant reshaping of the original melodic contour with respect to the underlying harmonic scheme.

- Leopold Mozart is notably frugal in his discussion of embellishment. Diminutions are hardly discussed, and those few rising and falling grace-note formulae that he does include in his chapter 9, sections 18–22,[4] are recommended only for use in solo playing. For Leopold, the performer's duty is to be able to read the notated score for its coded messages, knowing where the composer intends ornamentation (and applying it judiciously in such places) and where not (and in such places leaving well alone). For example, it is incorrect to add upper-note appoggiaturas in places where the main harmony note is already preceded by an appoggiatura, thus detracting from the dissonant effect already crafted by the composer. Leopold's stricture that the player should introduce no embellishments except those that do not spoil the melody or the harmony perhaps represents an extreme a case for the performance of Wolfgang's sonatas, but offers a useful check to the player.

---

    [2] Johann Joachim Quantz, *Versuch einer Anweisung die Flöte traversière zu spielen* (Berlin, 1752), trans. Edward R. Reilly as *On Playing the Flute*, 2nd edn (London and Boston, 1966), pp. 136–61.

    [3] C. P. E. Bach, *Versuch über die Wahre Art das Klavier zu spielen*, 2 vols (Berlin, 1753, 1762; vol. 1, 2nd edn, 1759), trans. and ed. William J. Mitchell as *Essay on the True Art of Playing Keyboard Instruments* (New York, 1949), pp. 79–146; Leopold Mozart, *Versuch einer gründlichen Violinschule* (Augsburg, 1756), trans. Editha Knocker as *A Treatise on the Fundamentals of Violin Playing*, 2nd edn (Oxford and New York, 1985), pp. 166–85 (especially pp. 177–82).

    [4] Mozart, *Fundamentals of Violin Playing*, pp. 177–82.

Specific questions for our embellishments of Mozart's sonatas include:

- Whether or not to repeat expositions with embellishments (and whether these should be diminutions or recompositions).
- Whether or not to embellish repetitions of exposition material within recapitulations (and whether these should be diminutions or recompositions).
- Whether or not to embellish reprises within ternary or more extended rondo structures (both in slow movements and in finales).
- Whether embellishments (again, either diminutions or recompositions) should be applied within phrases where these involve repetition of thematic elements (sequential writing, for instance, in which the first statement should be played as notated but subsequent ones successively embellished, changing the narrative content of the phrase from a 'static' presentation of ideas to a 'dynamic' trajectory).

Judgements that we might consider, as if from the listener's point of view, include additionally:

- Is the perception of a reprise exclusively grounded in the return of a melodic statement, or is its harmonic context also a key component?
- If *melodic reprise* is fundamental to the perception of a reprise *per se*, is it also necessary to the perception that its exact intervallic and rhythmic profile is retained?
- If so, is that exact intervallic and rhythmic profile *in its totality* – rather than just a reference to its first few notes – necessary to the perception?

For instance, in the finale of the C minor Sonata K.457, we might opt for solutions such as those offered in Examples 7.1a–d when playing the reprises. It is perhaps ultimately a matter of personal taste where (if at all) the recognition of a reprise breaks down (remembering that in Mozart's own variation sets, specific intervallic resemblance to the original theme is frequently not preserved for very long).

Extemporized embellishment is an aspect of Mozart performance practice especially associated with the playing of fortepianist Robert Levin. Anyone who has heard Levin's improvised cadenzas in performances of Mozart's piano concertos will have a sense of the primacy of performance that Levin brings to the occasion: his Mozart goes way beyond the notated text, realizing its potential differently each time with enviable creative flair. Cadenzas are a special case, of course. Here we are talking about a compositional act on the part of the performer of a rather different order from the invention of diminutions when a phrase is repeated. Mozart did not always notate these cadenzas; those that are notated demonstrate certain procedures which are among the techniques to be found in Levin's cadenzas. But his reading of Mozart's notated texts likewise opens up a world of signification that commands our attention as listeners. An example is

Example 7.1a–d   Sonata in C minor K.457/iii: suggested embellishments for
                reprises of the opening theme

(a)

(b)

(c)

(d)

his recording of the F major Sonata K.280, in particular its *Siciliana* Adagio.[5] Levin's repeats of the two sections of this sonata form include interventions of three principal kinds: generic ornaments (O), such as turns, trills and grace notes; diminutions (D); and recomposition (specifically in the form of *Eingänge* at appropriate cadential pauses). The listing in Table 7.1 (though not exclusive) gives some idea of their application.

Levin's embellishments here are both tasteful and purposeful: interventions drawing upon eighteenth-century principles and materials that may well have been applied in performances of Mozart's day. Broadly speaking, his approach contextualizes Mozart's notation as something not exhibiting fixed or finished meanings, but pregnant with potential meanings: his interpretation of the simply notated cadence in bar 42, for instance, turning it into an elaborate cadenza that suspends the regular pulse, unfolds into a several-octave register span and makes a rhetorical feature of this tonic cadence that has the twofold consequence of (i) local closure and (ii) recasting the following phrase as a new beginning. This it has previously been in the first half of the movement (cf. bar 11 – a continuation in the relative major, to which Levin previously appended a brief *Eingang*); but sounded for the final time, in the repeat of the second section, it attains far greater prominence through Levin's creative realization. Indeed, it probably exceeds that of the moment of recapitulation (bar 37). The effect – arguably – of Levin's remarkable cadenza is to mark out (retrospectively) bars 37–42 as an intervening tonic episode (an *action*, existing in real time, rather than simply a restatement fulfilling an abstract conceptual expectation within this form), following which

[5] *Mozart: Piano Sonatas K.279, K.280 & K.281 on Fortepiano*, vol. 1, Sony BMG Music Entertainment/Deutsche Harmonia Mundi, 2006 [82876 84237 2]. In the liner notes Levin touches on the role of improvisation within performances of Mozart's keyboard sonatas.

122   *Changing the System: The Music of Christian Wolff*

Table 7.1   Creative reinterpretations in Robert Levin's recording of K.280/ii

Bar	Feature	Comment
2	O	Enhancement of dissonant level
6	O	Enhancement of dissonant level
8	D; *Eingang*	Raises profile of cadential point
10–11	O	
12	D	
13–14	O	
15–16	D	
18–19	O	Recontextualizes Mozart's notated grace notes
20	O; D	
30–31	D	
32	*Eingang*	
33	D	
34	O	
36	D	Highlights structure (thematic recapitulation)
37–8	D	
40	O	
42	D; *Eingang*	The diminution (beat 1) is an extended cadenza
44	D	
45	O	
46	D	
47–8	O	
49–50	D	
53	O; D	Enhancement highlighting subsequent V pedal
54	D	Enhances already chromatic harmony

the chromatic harmonic journey of bars 43–57 is spotlighted as a continuation of the instability of the developmental section (bars 25–36), withholding eventual tonic resolution in bar 57 all the more expressively. Levin demonstrates convincingly here how performance practice can engage with Mozart's text, responding to the challenge to continue beyond its notated values. His actions as a performer creatively deforms the notated text in the sense that its constructed conceptual meanings are now made to coexist with a meaning that is not only of a different sort (a tonic episode, not simply a tonic restatement), but also inhabits a different (performative) dimension.[6]

Performances and recordings such as those of Levin remind us that the extemporization of embellishments in Mozart's piano sonatas is not just historically appropriate, but can also be a valuable tool for understanding them. It represents, in fact, a conflation of historical and performance perspectives, for if we play in a historically informed way, we certainly do not play just the same notes as the first time all over again whenever we observe a repeat; instead we add embellishments, a practice addressed in many contemporary performance treatises. When we extemporize embellishments, for instance in the repeats of a first-movement exposition, we engage creatively (of course) with Mozart's original notated text; but our creative engagement leaves behind also a commentary on its features, a trace of our understanding of its content and underlying principles of its organization.

Interrogating, for instance, the central repeat mark of the opening Allegro of the B flat Sonata K.570 (February 1789)[7] in relation to this historical context, the parameters for our understanding of what to do next in a performance will have to include the following grammatical ground-rules:

- The total length of the embellished repeat will be the same number of bars as that of the notated original.[8]
- The harmonic outline of 'Mozart's' text will be retained, traversing the same tonal path in the same relative proportions. For instance, at the opening, there will still be four bars of unchanging tonic harmony, followed by two pairs of two-bar alternations of dominant and tonic, covering 12 bars in total.

---

[6]   I am certainly not qualified to discuss the psychologically recognized tension that thus arises between the performative and the conceptual dimensions in this or similar cases. I merely record it here as an example of a *potential for meaning* within Mozart's sonatas which stems from this aspect of historically informed performance, and which Levin's behaviour highlights.

[7]   It is slightly presumptuous, perhaps, to think of this text, and the notated repeat, as 'Mozart's notation', since the autograph of this section (London, British Library, Add. MS 47861) is lacking; we rely on the first edition, therefore (*Sonata per il clavicembalo o piano-forte con l'accompagnemento d'un violino composta del Sigr. W. A. Mozart opera 40*, Vienna, Artaria, 1796), in which the notation of the slurring of the opening figure is different from that found in Mozart's *Verzeichnüss* (also in the British Library, Stefan Zweig collection, MS 63). In the *Verzeichnüss*, K.570 is described as being 'Eine Sonate auf Klavier allein'. At the risk of pedantry here, I will refer to Mozart's text as given in the first edition as 'Mozart's' text.

[8]   Unless it is felt that the dramatic textural and tonal rupture in the narrative at bars 21–2 would be made the more effective the second time around by extemporising a brief *Eingang* before the continuation with the lyrical E flat theme.

- However, the precise melodic, rhythmic and perhaps textural profile may depart somewhat from 'Mozart's' text, as indeed, Mozart departs from the original 'plain' thematic statements in his own sets of fully written-out variations. There may even be minor deviations from the precise harmonic contour, provided these make good sense in grammatical and harmonic terms and underline the basic outline.

Next, a detailed consideration of how this may be realized in practice. In addition to being a performance, our performance will also leave a trace of our particular understanding of 'Mozart's' text. (And note that it is only one among many alternative and provisional understandings, not *the* – by implication, one and only correct – understanding). Example 7.2 represents one way in which 'Mozart's' text may be varied in performance of the exposition repeat of K.570's opening movement. In arriving at the example, I have tried not to be exemplary for purposes of textbook illustration, but rather to present something of the sort that I might actually play. That is partly because there is a strong aesthetic dimension to the art of embellishment (and the fact that, for instance C. P. E. Bach and Türk fulminated against inappropriate embellishments that were part of the contemporary musical landscape implies that such aesthetic boundaries were already being regularly abused). The result should not, for instance, be unrelieved torrents of semiquavers, but should aim to recapture – but afresh – the contours of the original landscape. In particular, it is important to recognize the layout of the textural narrative and to complement, not obliterate, it. In the case of bars 35–40 of this movement, therefore, the outbreak of semiquavers may be understood as a textural culmination to this

Example 7.2   Sonata in B flat K.570/i: suggested embellishment of the opening
                theme when repeated

section in terms of the density of rhythmic movement; given that it is preceded by a section equally consistent in its (longer) note-values and slower-moving harmonies, for instance, that relativity ought perhaps to be retained in an embellished repeat. A similar observation may be made of the profile beginning at bar 13, launching out from the tonal scene-setting of the opening, and of bars 57–69.

One possibility at the repeat of the opening, which would be a historical kind of commentary on the text actually notated by Mozart in his *Verzeichnüss*, would be to play the slurring from the *Verzeichnüss* (namely, the first two bars slurred as a pair, followed by a separate slur over bar 3) as if that of the first edition had been used at the very start (or *vice versa*).

Embellishments and Structure

Central to the above introduction is that we should, as historically informed performers, bear closely in mind the effect of what we are doing when we interfere creatively with Mozart's scores. Remember that the Music is not the Score. The Score represents through visual means what the Music may be (not 'must be') about. The visual cannot hope wholly to capture that, of course, and we should not feel too bad about departing from visual representations of music (such as scores) in historically justifiable ways and for creatively innovative reasons. But we should take the trouble always to ask whether, by adding (that is, in embellishing or improvising) we are actually taking something away from the Music. When I improvise a different *da capo* in the Andante cantabile of the C major Sonata K.330, am I perhaps changing the overall structure of the movement? And if so, should I be worried about that? The middle section departs in various expressive ways from the opening, and, in a literal d*a capo* (a designation which Mozart writes in the autograph manuscript of this piece – he does not bother to write the notes out all over again) the middle section subsides back into the opening. The question here is what Mozart means by *da capo*. Does he mean a note-for-note repeat of the original? Or does he mean 'repeat basically the same music as the opening (but of course, not note-for-note the same)'? The weight of contemporary evidence strongly suggests the latter. There are significant differences between the two solutions. Play the *da capo* note-for-note the same, and you set up a pattern of departure and return. Improvise a new *da capo*, and that pattern of departure and return is nuanced in favour of an ongoing process of departure. The question for the player is not so much the relation of the original opening to the *da capo*, but of the middle section to the *da capo*. The degree of improvisation around the original themes and harmonies in the *da capo* will modify the narrative: the middle section may either subside back into home territory, or else progress into unexplored territory. It is worth noting here that for the first edition of this sonata (1784) Mozart added a little coda, which refers back (albet in the major key) to the end of the middle section. (This is not present in the autograph.) Now, if you play the *da capo* 'straight', it does seem a little odd to end the movement with a reference back to the middle section. But if you improvise a more elaborate *da capo*, taking the narrative into uncharted territory, the coda can have the useful effect of 'grounding' the movement at its close. That is not a scientifically tested theoretical position, just a speculation. But it does actually make the music *speak* in a particular way.

A similar paradox applies in refrain forms, such as the slow movement of the B flat Sonata K.570. The overall form here works as a series of statements of the main theme, alternating with episodes that introduce new material. Here the contrasting episodes may lose some of their contrasting effects if the successive returns to the refrain theme in between are embellished, rather than left plain. So should we perhaps leave these refrains alone – just as Mozart notated them – to function as moments of stable repose, punctuating the intervening episodes? If we embellish the refrains, we create a different structure of contrasting episodes running in parallel with a developing process of accretion in the refrains. An approach that largely leaves Mozart's refrains unembellished, while taking the opportunity for sensitive embellishment within the repeated sections of the episodes, is that of Ronald Brautigam (BIS-CD-837D).

K.309 Andante un poco Adagio: Reading between the Lines of Mozart's Texts

Speaking now as a performer, I find that the Andante un poco Adagio from Mozart's C major Sonata K.309 (composed in Mannheim during October–November 1777) remains something of a paradox. Whenever I play it (the opening 16 bars, for instance), I fail to engage with its notated text satisfyingly in the way I would ideally wish – namely, to embellish it. The problem is that Mozart seems to have written in all the embellishments already, leaving no room for the player to intervene. That troubles me, not because I take a cavalier attitude towards Mozart's notation, assuming that I can just add or subtract notes from it as I wish. Far from it. It is because I strongly believe that in Mozart's era performance was still connected to composition, still an extension of the creative process that subsequent developments in music historiography configured as a 'Work' in some sense – enshrined in notation, for instance, and apparently possessing some regulative qualities such as determining generic boundaries, or settings for its representation to a public which in turn brings certain expectations to the occasion, such as an expectation that the Work will be performed upon a stage by a professional pianist trained in a conservatoire.

For me as a *player* of this piece, engaging in the creative (meaning, really, compositional) process is vital. If I do not – if I just obey the instructions in the score – then I am not representing a whole dimension of what classical-period music was about: namely, extending the journey of the notated composition through *performance*. And that is very frustrating! Exploring and revisiting the acceptable boundaries of my desire to intervene creatively with this Andante is what I find so fascinating about the piece. Should I therefore intervene and embellish this text, perhaps beginning at bar 9 with the reappearance of the opening theme (Example 7.3)? At first sight, such embellishments might seem to fly in the face of Mozart's own guidance on the performance of this movement, which we find in a letter he wrote from Mannheim to his father back in Salzburg on 14 November 1777. Mozart observes that the Andante is highly expressive in character and consequently must be played strictly according to the notation with

Example 7.3   Sonata in C K.309/ii: suggested embellishment of the opening theme when repeated

all the exact shadings of *forte* and *piano*.[9] Looking at the score, one sees what Mozart meant. Almost every note is adorned with a dynamic mark or a phrasing, staccato, *crescendo* or *fp* indication. One could plausibly argue that Mozart means what he writes in K.309's Andante *prescriptively*, expecting the performer simply to *reproduce* his musical text as sound, thus separating the 'Work' from its subsequent representation, and the creator from the executant, whose function it is simply to play *what the composer wrote*.

But before we surrender to the *diktat* of the text, we ought to consider Mozart's remarks a little further. For a start, they appear in a *pedagogical* context. At the time, Mozart was teaching his Andante to Rosina Cannabich (daughter of the Mannheim Kapellmeister), and his remarks about accuracy of expression and exact shadings of *forte* and *piano* are actually introduced in the letter as an illustration of something Rosina would find difficult in playing this piece. We may therefore consider his notated text to be exemplary (to her) to a large extent, a record of how he trained her in appropriate ways of applying dynamic shading to particular turns

---

9   *Briefe*, 373: 33–51.

of phrase, and also of how to vary these dynamic twists and turns according to context. Perhaps, then, his notated embellishments may be regarded as exemplary too: ways in which phrases *may be* decorated on repetition. But to the experienced player, 'may be' is not necessarily 'must be'. Mozart, it seems, habitually embellished phrases in his own performances of his sonatas and concertos, and he occasionally sent his sister examples by post of how he embellished plainly notated phrases in his own works.[10] But those too are exemplary, not prescriptive embellishments, not 'must be', but 'may be'. When considering embellishments we should, surely, feel free to supply our own, *realizing the notation in the act of performance*, as he did. Or at least, we should consider that as a challenge, and only within certain limits. I shall explore some of those limitations now.

Managing the dynamics in relation to the localized stress patterns might be our starting-point. Was the unusual profusion of dynamics here, so precisely marked, perhaps Mozart's way of conveying to Rosina the importance of maintaining the relation of strong to weak beats within the triple-time bar, whatever the dynamic level? Grasping that principle counts for a lot within the sarabande character underlying this Andante. Sometimes the progression goes **STRONG**–WEAK–WEAK; sometimes it is WEAK–**STRONG**–WEAK. The dynamics sometimes reinforce these patterns, but sometimes cut across them: Note especially a couple of subtleties:

- Bar 3 only *implies* additional stress on beat 2 (where the highest point in the phrase occurs – there is no underlying harmony here).
- Bar 5 slips in a resolution in the left hand on just the quaver value (the slurred pair B♭–A from the half-beat of beat 2 onto beat 3), halving the unit of resolution in a kind of 'metrical counterpoint' with what is going on elsewhere in the bar.

The return in bars 9–10 to a pattern of WEAK–**STRONG**–WEAK may creatively be reinforced in performance by the kind of embellishment I applied earlier. But what about the third beat of bar 13? Should the player embellish this (as I did earlier) or leave well alone? At the beginning of bar 14 Mozart foreshortens the STRONG–WEAK pattern within just the first beat of the bar, playfully wrong-footing us if by now we had become accustomed to an underlying alternation of **STRONG**–WEAK–WEAK and WEAK–**STRONG**–WEAK. The pattern is slurred through the whole crotchet length (implying a slight *decrescendo*, within the *forte* dynamic marking if we properly apply contemporary performance-practice

---

[10]   For instance, the slow movement of the D major Piano Concerto K.451. The additional embellishments to the slow movement of the F major Sonata K.332 found in the first edition (Vienna, 1784) perhaps indicate how Mozart may have realized the plainer text of the autograph in his performances.

advice, for instance as given by Mozart's father in his 1756 violin treatise[11]), and this crotchet is arguably made to appear the longest unit of resolution locally if this 'rule of the slur' is applied, since on beat 3 of bar 13 the semiquaver pattern is subdivided into two slurred pairs, making the crotchet unit at the beginning of bar 14 follow on from two half-units. Notice that at the analogous upbeat point in bar 5, Mozart placed all four semiquavers under a single slur (a crotchet unit), and the continuation into bar 6 resolves STRONG–WEAK from beat 1 onto beat 2 (namely, two *beat* units). One might therefore claim that in bars 13–14, Mozart's careful dynamic placement and slurring *preserve the relative scansion from bars 5 into 6*, a point perhaps better felt in performance than explained on paper. So on a strict view, should no embellishment be added to the upbeat of bar 13? But the sense of half-units conveyed by Mozart's slurring of semiquaver pairs can still be captured by a precisely shaped embellishment pattern such as that shown in Example 7.3. Are we then free creatively to manipulate Mozart's notation in performance after all (provided we appreciate and preserve the subtle implications his notation may convey)?

Set against all this is the effect of playing accurately what Mozart wrote. Compare the articulation marks to the right-hand upbeats:

- At the end of bar 4, four staccato semiquavers.
- The end of bar 5, four semiquavers under a single slur.
- At the end of bar 6, two pairs of slurred semiquavers.
- But at the end of bars 20, 21 and 22, all the embellished versions of these upbeats are the same each time (eight demisemiquavers under a single slur).

Another illustration:

- The restatement of the opening theme beginning at bar 9 retains the slurred pairs of the opening (beginning ♩. ♪ and giving a distinctive scansion of ♪♪ ♩♩, ♪♪♩♩, ♪♪♪♪♪♪, ♩♩♩).
- But by the time these bars are embellished at bars 25–8, the original pairings have been sacrificed for longer slurs (*uniformly in crotchet-beat lengths*, and with markedly different scansion).

Something similar is going on too with dynamics. Compare bars 4–8 and 20–24 in particular:

---

[11]   Mozart, *Versuch*. Leopold states that 'the first of such united notes [i.e. those connected by a slur] must be somewhat more strongly stressed, but the remainder slurred on to it quite smoothly and more and more quietly' (chapter VII, part 1, § 20). See *Fundamentals of Violin Playing*, pp. 123–4, and Anthony Pay, 'Phrasing in Contention', *Early Music*, 24 (1996): 291–321.

- The upbeat at the end of bar 4 is marked *piano*.
- The end of the analogous bar 20 is *forte*.
- In bars 5–7, *piano*, *crescendo* to *forte*, thence *piano* at the cadence.
- But *forte–piano* (bar 21), *forte* (bar 22) and *piano* (bars 23–4).

All this suggests a subtle and deliberate contrast between the way these phrases are spoken each time, which in turn points to a way of organizing the larger-scale form in sound, as it is produced through the fingers and the instrument. Embellish bars 21–4 differently, with different articulations and dynamics, and you lose this larger effect. Ought we then to resist the temptation to embellish differently from how Mozart notated it in order to preserve an ever-so-subtle layer of his meaning?

But maybe what we have here is *precision on the local level enabling a larger-scale expressive flexibility*? Certainly, those local details require careful management in performance. But the payoff is the freedom for the player to organize creatively how all those large-scale variants of dynamic and articulation will balance out: *the way in which* the upbeats to bars 20, 21 and 22 are handled in relation to their analogues in bars 4, 5 and 6 is up to the player. Mozart's precise notation of the individual moments is an invitation to the player to act in a particular rhetorical way, to pronounce the vocabulary as a series of localized expressive gestures. Recipe, not regulation; tool, not rule. And of course, not all expressive voices will be the same: the gradation of a *crescendo*, the degree of contrast between *forte* and *piano*, the precise emphasis given to an *fp* – all these are issues that remain for the individual performer to determine, intelligently and creatively applying performance practice advice from Mozart's own time (one hopes). By following his markings carefully, one finds, paradoxically, freedom of expression.

That is the first paradox I find in K.309's Andante. But there is another at work in parallel here. On the one hand, Mozart bothers to overlay his score with a plethora of subtle expressive markings. On the other, the actual *sound* of this music is something else entirely: it sounds like an *improvisation*. Right from the start, with the searching quality of its rising opening bar, turning backwards and dissolving into nothing, it sounds as if it were being made up on the spot, playing with gestures typically associated with improvisation (from the Latin *improvisus* – literally unforeseen, in the sense of appearing to be unscripted, unplanned). These improvisatory gestures are easily recognizable (the following is not an exhaustive list):

- The reliance on conventional harmonic patterns as a generator of narrative continuity (e.g. bar 40, a descending sequence of suspensions, slightly embellished).
- Register contrast (e.g. bars 30–31).
- Texture contrast (e.g. bars 9–16).
- Dynamic contrast (eg. bars 47–53).
- Rhetorical use of silence (e.g. between phrases at bar 14, but more generally and subtly within phrases, giving the impression of disjunction or discontinuity, hinted at from the very beginning and becoming more

prominent at e.g. bars 28–32).

- Unexpected harmonic progressions (e.g. bars 70–71).
- Prominent contrast of note-values and their associated shapes (e.g. bar 63–end).
- Above all, the sheer *mobility* of this musical environment.

Mozart was noted as a brilliant improviser, of course, and his own concerts sometimes set fully-formed compositions alongside improvisations at the keyboard. For him, there was probably a less clear-cut distinction between process-based notated composition and the more transient improvisation which is, at least in part, a spontaneous application of what were once learnt processes, absorbed and filtered in the imagination over time and now able to be delivered *ad libitum*, the thought of the past becoming the action of the present. K.309's Andante is, I believe, one such case: effectively it is a notation of an improvisation.

It it then necessary, in order to represent that element, to observe Mozart's notated dynamics precisely in performance? Thus at bars 69–72, the sense of suspended metre portrayed by those delicately fractured offbeat quaver chords punctuated by silence depends for its effective realization on their being *piano* in contrast to the continuous textures (*forte*) either side, and also on the contrast of register implied, for, at the upbeat to bar 69, for the first and only time in this movement, the leading melody is transferred to the left hand, extending the span of the figure down to B♭ and throwing into sharp relief the higher tessitura (starting from f') on which the punctuated chords enter thereafter. The sense of interruption here is not in itself new (cf. bars 12–16 and 49–52). But here at bars 69–72, Mozart literally stretches time, extending the phrase by three whole beats by comparison with those earlier points and escaping momentarily the containing frame of the sarabande, before restoring a sense of equilibrium once more at bars 72–6 – the actual consequent to bars 12–16 and 49–52; and only once this phrase enters do we realize retrospectively that bars 69–72 were just an insertion, playing with our expectations as an improviser does.

One important lesson of K.309's Andante is something already stated several times earlier in this book: *the Music is not the Score*. In material ways, such as contrast of dynamic, of register and of texture, suspension of pulse and extension of phrase, Mozart represents in his precisely notated text the enigmatic language of the improvisatory, encoding a memory of what it once felt like to be improvising this work. Recapturing that is perhaps the greatest challenge to the player.

K.332 Adagio: Embellishment and Social Location

Embellishment and dynamics are not obvious candidates for exploring historical settings for Mozart's sonatas, yet both of these elements illuminate in surprising ways the inscription of historical practice within the musical text of a Mozart sonata. That is to say that the text is a trace of a particular behaviour that inhabits a specifically historical environment.

Mozart occasionally published his piano sonatas, normally several years after the original date of composition. When he did so, the text of the autograph (where that is known to survive) is typically elaborated, sometimes including additional dynamic markings and articulations, as in the case of K.284 in D, which was composed in 1775 and was published in Vienna in 1784 by Torricella as the second of *Trois sonates pour le clavecin ou piano forte. La troisième est accomp: d'un violon obblig: composées par Mr. W. A. Mozart, dediées a son Excellence Comtesse Therese de Kobenzl ... œuvre VII* (the other works being K.333 and K.454). This is surely because when he published them, he was aware that the texts representing the works were now aimed at a market – either locally in Vienna or further afield in Paris or London – of potential purchasers who had been exposed to the possibilities of the fortepiano and whose expectations had been conditioned as a result. In other words, he adapted the sonatas to take greater account of an appetite for keyboard music ideally suited to an instrument on which physical control of dynamic contrast, degrees of staccato and phrasing-off was suddenly possible, enabling the home pianist to participate fully in the articulate elegance of modern classical musical language. From the historical point of view, one might see this process as part of a gradual habilitation of keyboard music to the classical style, within which performance indications become central to the expression. In the case of the Adagio of K.332 in F, we have two rather different texts of the Adagio: (i) the autograph of c.1781 (Princeton University Library, William H. Scheide Collection) and (ii) the first edition published in Vienna in 1784 by Artaria as the third of *Trois sonates pour le claveçin ou pianoforte composées par W. A. Mozart, œuvre VI*. If we examine the text of the first edition, we find that, in comparison with the autograph, it considerably increases the degree of elaboration in the right-hand part in the thematic reprises, adds articulations and fills out the texture slightly (see especially bars 23, 24, 27, 30–31 and 34–5). None of these elaborations alters the prevailing harmonic progression, tonality or structure on the global level, but significantly changes the extent to which elaboration, slurring and staccato (though not dynamics in this case) bear the narrative load in relation to those underlying elements. This revised text may be read as bringing it into line with an emergent trend within Vienna during the 1780s towards public presentations of solo piano music in concerts by professional performers who were noted for their virtuosity, and who routinely improvised fantasias or variation sets in which melodic embellishment played a leading part (Beethoven was to join their ranks in the 1790s). The home pianists to whom the printed text of K.332 was aimed might aspire to that same condition of virtuosity by following the written-out embellishments of this printed text, and the sonata is to some extent generically reshaped in catering to that aspiration.

It is worth remembering that the harmonic basis is not structurally affected by the embellishments of the first edition. For all that the articulation and the placement of *sfp* marks slightly delays the arrival or modifies the emphasis of certain pitches, the underlying suggestion in the treble of bars 23–4 is still of a local scale-step descent, [g″]–f″–e♭″–d″–c‴, within which f″ is perhaps, in

Schenkerian terms, the most significant, being a dominant step: it is established rather surreptitiously in bars 21–2, and Mozart returns frequently to it in the remainder of the movement, ultimately releasing it through bars 36–8 leading to the trill on a minim c″. Nevertheless, close inspection reveals that the placement of dissonance within bars (and by extension, phrases) is sometimes altered subtly. For instance, in bar 31 the autograph retains consonance until the third beat's upwardly resolving ninth, whereas in the first edition Mozart's demisemiquavers on beat 1 inject mild dissonance from the start. That alters the effect of beat 3's ninth, which is arguably less prominent than in the original, the weight of dissonance and rhythmic intensity having been transferred to the beginning of the bar. To turn to the placement of dissonance on the level of the phrase, it is noticeable that whereas in bars 29, 30, 33 and 34, the autograph maintains the original form of bar 29 almost exactly (even down to matters of articulation), the first edition departs from that stable original straight away: none of these four bars is the same, whether in precise melodic or rhythmic shape, or in the placement of dissonance, whose sheer mobility here seems indissolubly wedded to articulation (that is, the physical production of the sound). One analytical interpretation of the difference might highlight the fact that the prominence of the pitch f′ in the autograph text (frequently repeated in a relatively unembellished context and typically emphasized by a staccato wedge) is diminished in the first edition (especially in relation to the progressive embellishment found in bars 33–4), leaving open the possibility that its organizing force does not remain so powerful within bars 21–38 as had formerly been the case (for instance, the power of e♭″ in bars 33–4 may on such a reading be thought greater in the first edition than in the autograph).

Turning now to motive forms, comparative analysis of the autograph and first edition texts of bars 21–39 reveals many differences of detail, suggesting an organizational approach to continuity derived from motivic transposition and rhythmic repetition. For instance, the printed edition's more elaborate fourth beat of bar 23 (right hand) may be derived by just such means from the two falling demisemiquavers at the end of beat 3 (the same is true in similar ways of bars 30, 33 and 34). This analytical process of generation is basically that outlined by Arnold Schoenberg in *Fundamentals of Musical Composition*.[12] This is a perfectly justifiable way of understanding what is going on in the primary musical text, assuming an underlying logic for the generation of material content and its internal organisation – a logical *process*, in other words. But in engaging with Mozart's score (his 'primary text'), the analysis uncovers, perhaps unconsciously, another dimension, which is to do with historical usage of a process and has resonances beyond the printed musical page and within the social flux of late eighteenth-century Viennese concert life, virtuosity, the relation between artistry and audience and the generic trajectory (perhaps synonymous with progress) of the sonata genre.

---

[12]   Arnold Schoenberg, *Fundamentals of Musical Composition*, ed. Gerald Strang and Leonard Stein (London, 1977). See chapter 3, 'The Motive', and specifically examples 16a and b (Beethoven, Sonata in B flat Op. 22/III), p. 12.

Realizing that the text of Mozart's Adagio is also socially located is an important aspect of the way we may understand it.

Comparison of Recorded Examples

Management of improvised embellishments in performance can significantly affect the resulting structure. Sensitively done, such embellishments enhance the listener's harmonic understanding of the movement (while simultaneously betraying the performer's reading), since melodic and rhythmic accretions will necessarily conform to the underlying harmonic outline. At the same time, there is an aesthetic dimension to the performer's management of the embellishments. This will most often affect the local terrain, for instance, the appropriateness of the particular melodic enhancement within the shape of the line at any point (including climactic moments within phrase shapes, whether it is to do with register or rhythmic or textural intensity) or the placement of certain kinds of embellishment such as non-harmonic melodic tones in order to point up moments of dissonance against the bass or else to underpin a sense of cadential significance. Beyond this, though, there is a sense in which improvised embellishments introduce a structural reading of the movement concerned which, when considered as a kind of 'counterpoint' to the notated score when listening to a performance or recording, demonstrates powerfully the capacity of historically informed playing to open up for us layers of understanding that are absent from Mozart's notation (an idea introduced at the start of this chapter in relation to Robert Levin's performances). While the comments in the following section, derived from close aural inspection of different recordings of two slow movements, are intended to develop here our understanding of how expressive playing affects our understanding of Mozart's sonatas, they do also illuminate an important current trend their reception history, namely a demonstration of the declining hegemony of the score as a primary artefact (transmitting what is assumed to be a definitive 'truth' about these pieces, somehow 'sealed' in the notation) and the transient performance as a subsidiary element in their transmission. All of the recordings examined below assume (to varying degrees) that the performer is expected to intervene creatively to the extent that the text is actually adapted by playing notes that Mozart never wrote, and which belong within the space that is the performance (which becomes, consequently, a 'text'). None of these performers – Ronald Brautigam, Andreas Staier and Tom Beghin – slavishly 'serves' the composer by faithfully obeying the notated text, but they instead take Mozart's text as a starting-point for exploring the potential of that text to be realized in action through a combination of Mozart's notation, eighteenth-century advice on performance practice and the sound-world of their different fortepianos

K.570 Adagio

Ronald Brautigam
Mozart: The Complete Piano Sonatas, BIS Records, 1996–2000 [BIS–CD–835/37; BIS-CD-837D, track 8]
Fortepiano by Paul McNulty, Amsterdam, 1992, after Anton Gabriel Walter, c.1795. Recorded at the Länna church, Sweden, 1996

Tom Beghin
Wolfgang Amadeus Mozart: Sonatas K.331 Alla Turca, K.570, Fantasia K.397, Adagio K.540, Klara Et'cetera, 2005 [KTC4015]
Fortepiano by Chris Maene, Ruisdale, 2005, after Anton Walter, 1782 owned by Mozart.[13] Recorded at Studio 12, Radio Canada, Montréal, 2005

Brautigam's interventions are minimal but telling (a feature of his overall approach to the complete recording of Mozart's sonatas). Rather than overlay each of the many repeated sections within this movement with embellishments, the strategy is to reserve these in the main for the episodes, leaving the rondo reprises of the opening section almost unadorned, and therefore establishing a contrasting separation between the episodes (the site of performer intervention) and the reprises. The result is a convincing counterpoint of stability or mobility which goes beyond the text in the creation of a narrative. Examples of Brautigam's interventions in the episodes (always referring to *repeats* of bars) include bar 13, beats 1 and 3 (non-harmonic demisemiquavers respecting the sequential shape of the figure, and repeated again at bar 21, thus retaining the structural outline of the episode); bar 15, beat 3, adding passing-note acciaccaturas; bar 22, beat 1, a turn; bar 31, between beats 1 and 2, a turn (repeated in the following bar, preserving the sequence); bar 43, a brief scalic *Eingang*, leading into the final reprise of the opening theme; bar 49, beat 1, a turn.

While Brautigam's actual interventions are few, they are paralleled by subtle distinctions in the precise tempo, the chord-weighting, the speed at which notated ornaments are played and the variation of emphasis across different beats of the bar in all the repeated sections, for instance the repeat of bar 1, where he introduces a significant hesitation between the two slurred groups; the repeat of bar 34, beats 2 and 4, where momentary pauses reinforce the separation between the end of the slur and the staccato semiquavers that follow; and the repeat of bar 35, beat 2, where slight pauses again stress the gear-change from a whole-beat slur to two half-beat

---

[13]   For this recording, Chris Maene built two different, interchangeable actions that Mozart's Walter piano is known to have had at various times, the *Stossmechanik* with hand-stops to operate the dampers and the *Prellmechanik* with knee-levers operating the dampers (an adaptation made by Walter himself to Mozart's instrument in about 1800, as mentioned above in Chapter 6). Throughout the CD, Tom Beghin experiments with the sound possibilities that may be drawn from these two different actions. The Adagio of K.570 is played on the *Prellmechanik* with knee-levers (added after Mozart's death).

slurs (also judiciously marking out the momentary dissonances against the bass on beat 2 just before the cadence).

Beghin is far more interventionist. At times, his embellishments amount to wholesale recomposition of Mozart's notated score, for instance in the repeat of bars 7 and 8, where the right hand becomes quite rhapsodic. In the first (C minor) episode, Beghin applies an embellishment at the repeat of bar 13, beats 1 and 3, similar to that of Brautigam at this point (the rhythm is the same, though the shape of Beghin's figure is slightly different and is doubled in thirds); when this moment returns for the last time (in the repeat of bar 21), Beghin treats us to a culminating virtuoso flourish of demisemiquavers in doubled thirds which highlights this as a climactic moment in his reading of the structure while simultaneously relating it (quantitatively, by degree) to the embellishment of bar 13's repeat. As his performance of the episode unfolds, so the density of embellishment applied to this figure grows, and his activity – especially his importation of virtuosity at the climactic bar 21 – defines the performance space memorably as a primary level equivalent in status to the notated text. Mozart's text is here creatively extended to include the gestural not simply as an agency for the representation of the 'Work', but as a mode of conveying understanding. Beghin's performance is itself a 'text'.[14]

Beghin's entire approach is overtly rhetorical in nature (as one might expect from the author of a recent study of rhetoric in the performance of Haydn),[15] maximizing the impact of local gesture by careful emphasis of the precise articulations (especially the separation between adjacent slurred groups throughout the opening phrase), building phrases by speaking their individual components, rather than moulding everything into a seamless legato, and, most notably, deliberately sacrificing all attempts at a steady tempo in order to allow this.[16]

K.330 Andante cantabile

Ronald Brautigam
Mozart: The Complete Piano Sonatas, BIS Records, 1996–2000 [BIS-CD-835/37; BIS-CD-837B, track 2]

---

[14]   It is a text that contains clear strategic planning in its application of rhapsodic, florid right-hand embellishment at cadence approaches (for instance, the repeat of bars 29–30), as also of sextuplet semiquavers to enhance repeats of ascending phrases (at bars 5, 18, 34 and 37, for instance). Uniquely, at bar 22, beat 4, Beghin introduces a sextuplet decoration in the left hand.

[15]   Tom Beghin and Sander M. Goldberg (eds), *Haydn and the Performance of Rhetoric* (Chicago, 2008).

[16]   The tempo varies considerably from section to section, even within individual phrases; if there is a notional tempo, it lies at roughly ♩ = c.42, though it increases to c.48–50 within even the first section of the opening theme, and the first episode is notably quicker (c.52). Brautigam's tempo, by comparison, is rather more consistent at about ♩ = 48 (recorded in a more reverberant acoustic).

Fortepiano by Paul McNulty, Amsterdam, 1992, after Anton Gabriel Walter, c.1795. Recorded at the Länna church, Sweden, 1996

Andreas Staier
Mozart: Piano Sonatas / Klaviersonaten K.330, 331 'Alla Turca', 332, Harmonia Mundi Records, 2005 [HMC 901856, track 2]
Fortepiano by Monika May, Marburg, 1986, after Anton Walter, c.1785. Recorded at Teldex Studios, Berlin, 2004

As in K.570, Brautigam's performance is remarkable for the scarcity of embellished repeats, though when these occur they do so purposefully. The repeat of bar 23 precedes the quaver d♭″ with a short grace note from above; a turn is added to the quaver a♭′ midway through the repeat of bar 24; a turn between beats 2 and 3 in bar 27 enhances the cadential repeat at the end of the first half; the most extensive embellishment (a descending succession of eight semiquavers decorating beats 2 and 3 in the repeat of bar 31: d♭″–c″–b♭′–a♭′–g′–f′–e♮′–f′) is positioned precisely to enhance a particularly attenuated harmonic moment; finally, ascending sextuplets and a grace note spanning an expressive falling sixth embellish bar 47 in the *da capo*. But that is certainly not the full extent of Brautigam's involvement with Mozart's notation. Typical of the subtlety of articulation that characterizes Brautigam's approach to Mozart is the way in which he draws maximum expressive effect from seemingly limited means in the repeated sections. Whereas the upbeat leading into bar 9 (that is, immediately following the central double bar) is played the first time with long grace notes, at the repeat these are played shorter and more accented, casting the crotchet–quaver g′–f♯′ at the beginning of bar 9 in a different light as a long resolution in contrast to its more pointed local preparation (and thereby attracting additional rhetorical emphasis) whereas before it had formed part of a more continuous, and apparently longer phrase. The short grace notes here have the effect of highlighting the local successions in the articulation rather more prominently than at first, showing two complementary readings of the phrase-shape. Embellishment, in Brautigam's performance, sits alongside subtle recasting of phrase-shapes, of melodic, rhythmic and harmonic intensity within phrases, one of the most telling of which is the delicate rubato and dynamic fade applied to the descending line in the repeat of bar 29, giving the two semiquavers, d♭″–c″, ever so slightly greater prominence within this shape and throwing the left-hand d♮′ at the end of the bar into relief, focusing our attention on the harmonic shifting back and forth between relatively dark and light regions (the *forte* phrase the immediately follows plunges us well and truly back into the darkness). Brautigam's reading is truly a rhetorical one, allowing, through minimal recalculation of the placement of his attacks, a world of delicate shading to emerge from this phrase.

Andreas Staier's account[17] finds different subtleties, relying on frequent light upward arpeggiation of left-hand chords in repeated sections to create novelty (for example at the beginning of the repeated bars 1, 4, 5, 6, as well as bars 56 and 58 of the *da capo*). As in Brautigam's reading (though differently placed), there are distinctions in the execution of notated grace notes too (those in bar 11, beat 3, are played first long, then short) and variation in the dynamic contours (a pronounced *crescendo* across bars 2 and 3, for instance). Beyond that, embellishment is restricted to details: care is always taken to preserve the existing melodic and harmonic profiles by the addition of grace notes, for instance (at the start of bar 14, before the quaver d♭″ in bar 23, at the start of bars 30, 34 and 42 – approaching the main note from the third below); turns (in bars 31, 41 – both times on the third quaver – 45 and 52 – both times on the last quaver – and to the cadence between beats 2 and 3 in bar 59); a sextuplet (the first beat of bar 27); and a trill added on the second quaver in bar 51. The most radical intervention is perhaps the deliberate syncopation against the left hand of the three quavers at the end of bar 50 in the *da capo*. Staier's approach to embellishment concentrates on the addition of sharply profiled melodic gestures in the main, extracting remarkable expressive value from the grace notes, which typically coincide with a melodic dissonance against the bass, drawing that feature of Mozart's narrative to our attention (and its frequent coincidence with a rhythmic impulse of long–short from beat 1 to beat 2). There is no doubt that Staier's embellishments engage creatively with Mozart's text, making distinctive and convincing use of contemporary gestures of ornament rather than extensive recomposition.[18] As an object-lesson in the performative power of ornament, Staier's reading is a 'text' that goes beyond Mozart's – more introspectively than, say, Beghin in K.570, though no less strikingly.

---

[17]   Somewhat quicker than Brautigam's at ♩ = c.58 (Brautigam is c.52) and noticeably drier acoustically.

[18]   By contrast, his performance of the opening movement does not hesitate to recompose quite extensively in the exposition repeat.

Chapter 8
Epilogue: Listening to Texts

What happens, in general terms, when we listen to a Mozart piano sonata, for instance the first movement of the B flat Sonata K.281 (1775)? I start from the premise that listening to a work such as this considers itself as an activity that involves an aural encounter with an object; that is, the piece of music is objectified in order to be the substance with which an encounter takes place. That involves a degree of philosophical context. What, for instance, is the nature of the thing so objectified? Is it, for instance, substantial material 'out there', external to the perception? Or is it an object constructed by the perceiver? If the object were wholly external its form would also be quite difficult to comprehend. Clearly Mozart wrote this sonata at a particular time and in a particular place. Moreover, he recorded the sonata in notated, reproducible form, and when a listener encounters the piece in a performance, what is happening is that a performer is enacting a physical encounter with the notated score in order to convert it into sound which the listener perceives. To that extent, the stimulus for the listener is external both in the sense that a composed piece of music is what is being attended to and in the sense that this particular encounter is a particular physical reproduction of a notated score. Nevertheless, it is impossible to exclude both the interpretation of the performer and that of the listener. That of the performer remains external to the listener, of course. But in the sense that that interpretation is interposed between the composition and the listener in any specific performance, then that external musical object experienced by the listener is no longer directly the work itself, but something mediated. Indeed, in such a situation, it is difficult to quantify what the work itself might consist of: rather, the listener's encounter is with an object not fixed, but fluid in kind. And what the listener perceives in any case is then interpreted personally in accordance with whatever paraphernalia and experiences are brought to a particular listening situation, perhaps subtly tailored to the appreciation of a particular musical style, perhaps not. In any event, it is difficult to see how the particular form that the object of the listening encounter takes in the listener's mind can be independent of the listener's concepts of, for instance, structure, whether on the level of movement form, phrase construction, cadence construction, motivic construction or any other parameter – any or all of which may indirectly have been built up in the listener's mind over time as a result of either listening to music or reading about its form in textbooks or both. Perhaps what is listened to, then, is not purely an encounter with an external musical object, but a continually shifting internal dialogue between what is heard on the particular occasion and structures for musical understanding stored in the listener's memory. All of this makes listening to Mozart's music quite a complicated activity.

The first movement of the B flat Sonata K.281 challenges the listener with a considerable variety of material within the exposition. The succession of melodic shapes, the scansion, the register, the dynamic level, the texture: all are in flux. In particular, the exposition is noteworthy for the variety of rhythmic content. Within the opening four-bar phrase, for instance, the right-hand part subdivides the crotchet beat successively into dotted quaver plus two demisemiquavers, sextuplet semiquavers, quaver plus quaver rest, two quavers, eight demisemiquavers and finally a quaver pair preceded by a grace note (and concluding with a beat's rest). Following the repeat of the opening figure, the patterning holds more consistently to demisemiquaver subdivisions until the secondary theme arrives in bar 17, though once the right hand has acquired that profile, the left-hand accompaniment takes on a more varied character. In such a modular narrative, and assuming that the listener's perception is nevertheless that the section 'hangs together', what provides that grounding is a sense of logical patterning. Mozart marries the exceptionally mobile motivic and rhythmic surface with an economical use of pattern repetition on the level of the phrase, invoking well-tried models such as antecedent–consequent (bars 1–4, 5–8), sequence (bars 12–14) and dialogue bars 12–13, 16). Profligacy of invention is regulated by frugality of pattern. The two exist in a satisfying equilibrium. Register, allied to dynamic pattern repetition and contrast, enhances the subtlety of Mozart's equation: the opening phrase, *forte*, recurs at bar 5 an octave lower, *piano*, but this consequent phrase climaxes with an arpeggiated leap back into the higher register, *forte*, in bar 7.

Phrase-elision also plays its part in the unfolding of this opening, and while it can be appreciated analytically within the notated score, it is in a live aural encounter that the device makes its presence most strongly felt. At two points, bar 8 and bar 12, the listener is challenged to decide between an end-point and a beginning, re-evaluating retrospectively in the light of the music's ongoing progress. Bar 8 may easily be heard as a resolution onto the tonic of the preceding phrase, in which case it is the chordal resolution from E flat to B flat from bar 9 to bar 10 that starts off the next phrase (chords move uniformly on the level of the bar at this point); assuming that to be the case, then the B flat harmony lasting until bar 12 is the balancing end of this phrase. And yet at precisely this point the pattern changes, both in the leading melodic (right-hand) part and in the accompaniment, suggesting that this moment is instead a beginning. Moreover, bar 13 (answering tonic harmony with a dominant reply) stands in a dialogic relation (*piano*) to its predecessor (*forte*), and is itself succeeded by a return to *forte*, reinforced in octaves in the left hand. Once this dialogue has been perceived, the listener, in his own ongoing dialogue between what is newly heard and the memory of what has already been heard (an aural analogy to navigation, as it were), may retrospectively renegotiate the status of bar 12. Bar 14, while clearly a continuation of the pattern begun two bars earlier, contributes something new, however: the semiquaver upbeat, repeated a bar later just before the dominant cadence. Seemingly a marginal feature, this more animated rhythmic resolution across the barline arguably cements a process of phrase contraction stretching back at least as far as bar 12. Bars 12 and 13 might plausibly be considered as a (sequential) pair forming a two-bar unit; the punctuation provided by the accompaniment at the end of bar 14 and bar 15 separates these out as individual one-bar units, and in bar 16 the contraction proceeds yet a further stage, to the half-bar (right hand answered by left). Once again, the realization of this localized space as a steady contraction from two-bar to one-bar and then half-bar units is something attained retrospectively in the act of listening, continually mapping each unfolding event against memory. In fact the process of contraction perceived in bars 12–16 may actually serve to define bars 8–17 as a unit, for bars 12–13 could be regarded as the third term in a succession of two-bar units beginning at bar 8, always moving harmonically at the rate of one chord per bar (B flat–E flat; B flat–E flat; B flat–F), in which case the elision in bar 8 involves a beginning rather than an end.

Retrospective redefinition of such a broad musical space may be pushing the credibility of listening as understanding beyond a reasonable limit. But my point here is to suggest that the act of listening is to some extent an act capable of rendering musical space intelligible in meaningful ways. It is a different act from analysing a notated score in that, being 'live', the aural encounter with a performance draws the listener into the experience, the forming of a shape in the imagination happening in real time as the music unfolds and in tandem with it. That it happens against a pre-formed template of understanding does not diminish the value of that act, but situates it as a practice that is socially determined in various ways. For instance, it is a practice that carries with it a social trace (in forming such judgements, the listener applies certain learned structures of understanding, thus creating a space for himself in the reception history of the work listened to – identifying himself as a person with a certain sort of educational background, for example one gained from the study of composition textbooks). It is also an act that entails the social production of meaning. Listening to a performance of K.281 happens in certain contexts. In Mozart's day, the sonata was typically a domestic genre, but by as early as the autumn of 1777 in Augsburg, he was playing this and other sonatas from the same set in his concerts, which were to some extent, public affairs (for instance, his concerts in Augsburg in October 1777 were advertised in the local press). Listening to him do so was a public act within which listeners of a variety of backgrounds may have focused principally on the element of virtuosity, the contrasting characters, dynamics and textures that could be portrayed at the keyboard (especially a Stein fortepiano, which Mozart adored at this stage in his career). In the generations after his death, listening would have produced a different set of meanings (for instance, perplexity at the sheer variety of motivic content within such a short exposition, the lack of relation between the development section and the exposition – in particular, the lack of any *development* as such). Those meanings would have been determined to some degree by comparison with the solo piano sonatas of Beethoven (and supporting theoretical constructs for their understanding), in which the size, emotional scope and sheer technical difficulty made these mighty works the preserve of the seasoned professional pianist, and against which K.281 would seem a mere trifle.

The listener listens and forms an understanding in a social context. It is also a historical context. The nineteenth-century listener listened from a different vantage-point from his eighteenth-century forbears, one profoundly and irreversibly affected by Beethoven's impact on the way in which and purposes for which music was conceived, performed and valued. For twentieth-century and twenty-first-century listeners, the vantage-points have become yet more varied and include the radical innovation of listening not to a live performance but to a recording – on the face of it a repeatable experience in which everything is always the same in its digitized perfection. But this is never really the case; for each time we listen – and this is equally true of listening to a live performance, whether now or in Stravinsky's day, or Busoni's or Liszt's, or Schumann's, or Beethoven's or Mozart's own – we listen against a slightly different template of memory. We get to know the work better (or differently) on repeated hearings, the space occupied by the novelty, or anxiety, or frustration, or incomprehension, or inexperience steadily diminishing along the way. The environment in which we listen changes each time. Each time afresh we inscribe something else of ourselves onto the listening experience and onto Mozart's sonatas. Mozart himself was once a listener, of course: his scores (of K.281, for instance) inscribe the act of Mozart listening to himself thinking. They are not themselves the Music; rather, they are a kind of choreography whose pitches, durations, articulations, dynamics, tempos, characters, textures and gestures unite composer, performer and listener in creative and re-creative musical *action*.

Bibliography

Primary Musical Sources of Mozart's Sonatas

Chefs d'oeuvre de Mozart: A New and Correct Edition of the Piano Forte Works (with & without Accpts.) of this Celebrated Composer (London, 1836).

Mozart: An Entirely New and Complete Edition of the Piano Forte Works, with and without Accompts. of this Celebrated Composer, Humbly Dedicated by Express Permission to Her Most Gracious Majesty, the Queen. Edited by Cipriani Potter (London: Coventry, 1848).

K.310

Sonate pour le claveçin ou piano-forte composé par W. A. Mozart oeuvre 20 a Vienne chez Artaria et comp. (Vienna: Artaria, 1792).

Sonate sentimentale, pour le piano-forte ... revisé par J[ohann] B[aptist] Cramer, 'Morceaux characteristiques et brillantes', No. 7 (London: Cramer & Co., c.1860).

K.330

Sonate pour le forte-piano composé par W. A. MOZART (Leipzig: Hoffmeister and Kühnel, 1803).

Trois sonates pour le claveçin ou pianoforte composées par W. A. Mozart, œuvre VI (Vienna: Artaria, 1784).

K.333

Due sonate per il clavicembalo o forte piano ... opera 7 (Vienna: Artaria, 1787).

Trois sonates pour le clavecin ou pianoforte. La troisième est accomp: d'un violon obblig: composées par Mr. W. A. Mozart, dediées a son Excellence Comtesse Therese de Kobenzl ... œuvre VII (Vienna: Torricella, 1784).

K.545

Sonate facile pour le pianoforte composée par W. A. Mozart, œuvre posthume (Vienna: Bureau d'Arts et d'Industrie, 1805).

Sonate facile pour piano-forté composée par W. A. Mozart a Vienne au mois de juin 1788 (Offenbach am Main, 1805).

Selected Modern Editions of Mozart's Sonatas

Mozart: Sonatas for the Pianoforte, ed. Stanley Sadie and Denis Matthews (London: Associated Board of the Royal Schools of Music, 1970–81).
Mozart: Violin Sonatas / Violinsonaten, vol. 3: *K.454, K.481, K.526, K.547; Variations / Variationen K.359 & K.360*, ed. Cliff Eisen (London, Frankfurt am Main, Leipzig and New York: Peters, 2006).
W. A. Mozart: Pianoforte Sonatas, ed. York Bowen and Aubyn Raymar (London: Associated Board of the Royal Schools of Music, 1931).
Wolfgang Amadeus Mozart: Piano Sonatas, ed. Wolfgang Plath and Wolfgang Rehm, Urtext taken from *Wolfgang Amadeus Mozart: Neue Ausgabe sämtliche Werke*, issued by the Internationale Stiftung Mozarteum Salzburg, series IX, *Klaviermusik*, Werkgruppe 25 (Kassel: Bärenreiter, 1986). [Also available as *Wolfgang Amadeus Mozart: Neue Ausgabe sämtliche Werke: Taschenpartitur-Ausgabe*, vol. 20: *Klaviermusik*].

General Listing of Works Cited

Adam, Louis, *Méthode de piano du Conservatoire* (Paris, 1805).
Agawu, V. Kofi, *Playing with Signs: A Semiotic Interpretation of Classic Music* (Princeton: Princeton University Press, 1991).
Allanbrook, Wye J., 'Two Threads through the Labyrinth: Topic and Process in the First Movements of K.322 and K.333', in Wye J. Allanbrook, Janet M. Levy and William P. Mahrt (eds), *Convention in Eighteenth- and Nineteenth-Century Music: Essays in Honor of Leonard G. Ratner* (Stuyvesant, NY: Pendragon, 1992), pp. 125–71.
Auslander, Philip, *From Acting to Performance: Essays in Modernism and Postmodernism* (London: Routledge, 1997).
Bach, C. P. E., *Sechs Sonaten für Klavier mit veränderten Reprisen* (Berlin, 1760).
Bach, C. P. E., *Versuch über die Wahre Art das Klavier zu spielen*, 2 vols (Berlin, 1753, 1762; vol. 1, 2nd edn, 1759); trans. and ed. William J. Mitchell as *Essay on the True Art of Playing Keyboard Instruments* (New York: Eulenburg, 1949).
Badura-Skoda, Eva and Paul, *Interpreting Mozart on the Piano* (New York and London: Barrie & Rockliffe, 1962).
Baker, Nancy K, 'Heinrich Koch and the Theory of Melody', *Journal of Music Theory*, 20 (1976): 1–48.
Baker, Nancy K, '"Der Urstoff der Musik": Implications for Harmony and Melody in the Theory of Heinrich Christoph Koch', *Music Analysis*, 7 (1988): 3–30.
Baker, Nancy K., and Christensen, Thomas (eds), *Aesthetics and the Art of Composition in the German Enlightenment: Selected Writings of Johann*

Georg Sulzer and Heinrich Christoph Koch (Cambridge: Cambridge University Press, 1996).

Barnhart, Robert K. (ed.), *The Chambers Dictionary of Etymology* (New York: Chambers, 2005).

Barthes, Roland, 'The Death of the Author', in *Image, Music, Text*, trans. Stephen Heath (London: Fontana/Collins, 1977), pp. 142–8.

Beghin, Tom, 'Delivery, Delivery, Delivery!', in Tom Beghin and Sander M. Goldberg (eds), *Haydn and the Performance of Rhetoric* (University of Chicago Press, 2007), pp. 131–71.

Beghin, Tom, 'Haydn as Orator: A Rhetorical Analysis of his Keyboard Sonata in D major, Hob. XVI:42', in Elaine Sisman (ed.), *Haydn and his World* (Princeton: Princeton University Press, 1997), pp. 201–54.

Beghin, Tom and Goldberg, Sander M. (eds), *Haydn and the Performance of Rhetoric* (University of Chicago Press, 2007).

Benjamin, Walter, *The Work of Art in the Age of Mechanical Reproduction*, trans. J. A. Underwood (London: Penguin, 2008).

Bent, Ian, 'Analytical Thinking in the First Half of the Nineteenth-Century', in Edward Olleson (ed.), *Modern Musical Scholarship* (London: Oriel Press, 1978), pp. 151–66.

Bilson, Malcolm, 'Execution and Expression in the Sonata in E flat, K.282', *Early Music*, 20 (1992): 237–43.

Bilson, Malcolm, 'Interpreting Mozart', *Early Music*, 12 (1984): 519–22.

Bilson, Malcolm, 'Some General Thoughts on Ornamentation in Mozart's Keyboard Works', *Piano* Bilson, Michael, 'The Viennese Fortepiano of the Late 18th Century', *Early Music*, 8 (1980): 158–62.

Quarterly, 95 (1976): 26.

Bonds, Mark Evan, *Wordless Rhetoric: Musical Form and the Metaphor of the Oration* (Cambridge, Mass.: Harvard University Press, 1991).

Braunbehrens, Volkmar, *Mozart in Vienna*, trans. Timothy Bell (Oxford: Oxford University Press, 1991).

Brown, Clive, 'Dots and Strokes in Late 18th- and 19th-Century Music', *Early Music*, 21 (1993): 192–230.

Burnham, Scott, 'A. B. Marx and the Gendering of Sonata Form', in Ian Bent (ed.), *Music Theory in the Age of Romanticism* (Cambridge: Cambridge University Press, 1996), pp. 163–86.

Burnham, Scott (ed. and trans.), *Musical Form in the Age of Beethoven: Selected Writings on Theory and Method* (Cambridge: Cambridge University Press, 1997).

Caplin, William E., *Classical Form: A Theory of Formal Functions for the Instrumental Music of Haydn, Mozart, and Beethoven* (New York: Oxford University Press, 1998).

Carlson, Marvin, *Performance: An Introduction* (London: Routledge, 1996).

Churgin, Bathia, 'Francesco Galeazzi's Description (1796) of Sonata Form', *Journal of the American Musicological Society*, 21 (1968): 181–99.

The Concise Oxford Dictionary of Current English. Based on the Oxford English Dictionary and its Supplements, 6th edn (Oxford: Oxford University Press, 1980).

Counsell, Colin, and Wolf, Laurie (eds), *Performance Analysis: An Introductory Coursebook* (London: Routledge, 2001).

Czerny, Carl, *School of Practical Composition* (London, 1848).

Czerny, Carl, *Vollständiges Lehrbuch der musikalischen Composition*, 4 vols (Vienna, 1832–4).

Daube, Johann Friedrich, *Der musikalische Dilettant* (Vienna, 1773); trans. Susan P. Snook-Luther as *The Musical Dilettante: A Treatise on Composition by J. F. Daube* (Cambridge: Cambridge University Press, 1992).

Derrida, Jacques, *Writing and Difference* (Chicago: Chicago University Press, 1983).

Deutsch, Otto E., *Mozart: Die Dokumente seines Lebens* (Kassel: Bärenreiter, 1961); trans. Eric Blom, Peter Branscombe and Jeremy Noble as *Mozart: A Documentary Biography* (London: Barrie & Rockliffe, 1965, repr. 1990).

Eisen, Cliff, *New Mozart Documents: A Supplement to O. E. Deutsch's Documentary Biography* (Stanford: Stanford University Press, 1991).

Eisen, Cliff, 'The Old and New Mozart Editions', *Early Music*, 19 (1991): 513–32.

Fish, Stanley, 'Interpreting the Variorum', *Critical Inquiry*, 2 (1976): 465–85.

Fish, Stanley, *Is There a Text in this Class? The Authority of Interpretive Communities* (Harvard: Harvard University Press, 1980).

Forte, Allen, and Gilbert, Stephen, *Introduction to Schenkerian Analysis* (New York and London: Norton, 1982).

Gadamer, Hans-Georg, *Truth and Method*, 2nd rev. edn, trans. J. Weinsheimer and D. G. Marshall (New York: Crossroad Press, 1989).

Galeazzi, Francesco, *Elementi teorico-practici di musica*, 2 vols (Rome, 1791, 1796).

Goehr, Lydia, *The Imaginary Museum of Musical Works: An Essay in the Philosophy of Music* (Oxford; Oxford University Press, 1992).

Gritten, Anthony, and King, Elaine (eds), *Music and Gesture* (Aldershot: Ashgate, 2006)

Haberkamp, Gertraut, *Die Erstdrücke der Werke von W. A. Mozart* (Tützing: Schneider, 1986).

Halliwell, Ruth, *The Mozart Family: Four Lives in a Social Context* (Oxford: Oxford University Press, 1998).

Haynes, Bruce, *The End of Early Music* (New York: Oxford University Press, 2007).

Heathfield, Adrian, *Live: Art and Performance* (London: Tate Publishing, 2004).

Heidegger. Martin, *Gesamtausgabe*, vol. 2, ed. F. W. von Herrmann (Frankfurt am Main: Klostermann, 1977).

Heidegger, Martin, *Sein und Zeit* (1927); trans. John Macquarrie and Edward Robinson as *Being and Time* (London: SCM Press, 1962).

Hepokoski, James, and Darcy, Warren, *Element of Sonata Theory: Norms, Types and Deformations in the Late-Eighteenth-Century Sonata Form* (Oxford: Oxford University Press, 2006).

Hosler, Bellamy, *Changing Aesthetic View of Instrumental Music in Eighteenth-Century Germany* (Ann Arbor: University of Michigan Press, 1981).

Hoyt, Peter A., 'The Concept of 'Développement' in the Early Nineteenth Century', in Ian Bent (ed.), *Music Theory in the Age of Romanticism* (Cambridge: Cambridge University Press, 1996), pp. 141–62.

Huxley, Mike, and Witts, Noel (eds), *The 20th Century Performance Reader* (London: Routledge, 2002).

Ingarden, Roman, *The Work of Music and the Problem of its Identity*, trans. A. Czerniawski, ed. Jean G. Harell (Berkeley and Los Angeles: Palgrave Macmillan, 1986).

Irving, John, 'Deconstructing Topics: Tracing their Status in the Allegro of Mozart's Piano Sonata, KV332', *Mozart Studien*, 15 (2006): 269–76.

Irving, John, *Mozart's Piano Sonatas: Contexts, Sources, Style* (Cambridge: Cambridge University Press, 1997).

Irving, John, review of William Kinderman, *Mozart's Piano Music* (Oxford and New York: Oxford University Press, 2006), *Music and Letters*, 89 (2008): 467–72.

Iser, Wolfgang, *The Act of Reading: A Theory of Aesthetic Response* (Baltimore: Johns Hopkins University Press, 1978).

Jauss, Hans-Robert, *Aesthetic Experience and Literary Hermeneutics*, trans. Michael Shaw (Minneapolis: University of Minnesota Press, 1982).

Kant, Immanuel, *Kritik der Urteilskraft* (Berlin, 1790); trans. Werner S. Pluhar as *Critique of Judgment* (Indianapolis: Hackett, 1987).

Kaye, Nick, *Postmodernism and Performance* (London: Routledge, 1994).

Kaye, Nick, *Site-Specific Art: Performance, Place and Documentation* (London: Routledge, 2000).

Keefe, Simon P., *Mozart's Piano Concertos: Dramatic Dialogue in the Age of Enlightenment* (Woodbridge: Boydell Press, 2001).

Keefe, Simon P., *Mozart's Viennese Instrumental Music: A Study of Stylistic Re-Invention* (Woodbridge: Boydell Press, 2007).

Keefe, Simon P., 'Mozart's Late Piano Sonatas (K.457, 533, 545, 570, 576): Aesthetic and Stylistic Parallels with his Piano Concertos', in Dorothea Link and Judith Nagley (eds), *Words about Mozart: Essays in Honour of Stanley Sadie* (Woodbridge: Boydell & Brewer, 2005), pp. 59–75.

Keller, Hans, 'The Chamber Music', in Donald Mitchell and H. C. Robbins Landon (eds.), *The Mozart Companion* (London: Faber and Faber, 1956), pp. 90–137.

Kinderman, William, *Mozart's Piano Music* (Oxford and New York: Oxford University Press, 2006).

Koch, Heinrich Christoph, *Musicalisches Lexicon* (Frankfurt am Main, 1802).

Koch, Heinrich Christoph, *Versuch einer Anleitung zur Composition*, 3 vols (Leipzig and Rudolstadt, 1782, 1787, 1793); ed. and trans. Nancy K. Baker as *Heinrich Christoph Koch: Introductory Essay on Composition – The Mechanical Rules of Melody, Sections 3 and 4* (New Haven and London: Yale University Press, 1983).

Köchel, Ludwig Ritter von, *Chronologisch-thematisches Verzeichnis sämmtliche Tonwerke Wolfgang Amadè Mozarts. Nebst Angabe der verloren gegangenen, angefangenen, übertragenen, zweifelhaften und unterschobenen Compositionen desselben.* (Leipzig: Breitkopf & Hartel, 1862); 3rd edn, ed. Alfred Einstein (Leipzig: Breitkopf & Hartel, 1937); 6th edn, ed. Franz Giegling, Alexander Weinmann and Gerd Sievers (Wiesbaden: Breitkopf & Härtel, 1964).

Kollmann, August C. F., *An Essay on Practical Musical Composition* (London, 1799).

Komlós, Katalin, *Fortepianos and their Music: Germany, Austria and England, 1760–1800* (Oxford: Oxford University Press, 1995).

Komlós, Katalin, '"Ich praeludierte und spielte Variazionen": Mozart the Fortepianist', in Larry R. Todd and Peter Williams (eds), *Perspectives on Mozart Performance* (Cambridge: Cambridge University Press, 1991), pp. 27–53.

Komlós, Katalin, 'Mozart the Performer', in Simon P. Keefe (ed.), *The Cambridge Companion to Mozart* (Cambridge: Cambridge University Press, 2003), pp. 215–26.

Küster, Konrad, *Mozart: A Musical Biography*, trans. Mary Whittall (Oxford: Oxford University Press, 1996).

Latcham, Michael, 'The Check in Some Early Pianos and the Development of Piano Technique around the Turn of the 18th Century', *Early Music*, 21 (1993): 28–42.

Latcham, M. R., 'The Pianos of Johann Andreas Stein', *The Galpin Society Journal*, 51 (1998): 114–53.

Latcham, Michael, 'Mozart and the Pianos of Gabriel Anton Walter', *Early Music*, 25 (1997): 382–400.

Latcham, Michael, 'Pianos and Harpsichords for Their Majesties', *Early Music*, 36 (2008): 359–96.

Lester, Joel, *Compositional Theory in the Eighteenth Century* (Cambridge, Mass.: Harvard University Press, 1992).

Levin, Robert D., 'Improvised Embellishments in Mozart's Keyboard Music', *Early Music*, 20 (1992): 221–33.

Levin, Robert D., 'Mozart's Solo Keyboard Music', in Robert L. Marshall (ed.), *Eighteenth-Century Keyboard Music* (New York: Schirmer, 1994), pp. 282–319.

Levin, Robert D., 'Mozart's Solo Piano Music', in Robert L. Marshall (ed.), *Eighteenth-Century Keyboard Music* (New York: Schirmer, 1994), pp. 308–49.

Levin, Robert D., 'Performance Practice in the Music of Mozart', in Simon P. Keefe (ed.), *The Cambridge Companion to Mozart* (Cambridge: Cambridge University Press, 2003), pp. 227–45.

Levin, Robert D., 'The Instrument of Choice', http://www.youtube.com/watch?v=RWKbOGMqDVw (You Tube video, accessed May 2009).

Levin, Robert D., 'Mozart and the Three-Card Monty', http://www.youtube.com/watch?v=kPuxV0xXEc8&feature=related (You Tube video, accessed May 2009).

Levin, Robert D., 'Robert Levin on the Mozart Piano Sonatas', http://www.youtube.com/watch?v=RWKbOGMqDVw (You Tube Video, accessed May 2009).

Löhlein, Georg, *Clavier-Schule*, 5th edn, rev. J. G. Witthauer (Leipzig and Züllichau, 1791).

Marguerre, Karl, 'Mozarts B-Dur-Sonate KV570 "auf das Klavier allein"', *Musica*, 15 (1971): 361–3.

Marx, Adolph Bernhard, *Die Lehre von der musikalischen Komposition, praktisch-theoretisch*, vols 3 and 4 (Leipzig, 1838, 1845); 5th edn (Leipzig, 1879). See also Burnham.

Mather, Betty Bang, and Lasocki, David, *The Art of Preluding, 1700: For Flutists, Oboists, Clarinettists and Other Performers* (New York: McGinnis & Marx, 1980).

Maunder, Richard, 'Mozart's Keyboard Instruments' *Early Music*, 20 (1992): 207–19.

Maunder, Richard, *Keyboard Instruments in Eighteenth-Century Vienna* (Oxford: Oxford University Press, 1995).

Maunder, Richard, and Rowland, David, 'Mozart's Pedal Piano', *Early Music*, 23 (1995): 287–96.

Momigny, Joseph-Jérome de, *Cours complet d'harmonie et de composition* (Paris, 1803–6).

Morrow, Mary Sue, *Concert Life in Haydn's Vienna: Aspects of a Developing Musical and Social Institution* (Stuyvesant, NY: Pendragon Press, 1988).

Morrow, Mary Sue, *German Music Criticism in the Late Eighteenth Century: Aesthetic Issues in Instrumental Music* (Cambridge: Cambridge University Press, 1997).

Morrow, Mary Sue, 'Mozart and Viennese Concert Life', *The Musical Times*, 126 (1985): 453–4.

Mozart: Briefe und Aufzeichnungen Gesamtausgabe, ed. Wilhelm A. Bauer, Otto Erich Deutsch and Joseph H. Eibl, Internationale Stiftung Mozarteum, Salzburg, 7 vols (Kassel, Basel, London and New York: Bärenreiter, 1962–75) [*Briefe*].

Mozart family, *The Letters of Mozart and his Family*, ed. and trans. Emily Anderson, 3rd edn, ed. Stanley Sadie and Fiona Smart (London: Macmillan, 1985).

Mozart, Leopold, *Versuch einer gründlichen Violinschule* (Augsburg, 1756); trans. Editha Knocker as *A Treatise on the Fundamentals of Violin Playing*, 2nd edn (Oxford and New York: Oxford University Press, 1985).

Neumann, Frederick, 'Dots and Strokes in Mozart', *Early Music*, 21 (1993): 429–35.

Neumann, Frederick, *Ornamentation and Improvisation in Mozart* (Princeton: Princeton University Press, 1986).

The New Grove Dictionary of Music and Musicians, 6th edn (London: Macmillan, 1980); rev. as *The Revised New Grove Dictionary of Music and Musicians* (London: Macmillan, 2001), http://www.oxfordmusiconline.com.

Norris, Christopher, *Derrida* (London: Fontana, 1987).

Oldman, C. B., 'Cipriani Potter's Edition of Mozart's Pianoforte Works', in Walter Gerstenberg, Jan La Rue and Wolfgang Rehm (eds), *Festschrift Otto Erich Deutsch* (Kassel: Bärenreiter, 1963), pp. 120–27.

Pay, Antony, 'Phrasing in Contention', *Early Music*, 24 (1996): 291–321.

Peter, P. H., '*The Life and Work of Cipriani Potter (1792–1871)*' (dissertation, Northwestern University, 1972).

Phelan, Peggy, *Unmarked: The Politics of Performance* (London: Routledge, 1993).

Plath, Wolfgang, 'Beiträge zur Mozart-Autographie II: Schriftchronologie 1770–1780', *Mozart Jahrbuch* (1976–7): 131–73.

Portmann, Johann, *Leichtes Lehrbuch der Harmonie, Composition, und des General-basses* (Darmstadt, 1789).

Quantz, Johann Joachim, *Versuch einer Anweisung die Flöte traversière zu spielen* (Berlin, 1752); trans. Edward R. Reilly as *On Playing the Flute*, 2nd edn (London and Boston: Faber & Faber, 1966).

Ratner, Leonard G., *Classic Music: Expression, Form, Style* (New York: Schirmer Books, 1980).

Ratner, Leonard G., 'Eighteenth-Century Theories of Musical Period Structure', *The Musical Quarterly*, 42 (1956): 439–54.

Ratner, Leonard G., 'Harmonic Aspects of Classical Form', *Journal of the American Musicological Society*, 2 (1949): 159–68.

Ratner, Leonard G., 'Topical Content in Mozart's Piano Sonatas', *Early Music*, 19 (1991): 615–19.

Reicha, Antoine, *Traité de haute composition musicale*, 2 vols (Paris, 1824–6).

Reicha, Antoine, *Traité de mélodie* (Paris, 1814).

Réti, Rudolph, *The Thematic Process in Music* (London: Faber & Faber, 1961).

Riepel, Joseph, *Anfangsgründe zur musikaliechen Setzkunst* (Regensburg and Vienna, 1752, 1768).

Rosen, Charles, *The Classical Style: Haydn, Mozart, Beethoven* (New York and London: Faber and Faber, 1971).

Rosen, Charles, *Sonata Forms* (New York and London: Norton, 1988).

Rosenblum, Sandra P., *Performance Practices in Classic Piano Music: Their Principles and Applications* (Bloomington and Indianapolis: Indiana University Press, 1988).

Rowland, David (ed.), *The Cambridge Companion to the Piano* (Cambridge: Cambridge University Press, 1998).

Samson, Jim, 'Analysis in Context', in Nicholas Cook and Mark Everist (eds), *Rethinking Music* (Oxford: Oxford University Press, 1999), pp. 35–54.

Samson, Jim, 'The Musical Work and Nineteenth-Century History', in Jim Samson (ed.), *The Cambridge History of Nineteenth-Century Music* (Cambridge, Cambridge University Press, 2002), pp. 3–28

Sanders, C. (ed.), *The Cambridge Companion to Saussure* (Cambridge: Cambridge University Press, 2004).

Saussure, Ferdinand de, *Cours de linguistique générale*, ed. C. Bally and A. Sechehaye with the collaboration of A. Riedlinger (Lausanne and Paris: Payot, 1916); trans. W. Baskin as *Course in General Linguistics* (Glasgow: Fontana/Collins, 1977).

Schönfeld, Johann Ferdinand von, *Jahrbuch der Tonkunst von Wien und Prag* (1796); facsimile ed. Otto Biba (Munich: Katzbichler, 1976).

Schoenberg, Arnold, 'Brahms the Progressive', in *Style and Idea: Selected Writings of Arnold Schoenberg*, ed. Leonard Stein and Leo Black (London and Boston: Faber and Faber, 1975; rev. edn 1985), pp. 398–441.

Schoenberg, Arnold, *Fundamentals of Musical Composition*, ed. Gerald Strang and Leonard Stein (London: Faber, 1977).

Scruton, Roger, *The Aesthetics of Music* (New York: Oxford University Press, 1997).

Shamgar, Beth, *The Retransition in the Piano Sonatas of Haydn, Mozart and Beethoven*. (PhD dissertation, University of New York, 1978).

Siegmund-Schulze, Walther, 'Zur Datierung von Mozarts Klaviersonaten KV 330–333', in D. Berke and H. Heckman (eds) *Festschrift Wolfgang Rehm zum 60. Geburtstag* (Kassel, Basel, Tours and London: Bärenreiter, 1989), pp. 93–4.

Sim, Stuart, *Derrida and the End of History* (Cambridge: Icon Books, 1999).

Somfai, László, 'Mozart's First Thoughts: The Two Versions of Mozart's Sonata in D major, K.284', *Early Music*, 19 (1991): 601–13.

Strohm, Reinhard, 'Looking Back at Ourselves: The Problem with the Musical Work-Concept', in Michael Talbot (ed.), *The Musical Work: Reality or Invention?* (Liverpool: University of Liverpool Press, 2000), pp. 128–52.

Sulzer, Johann Georg, *Allgemeine Theorie der schönen Künste* (Leipzig, 1771–5).

Talbot, Michael, 'The Work-Concept and Composer-Centredness', in Michael Talbot (ed.), *The Musical Work: Reality or Invention?* (Liverpool: University of Liverpool Press, 2000), pp. 168–86.

Tarling, Judy, *The Weapons of Rhetoric* (St Albans: Corda Music, 2004).

Till, Nicholas, *Mozart and the Enlightenment* (London and Boston: Faber & Faber, 1991).

Todd, Larry R., and Williams, Peter (eds), *Perspectives on Mozart Performance* (Cambridge: Cambridge University Press, 1991).

Türk, Daniel Gottlob, *Clavierschule* (Leipzig, 1789); trans. and ed. Raymond Haggh as *School of Clavier Playing or Instructions in Playing the Clavier for Teachers & Students* (Lincoln, Nebr., and London: University of Nebraska Press, 1982).

Tyson, Alan, 'The Date of Mozart's Piano Sonata in B flat, K.333/315c: The "Linz" Sonata?', in M. Bente (ed.), *Musik – Edition – Interpretation: Gedankschrift Günther Henle* (Munich: Henle, 1980), pp. 447–54.

Tyson, Alan, *Mozart: Studies of the Autograph Scores* (Harvard and London: Harvard University Press, 1987).

Tyson, Alan (ed.), *Wolfgang Amadeus Mozart: Fantaisie und Sonate c-moll für Klavier, KV 475 + 457. Faksimile nach dem Autograph in der Biblioteca Mozartiana Salzburg*, introduction by Wolfgang Plath and Wolfgang Rehm (Salzburg: Bärenreiter, 1991).

Tyson, Alan (ed.), *Wolfgang Amadeus Mozarts Werke: Wasserzeichen-Katalog*, 2 vols. *Neue Mozart-Ausgabe*, supplementary vols X/33/2 (Salzburg: Bärenreiter, 1996).

Webster, James, 'The Rhetoric of Improvisation in Haydn's Keyboard Music', in Tom Beghin and Sander M. Goldberg (eds), *Haydn and the Performance of Rhetoric* (University of Chicago Press, 2007), pp. 172–212.

Wolf, Eugene, K., 'The Rediscovered Autograph of Mozart's Fantasy and Sonata in C minor, K.475/457', *The Journal of Musicology*, 10 (1992): 3–47.

Wolff, Christoph, 'Musikalische "Gedankenfolge" und "Einheit des Stoffes": Zu Mozarts Klaviersonate in F-dur (KV533 & 494)', in H. Danuser, H. de la Motte-Haber, S. Leopold and N. Miller (eds), *Das musikalische Kunstwerk: Geschichte, Ästhetik, Theorie: Festschrift Carl Dahlhaus zum 60. Geburtstag* (Laaber: Laaber, 1988), pp. 441–53.

Wyzewa, Théodore de, and Saint-Foix, Georges de, *Wolfgang-Amédée Mozart: sa vie musicale et son œuvre*, 5 vols (Paris: Desclée de Brouwer, 1912–46).

Zimmermann, Ewald, 'Eine neue Quelle zu Mozarts Klaviersonate KV 209 (284b)', *Die Musikforschung*, 11 (1958): 490–93.

Discography

Tom Beghin
Wolfgang Amadeus Mozart Sonatas K.331 Alla Turca, K.570, Fantasia K.397, Adagio K.540, Klara Et'cetera, 2005 [KTC4015].

Ronald Brautigam
Mozart: The Complete Piano Sonatas, BIS Records, 1996–2000 [BIS-CD-835/37].

Robert Levin
Mozart: Piano Sonatas K.279, K.280 & K.281 on Fortepiano, vol. 1, Sony BMG Music Entertainment/Deutsche Harmonia Mundi, 2006 [82876 84237 2].

Alexei Lubimov
Mozart: Complete Piano Sonatas, Warner Classics and Jazz/ERATO, 2008 [2564 69694-3].

Andreas Staier
Mozart: Piano Sonatas / Klaviersonaten K.330, 331 'Alla Turca', 332, Harmonia Mundi Records, 2005 [HMC 901856].

Andreas Staier and Christina Schornsheim
Mozart am Stein vis-à-vis, Harmonia Mundi Records, 2007 [HMC 901941].

Index

Adam, Louis 47–52
amateur pianists 132
analysis, musical 3–7, 10, 14–15, 46
appoggiaturas 118
Artaria (music publisher) 54–5, 59–63, 77,
    84, 132
Augsburg, Mozart's visit to (1777) 108–9
autograph scores 47–52, 55–7, 60, 84, 97,
    110, 125, 132

Bach, Carl Philipp Emanuel 118, 124
Bach, Johann Sebastian 9
Barthes, Roland 22
Beecke, Ignaz von 112
Beethoven, Ludwig van 1, 40, 45, 64,
    72–3, 99, 101, 132, 141–2
Beghin, Tom 134–6
bel canto style 67–8
Bossler, Philipp Heinrich 84
Brautigam, Ronald 5, 57, 126, 134–8
Bureau d'Arts et d'Industrie, Vienna 88

cadenzas 119, 121
Cannabich, Rosina 68, 109, 112, 127–9
Chopin, Frédéric 46
Clementi, Muzio 73
concert music and concert culture 8, 45,
    106, 141
counterpoint 79, 106–7, 115, 134
Cramer, Johann Baptist 9, 72–4, 101
cultural traditions 4–6
Czerny, Carl 9, 32, 34, 40

da capo style 125–6
dance-types 9
Darcy, Warren 3, 24
Derrida, Jacques 96
dialogue textures 115–16
différance concept 96
Dürnitz, Thaddeus von 55, 110
Dusek, Jan Ladislav 101

dynamic contrast on a forte-piano 114
dynamic markings in scores 48, 55–8,
    72–4, 84–5

editions of Mozart's piano sonatas 53–4,
    59, 68, 132
embellishment of Mozart's texts 55, 58, 64,
    67, 117–38
    and musical structure 125–6
empirical approaches to music 11, 14
ethical choices and con-sequences 40–46
evenness of touch on a fortepiano 113–14

finale movements 84
'finger pedalling' 108
fingering 46–52
first editions of Mozart's piano sonatas
    53–5, 60, 77, 84, 89
Fish, Stanley 24, 26, 29
fortepiano sound 2, 4–5, 7, 43, 57, 82, 84,
    101, 105–16
freedom of (musical) ex-pression 130
'fusion of horizons' 24–6, 29, 32, 38, 52

Gadamer, Hans-Georg 24–7, 29, 52
Galeazzi, Francesco 30
genre 9
Goehr, Lydia 7, 88, 100
grace-notes 117–18

harpsicord sound 110–11
Haydn, Joseph 136
Heidegger, Martin 26–7
Hepokoski, James 3, 24
historically-informed play-ing 123, 125,
    134
Hoffmeister and Hoffmeis-ter & Kühnel
    (music pub-lishers) 60–62, 84

improvisation 78–80, 126, 130–31
Ingarden, Roman 53